Power Graphics Programming

Michael Abrash

Que® Corporation
Carmel, Indiana

Programmer's Journal™
Springfield, Oregon

Power Graphics Programming

Copyright © 1989 by Que ® Corporation

Library of Congress Catalog Number: 89-61809

ISBN: 0-88022-500-9

93 92 91 90 89   8 7 6 5 4 3 2 1

Interpretation of the printing code: the rightmost double-digit number is the year of the book's printing; the rightmost single-digit number, the number of the book's printing. For example, a printing code of 89-4 shows that the fourth printing of the book occurred in 1989.

The material in this book originally appeared in the "On Graphics" column in Programmer's Journal™, *The Resource Journal for IBM Micro Programmers, between January 1987 and October 1989.*

Dedication

Dedicated to Steve Feldman, my friend and mentor.

Publishing Manager

Allen L. Wyatt, Sr.

Indexer

Brown Editorial Service

Cover Design

Dan Armstrong

For *Programmer's Journal* ™

Publisher

Elizabeth Oakley

Managing Editor

Robert E. Wanetick

Production Art

Ralph Bentley

About the Author

Michael Abrash

Michael Abrash is a senior software engineer for Orion Instruments, Inc., of Redwood City, California, where he is working on the design of advanced PC-based test instrumentation. He is the author of dozens of articles on PC programming and writes the "On Graphics" column for *Programmer's Journal*. This is his fifth book about the IBM PC.

Content Overview

Table of Contents

Acknowledgments

Thanks to the staff of *Programmer's Journal* for their patience and support over the years. Special thanks to Bob Wanetick and Ralph Bentley, for pulling this book together, and to Liz Oakley, for making the project a reality. Thanks also to the fine editors I've worked with at *PJ* over the years: Robert Keller, Erin O'Connor, and Steve Baker. As always, thanks to Shay and Emily for their patience and support. Finally, thanks to all the readers of "On Graphics"; without their enthusiastic support, this book could never have been possible.

Trademark Acknowledgments

Introduction

Simply put, this is a book about how to write excellent graphics programs for the EGA and VGA, surely both the most important and challenging graphics adapters on the market today. There are books aplenty about graphics, but no others that I know of that explore the EGA and VGA by delving into a series of hands-on, code-intensive applications, as this one does. This book shows the EGA and VGA in high-performance action, with lots of working code and plenty of theory to back the code up.

In order to understand why the EGA and VGA are both exceptional and difficult for the uninitiated to work with, and to see why this book offers a unique perspective on EGA and VGA graphics, a brief history lesson is in order.

Graphics: A Bit of History

Graphics are surely near the top of any list of the blessings of the microcomputer revolution. Fifteen years ago, $50,000 terminals attached to multimillion-dollar mainframes were required to produce monochrome wire-frame drawings; nowadays, a $2,000 computer can draw solid, 256-color pictures in just a few seconds.

It's not just cost that makes microcomputer graphics so wonderful, though. Graphics are, simply put, fun. That's not necessarily true of most microcomputer applications—have you ever heard someone "ooooh" and "ahhhh" at a spreadsheet? Has anyone ever woken you up in the middle of the night because he absolutely had to show *someone* this stunning word processor they just got? Do you know anyone who pours quarters into her favorite database at the local arcade?

Of course not. Each of these applications is useful and worthy, and they help justify the cost of a microcomputer—but they don't pack the sheer enjoyment that graphics offers. Heck, ten years ago I spent many sleepless nights creating a video game on a CP/M computer with 160-by-72 resolution—in monochrome, no less—and when I finished, people in my office lined up to play it. Nowadays, with 640-by-480 resolution taken for granted and the availability of 256 colors, graphics are more appealing than ever.

What's more, graphics are clearly the wave of the future. Our eyes are our highest-bandwidth input devices, and virtually all modern-day user interfaces acknowledge that by relying heavily on graphics. All in all, graphics are the most enjoyable and among the most important aspects of microcomputing.

How "On Graphics" Came to Be

The advent of the IBM PC was key in bringing about high-quality microcomputer graphics. The PC offered a widely accepted microcomputer graphics standard, assuring developers of a broad-enough customer base to justify the costs of software development. The only problem with the PC was that it offered too *many* standards: the Color/Graphics Adapter (CGA), the Hercules Graphics Card (HGC), the Enhanced Graphics Adapter (EGA), and the Video Graphics Array (VGA). The profusion of standards confused many people; worse, the later and more powerful entries, the EGA and VGA, proved to be quite difficult to program, owing to both the inherent complexity of the hardware and the lack of useful documentation. And yet, it was precisely the EGA (and later the VGA) that developers most wanted to work with, for these adapters offered resolutions and color capabilities far surpassing those of their predecessors.

Enter the "On Graphics" column in *Programmer's Journal*. In January 1987, the EGA was starting to hit its stride, but few people knew how to program it well, and I had seen no books or articles on EGA programming. I had worked extensively with the EGA and was eager to share my knowledge; the question was how best to do that. Books take months to write and more months to get into print—if I were to write a book, it would be over a year before my EGA programming techniques actually benefited anyone. An article would be a much quicker outlet; alas, it was clear that the EGA was far too vast a topic for a single article. Fortunately, *Programmer's Journal* recognized the enormous demand for graphics information, and thus the "On Graphics" column was born.

For the past three years, I've been leading the readership of *Programmer's Journal* on a grand journey of exploration. We started with the EGA; just as we got that under our belts, the VGA came along, adding a potpourri of new resolutions, colors, and features. Happily, everything we'd learned retained its value on the VGA and, in fact, gained new value as the VGA confirmed EGA-style graphics as a standard. "On Graphics" has been exploring the VGA ever since and probably will continue to do so for quite a while: The VGA seems likely to be the PC-graphics standard for a good long time, in light of IBM's decision to put the VGA right on the motherboards of all of its Micro Channel computers.

What Makes "On Graphics" Special

The "On Graphics" column isn't your standard cut-and-dried reference work. Instead, it's a hands-on, case-study exploration of the EGA and VGA. The only way to truly learn about hardware as complex as the EGA and VGA is to get right in there and work with it, and that's the approach I've followed in *Power Graphics Programming*. Every column contains working code that illustrates a useful feature of the EGA or VGA, along with the theory behind the code and an overview of how that feature fits into the overall architecture of the adapters. Piece by piece, *Power Graphics Programming* builds up a functional picture of the EGA and VGA, from write modes and color control clear through animation and undocumented high-resolution 256-color modes.

Power Graphics Programming doesn't cover *all* EGA and VGA features—that would take several volumes and would surely bore you to death with details. Instead, it covers a broad spectrum of EGA/VGA applications, illustrating useful features in the process. The idea is that you get working code and hands-on examples, all the while adding to your store of knowledge about these powerful but complex adapters.

This book is not intended to be your only reference on the EGA and VGA. In fact, it's not intended to be a reference at all; it's more a "user's guide," designed to complement a thick, dry EGA/VGA reference book with juicy real-world applications and lots of working code. Use this book to get a feel for what the EGA and VGA can do and to get excited about the possibilities; then use a reference book to answer any questions you may still have.

In short, *Power Graphics Programming* gets you started with EGA and VGA graphics programming and then shows you just how enormous the potential of those adapters is. Don't think, though, that this is a beginner's book—it "gets you started" with EGA/VGA programming, not programming in general. The readership of *Programmer's Journal* is highly sophisticated, and *Power Graphics Programming* is written to match, with terse explanations of basic programming concepts and lots of high-performance assembler code. I've always assumed that the average "On Graphics" reader is learning to program the EGA/VGA but is also an excellent programmer in general. This, along with the longevity of "On Graphics," has freed me to discuss advanced topics of the sort rarely found in magazines (or, for that matter, in books).

"On Graphics" is special for another reason. It's a forum for a two-way exchange of ideas. Naturally, it's a little one-sided: *someone* has to write the column on a regular basis! However, the readers write a surprisingly large portion of the column, either directly through letters or indirectly through questions that I answer. To me, the ongoing interchange with readers is the most satisfying aspect of the column, and it's a large part of the reason I've continued to write "On Graphics" over the years, no matter what deadlines and crises loom on other projects.

What You'll Need

The tools you'll need to use the code in this book are few. You'll need the Microsoft Macro Assembler version 5.0 or higher, or a compatible assembler (Turbo Assembler will do fine). You'll need a linker that supports your assembler. You'll also need a text editor to enter the code; alternatively, you can use the order form in this book to order all code in diskette form. Finally, you'll need Turbo C to compile a few listings toward the end of the book; however, the code can readily be converted for compiling with Microsoft C as well.

What You'll Find Inside

This book contains 13 installments of the "On Graphics" column, which appeared in *Programmer's Journal* issues from January/February 1987 through September/October 1989. The text and code in this book is substantially the same as that which appeared in the magazine; however, I've changed both text and code as needed to correct, improve, or clarify. That's not to say that either the text or the code is perfect—in particular, my experience is that there's no code that can't be made better. However, to the best of my knowledge, the code works properly and performs well, and the information contained in this book is correct. I would be glad to hear of any errors you may find.

Within this book you will find commentary here and there, including reviews and industry notes. This commentary is of particular interest for the perspective it offers on the rapid development of PC graphics. Mostly, though, the "On Graphics" column offers solid, well-explained code for the EGA and VGA, and that's what you'll find in abundance herein. As I've said, the EGA/VGA standard is more firmly entrenched now than it was when I started "On Graphics," and my guess is that the VGA will be with us through the turn of the century. Consequently, the code in this book is as relevant now as it was when it was written—and is perhaps even more important now, given the rapid acceptance of the VGA standard.

Two themes run through this book. One is that performance and graphics are inextricably intertwined; speed is as important to the user as resolution and number of colors. Consequently, I not only explain how to use the various features of the EGA and VGA, but I also take the time to show how to get high performance out of those features.

The second theme is this: Before you can write great graphics code, you must first understand the graphics hardware thoroughly. Once you've achieved that understanding, you can readily mix and match features and put those features to creative use in your programs. Again and again in this book we will see that graphics code written with a deep understanding of the hardware of the EGA and VGA handily outperforms run-of-the-mill graphics code, sometimes by stunning margins.

I hope you enjoy this book as much as I've enjoyed writing "On Graphics."

—Michael Abrash

Sunnyvale, Calif., 1989

CHAPTER 1

Inside the EGA

In 1986, when I sat down to write my first article on graphics for *Programmer's Journal*—the first installment of "On Graphics," which you're about to read—it was clear that the EGA was on its way to becoming the next PC-graphics standard. Unfortunately, few people knew how to program the EGA effectively at the time, and virtually no useful references were available to the average programmer. Consequently, I selected the EGA as my first graphics topic. After a few articles on the EGA, I planned to discuss the Color/Graphics Adapter, the Hercules Graphics Card, and the powerful Intel and TI graphics coprocessors that were just coming out—thus covering the spectrum of the PC graphics marketplace.

It didn't work out that way—but no one seems to be disappointed.

I never imagined that I would still be writing about the EGA (and its descendant, the VGA) three years later. Then again, I never imagined that there would be such tremendous reader interest in the EGA, that it would be such an overwhelming market success, or that the next graphics standard—the VGA—would be enough like the EGA so that I could switch smoothly from one to the other without missing a beat. And, to be honest, I underestimated the rich feature set of the EGA, which has proven to contain one unexpected gem after another—and how could I have imagined the VGA, with its undocumented 256-color modes and its myriad improvements on the EGA?

Anyway, it all started here, with installment 1. As I write this introduction to the chapter, three years later, I'm still taking *Programmer's Journal* readers on a tour of the EGA and VGA—and there are plenty of wonders yet to see.

I'd like to make a few updates to installment 1, given the benefit of hindsight. First (and most important), the Attribute Controller Index and Data registers of the VGA are accessible only at I/O port 3C0h, unlike the EGA, which makes those registers available at both 3C0h and 3C1h. Consequently, word OUTs to these registers should never be used. I've updated Listing 1.1 to reflect this. On the other hand, word OUTs to other EGA and VGA registers are now widely used, with no apparent ill effects; it has been years since I've heard of any computer on which word OUTs didn't work properly, and I use them myself whenever possible.

Second, there is now at least one assembler that is an excellent replacement for the Microsoft Macro Assembler: TASM, Borland's Turbo Assembler. TASM is much faster than MASM and, in my experience, has fixed MASM's bugs without losing compatibility.

Third, note that the smooth panning performed by Listing 1.1 may appear jerky on some clone EGAs or VGAs, owing to minor hardware differences from the IBM adapters. Such is the price we pay for the intense competition and open architecture that mark the PC-compatible arena—and for the incredible diversity and astonishingly low costs that competition and openness make possible. On balance, that's a price well worth paying.

Finally, I ended this first column by asking readers for solutions to two of my pet programming peeves, not knowing whether the readership of *Programmer's Journal* was either skilled enough or public-minded enough to help out. The answer proved to be a resounding *Yes!* on both counts. Excellent answers to my questions may be found in Chapters 3 and 4.

With that, let's begin. I take you back in time to January 1987, near the dawn of the EGA era . . .

Installment 1: In which we begin to learn about the most unusual, but most rewarding, EGA.

This is the first of a series of articles about graphics. Actually, it's about more than just graphics—it's about algorithms and assembly language programming and all manner of tricks for putting IBM PC-family microcomputers through their paces. Still, the focus will be on graphics of the EGA/CGA/Hercules sort, all the while keeping an eye on higher-performance boards that have the potential to become standards someday soon. If there's any particular area you'd like to see covered or interesting findings you'd like to share, let me know.

I'm going to start with a look at the Enhanced Graphics Adapter (EGA). The CGA and Hercules boards are pretty simple, and a great deal has been written about how to program them. The EGA, on the other hand, is a difficult board to program efficiently (the more so because IBM's documentation is hard to obtain and harder to understand), and little information about programming the EGA has seen print. The EGA's tremendous potential—far greater than that of the CGA—makes it well worth knowing about, and that's what the next few articles will be about.

The EGA

Although the EGA is fast becoming the standard graphics adapter in the IBM PC marketplace, it has not met with universal approval. The knock against the EGA is that its performance is inadequate. True, the EGA is not an ultra-high-resolution board, but it offers a solid price/performance ratio. Sixteen colors at a resolution of 640 by 350, complete with a monitor and decent compatibility with older software for under $800 is a pretty good deal—that's about what I paid for 320 by 200 in four colors just four years ago. (I'm talking about EGA clones, of course—the IBM EGA and monitor are greatly overpriced.) In my opinion, the EGA provides adequate resolution and color for the majority of PC applications at a price most users can afford.

There's another facet of graphics performance, though, and that's the speed at which programs can update the screen. Bit-mapped graphics tend to be slow when handled by the main processor, as witness Microsoft Windows, which really requires an AT for decent speed—or, for that matter, the Macintosh, which expends much of the power of an 8-MHz 68000 in supporting a bit-mapped interface. The time spent in bit-map manipulation goes up rapidly as the size of the bit map and the complexity of controlling it increase. The EGA's bit map is 16 times as large as the CGA's, and although the EGA has many useful features built in, those features are controlled by dozens of registers. The result: It's hard to produce fast graphics on the EGA.

Hard, but not impossible—and that's why I like this odd board. It's a throwback to an earlier generation of micros, when inventive coding and a solid understanding of the hardware were the best tools for improving performance. Increasingly, faster processors and powerful coprocessors are seen as the solution to the sluggish software produced by high-level languages and layers of interfacing and driver code, and that's surely a valid approach. However, there are hundreds of thousands of EGAs installed right now, with no coprocessors to help and hardly an 80386 in sight. What's more, because the EGA is an 8-bit device, and because of display-memory wait states, an AT isn't as much of a help as you'd expect. The upshot is that only a good, low-level coder who understands the EGA can push the board to its potential.

I'll be exploring the EGA by selecting a specific algorithm or feature and implementing code to support it on the EGA, examining aspects of the EGA architecture as they become relevant. You'll get to see EGA features in context—where they are more comprehensible than in IBM's somewhat arcane documentation—and you'll get working code to use or to modify to meet your needs. If there's a particular aspect of the EGA that you'd like to read about, send me a letter and I'll try to work it in.

The prime directive of EGA programming is that there's rarely just one way to program the EGA for a given purpose. Once you understand the tools the EGA provides, you'll be able to combine them to generate the particular synergy your application needs. My EGA routines are intended not to be taken as gospel, nor to show "best" implementations, but rather to start you down the road to understanding the EGA.

Let's begin.

An Introduction to the EGA

Most discussions of the EGA start out with a traditional "Here's a block diagram of the EGA" approach, with lists of registers and statistics. I'll get to that eventually, but you can find it in IBM's EGA documentation and several other magazines. Besides, it's numbing to read specifications and explanations, and the EGA is an exciting board. It's the sort of board that makes you want to get your hands dirty under the hood, to write some nifty code just to see what the board can do. What's more, the best way to understand the EGA is to see it work. So, let's jump right into an example of the EGA in action, getting a feel for the EGA's architecture in the process.

Listing 1.1 [presented at the end of this chapter] is a sample EGA program that pans around an animated, 16-color, high-resolution (640-by-350) playfield. There's a lot packed into this code; I'm going to take advantage of the technically high level of *PJ* readership and assume you can figure out the non-EGA aspects for yourself. I'm not going to explain how the ball is animated, for example. (For an introduction to animation, see "Animation Techniques for the IBM PC," by Michael Abrash and Dan Illowsky, in *PC Tech Journal,* July 1986.) What I *will* do is cover each of the EGA features used in this program—virtual screen, vertical and horizontal panning, color-plane manipulation, multiplane block copying, and page flipping—at a conceptual level, letting the code itself demonstrate the implementation details.

Some Background

A little background is necessary before we can begin to examine Listing 1.1. The EGA is built around four VLSI (Very Large Scale Integration) chips, named the CRT Controller (CRTC), the Sequence Controller (SC), the Attribute Controller (AC), and the Graphics Controller (GC). There are two GCs per EGA, since each GC controls two of the EGA's four planes of memory. Some EGA-compatible chip sets combine several of these chips into a single chip or shuffle specific functions among chips, but the programming interface always looks the same, since otherwise the chip set would not be EGA compatible.

Each of these chips has a sizable complement of registers. It is not particularly important that you understand why a given chip has a given register; all the registers together make up the programming interface, and it is the entire interface that is of interest to the EGA programmer. However, the means by which most EGA registers are addressed makes it necessary for you to remember which registers are in which chips.

Most EGA registers are addressed as *internally indexed* registers. The internal address of the register is written to a given chip's index register, and then the data for that register is written to the chip's data register. For example, GC register 8, the Bit Mask register, is set to 0FFh by writing 8 to port 3CEh, the GC Index register, and then writing 0FFh to port 3CFh, the GC Data register. Internal indexing makes it possible to address the 9 GC registers through only two ports and allows the entire EGA programming interface to be squeezed into fewer than a dozen ports. The downside is that two I/O operations are required to access most EGA registers.

The ports used to control the EGA are shown in Table 1.1. The CRTC, SC, and GC Index registers are located at the addresses of their respective Data registers plus 1. However, the AC Index and Data registers are located at the same address, 3C0h. The function of this port toggles on every OUT to 3C0h and resets on every read from the Input Status 1 register (3DAh when the EGA is in color modes, 3BAh in monochrome modes). Note that all CRTC registers are addressed at either 3DXh or 3BXh, the former in color modes and the latter in monochrome modes. This provides compatibility with the register addressing of the color/graphics and monochrome adapters.

Table 1.1   *The ports through which the EGA is controlled. These are the official addresses, but some EGA registers are incompletely decoded and can be addressed at several addresses. Most important, the AC Index/Data register can be addressed at 3C1h as well as at 3C0h.*

Register	Address
AC Index/Data register	3C0h (write only)
Input Status 0 register	3C2h (read only)
SC Index register	3C4h (write only)
SC Data register	3C5h (write only)
Graphics 2 Position register	3CAh (write only)
Graphics 1 Position register	3CCh (write only)
GC Index register	3CEh (write only)
GC Data register	3CFh (write only)
CRTC Index register	3B4h/3D4h (write only)
CRTC Data register	3B5h/3D5h (write only)
Input Status 1 register/ AC Index/Data reset	3BAh/3DAh (read only)
Feature Control	3BAh/3DAh (write only)

The method used in the EGA BIOS to set registers is to point DX to the desired index register, load AL with the index, perform a byte OUT, increment DX to point to the data register (except in the case of the AC, where DX remains the same), load AL with the desired data, and perform a byte OUT. A handy shortcut is to point DX to the desired index register, load AL with the index, load AH with the data, and perform a word OUT. Since the high byte of word OUT values goes to port DX+1, this is equivalent to the first method but is considerably faster. This even works for the AC, since the AC Index and Data registers are decoded at both 3C0h and 3C1h; however, be sure that the AC Index or Data register is set to index mode before programming the AC with a word OUT (you can ensure this by first reading the Input Status 1 register to reset AC addressing).

How safe is this method of addressing EGA registers? I have run into accelerator boards that had trouble with word OUTs; however, all such problems I am aware of have been fixed. Moreover, Microsoft Windows uses word OUTs, even to the AC, and so any clone computer or EGA that doesn't support word OUTs could scarcely be considered a clone at all.

A speed tip: The setting of each chip's index register remains the same until it is reprogrammed. This means that in cases where you are setting the same internal register repeatedly, you can set the Index register to point to that internal register once and then write to the Data register multiple times. For example, the Bit Mask register (GC register 8) is set repeatedly inside a loop when drawing a line. The standard code for this is

```
mov   dx,03ceh    ;point to GC Index register
mov   al,8        ;internal index of Bit Mask register
out   dx,ax       ;AH contains Bit Mask register setting
```

Alternatively, the GC Index register could initially be set to point to the Bit Mask register with

```
mov   dx,03ceh    ;point to GC Index register
mov   al,8        ;internal index of Bit Mask register
out   dx,al       ;set GC Index register
inc   dx          ;point to GC Data register
```

and then the Bit Mask register could be set repeatedly with the byte-size OUT instruction,

```
out   dx,al       ;AL contains Bit Mask register setting
```

which is four cycles faster than a word-sized OUT and which does not require AH to be set, freeing up a register. Be aware, however, that this method works only if the GC Index register remains unchanged throughout the loop.

Linear Planes and True EGA Modes

The EGA's memory is organized as four 64K planes, for a total of 256K bytes of display memory. (The base model from IBM comes with only 16K per plane, but this configuration doesn't support the 16-color, high-resolution mode. So far as I can tell, this version of the EGA is about as widely used as the PC's cassette port, and so I will discuss only 256K EGA operation.) Each of the planes is a linear bit map; that is, each byte from a given plane controls eight adjacent pixels on the screen, the next byte controls the next eight pixels, and so on to the end of the scan line. The next byte then controls the first eight pixels of the next scan line, and so on to the end of the screen. This will no doubt come as a relief to programmers weary of compensating for the CGA's two-bank architecture and the Hercules Graphics Card's four-bank architecture.

The EGA adds a powerful twist to linear addressing: The logical width of the screen in EGA memory need not be the same as the physical width of the display. The programmer is free to define all or part of the EGA's large memory map as a logical screen of up to 4096 pixels in width and then use the physical screen as a window onto any part of the logical screen. What's more, a virtual screen can have any logical height up to the capacity of EGA memory. Such a virtual screen could be used to store a spreadsheet or a CAD/CAM drawing, for instance. As we will see shortly, the EGA provides excellent hardware for moving around the virtual screen; taken together, the virtual screen and the EGA's smooth panning capabilities can generate very impressive effects.

All four linear planes are addressed in the same 64K memory space, starting at A000:0000. Consequently, there are four bytes at any given address in EGA memory; the plane or planes accessed at any given time depends on the settings of the EGA's registers. The EGA provides special hardware to assist the CPU in manipulating all four planes, in parallel, with a single memory access; the programmer doesn't have to spend a great deal of time switching between planes. Astute use of this EGA hardware allows EGA software to equal the performance of CGA software, even though the EGA bit map is much larger than the CGA bit map.

Each memory plane provides one bit of data for each pixel. The bits for a given pixel from each of the four planes are combined into a nibble that serves as an address into the EGA's palette RAM, which maps the 1 of 16 colors selected by display memory into any one of 64 colors, as shown in Figure 1.1. All 64 mappings for all 16 colors are independently programmable. Given the default palette RAM settings, plane 0 contains the blue component of each pixel and so is called the "blue" plane; similarly, plane 1 is known as the "green" plane, plane 2 is known as the "red" plane, and plane 3 is known as the "intensity" plane.

The EGA BIOS supports several graphics modes (modes 4, 5, and 6) in which EGA memory appears not to be organized as four linear planes. These modes exist for CGA compatibility only and are not true EGA graphics modes; use them when you need CGA-type operation, and ignore them the rest of the time. The EGA's special features are most powerful in true EGA modes, and it is on these modes (modes 0Dh, 0Eh,

0Fh, and 10h) that I will concentrate. EGA text modes, which feature soft fonts, are another matter entirely, to be explored separately at a later date.

With that background out of the way, we can get on to the sample EGA program shown in Listing 1.1. I suggest you run the program before continuing, since the explanations will mean far more to you if you've seen the features in action.

Smooth Panning

The first thing you'll notice upon running the sample program is the remarkable smoothness with which the display pans from side to side and up and down. The display's ability to pan at all is made possible by two EGA features: the 256K bit map and the virtual-screen capability. Even the most memory-hungry of the EGA modes, mode 10h, uses only 28K per plane, for a total of 112K out of the total 256K of EGA memory. Consequently, there is room enough in EGA memory to store more than two full screens of video data. In the sample program, memory is organized as two virtual screens, each with a resolution of 672 by 384, as shown in Figure 1.2. The area of the virtual screen actually displayed at any given time is selected by setting the display-memory address at which

---

Fig. 1.1   *Video-data path from EGA display memory to video connector.*

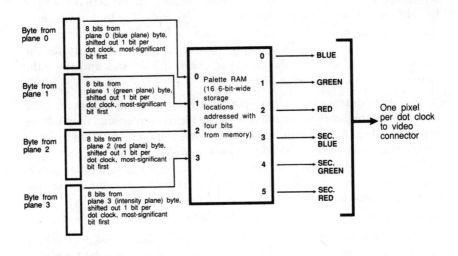

to begin fetching video data, by way of the start-address registers (Start Address High, CRTC register 0Ch, and Start Address Low, CRTC register 0Dh). Together, these registers make up a 16-bit display-memory address at which the CRTC begins fetching data at the beginning of each video frame. Increasing the start address causes higher-memory areas of the virtual screen to be displayed. For example, the Start Address High register could be set to 80h and the Start Address Low register could be set to 00h in order to cause the display screen to reflect memory starting at offset 8000h in each plane, rather than at the default offset of 0.

The logical height of the virtual screen is defined by the amount of EGA memory available. As the EGA scans display memory for video data, it progresses from the start address toward higher memory one scan line at a time until the frame is completed. Consequently, if the start address is increased, lines farther toward the bottom of the virtual screen are displayed; in effect, the virtual screen appears to scroll up on the physical screen.

The logical width of the virtual screen is defined by the Offset register (CRTC register 13h), which allows redefinition of the number of words of display memory considered to make up one scan line. Normally, 40 words of display memory constitute a scan line; after the CRTC scans these 40 words for 640 pixels' worth of data, it advances 40 words from the start of that scan line to find the start of the next scan line in memory. This means that displayed scan lines are contiguous in memory. However, the Offset register can be set so that scan lines are logically wider (or narrower, for that matter) than their displayed width. The sample program sets the Offset register to 2Ah, making the logical width of the virtual screen 42 words, or $42 \times 2 \times 8 = 672$ pixels, as contrasted with the actual width of the high-resolution screen—40 words, or 640 pixels. The logical height of the virtual screen in the sample program is 384; this is accomplished simply by reserving 84×384 contiguous bytes of EGA memory for the virtual screen, where 84 is the virtual-screen width in bytes and 384 is the virtual-screen height in scan lines.

The start address is the key to panning around the virtual screen. The start address registers select the row of the virtual screen that maps to the top of the display; panning down a scan line requires only that the start address be increased by the logical scan-line width in bytes, which is equal to the Offset register times 2. The start-address registers select the column that maps to the left edge of the display as well, allowing horizontal panning, although in this case only relatively coarse, byte-sized adjustments—panning by eight pixels at a time—are supported.

Smooth horizontal panning is provided by the Horizontal Pel Panning register, AC register 13h, working in conjunction with the start address.

Up to seven pixels' worth of single-pixel panning of the displayed image to the left is performed by increasing the Horizontal Pel Panning register from 0 to 7. This exhausts the range of motion possible via the Horizontal Pel Panning register in most modes; the next pixels' worth of smooth panning is accomplished by incrementing the start address by 1 and resetting the Horizontal Pel Panning register to 0. Smooth horizontal panning should be viewed as a series of fine adjustments in the 8-pixel range between coarse, byte-sized adjustments.

A horizontal panning oddity: Alone among EGA modes, monochrome EGA text mode displays nine rather than eight dots for each time video data is read from display memory. Smooth panning in this mode requires

---

Fig. 1.2   *Organization of EGA memory in sample program. Space is reserved for two 672-by-384 virtual pages and for images of the ball and the blank.*

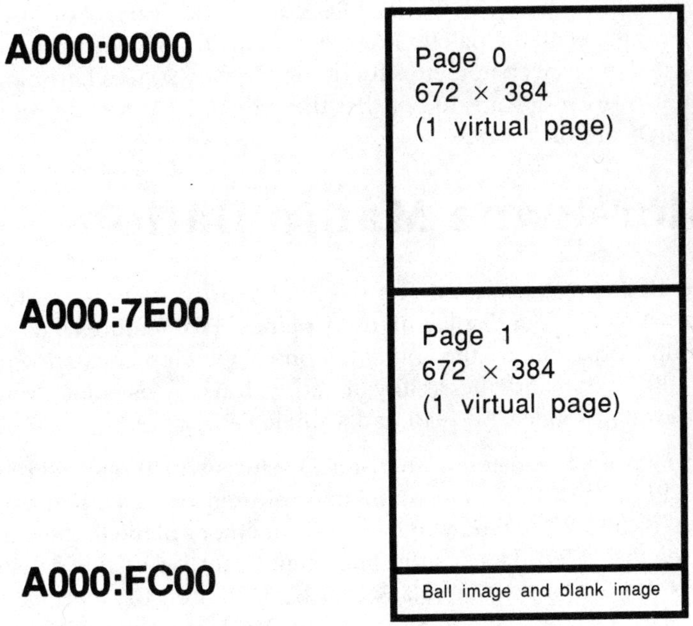

A000:0000

> Page 0
> 672 × 384
> (1 virtual page)

A000:7E00

> Page 1
> 672 × 384
> (1 virtual page)

A000:FC00

> Ball image and blank image

cycling the Horizontal Pel Panning register through the values 8, 0, 1, 2, 3, 4, 5, 6, and 7. The value 8, not 0, is the "no panning" setting.

The one annoying quirk about programming the AC is that when the AC Index register is set, only the lower five bits are used as the internal index. The next-most-significant bit, bit 5, controls the source of the video data sent to the monitor by the EGA. When bit 5 is set to 1, the output of the palette RAM, derived from display memory, controls the displayed pixels; this is normal operation. When bit 5 is 0, video data does not come from the palette RAM, and the screen becomes a solid color. The only time bit 5 of the AC Index register should be 0 is during the setting of a palette RAM register, since the CPU is able to write to palette RAM only when bit 5 is low. Immediately after setting palette RAM, however, 20h should be written to the AC Index register to restore normal video; at all other times, bit 5 should be set to 1.

By the way, palette RAM can be set via the BIOS video interrupt (interrupt 10h), function 10h. Whenever an EGA function can be performed reasonably well through a BIOS function, as it can in the case of setting palette RAM, it should be, both because there is no point in reinventing the wheel and because the BIOS may well mask incompatibilities between the IBM EGA and EGA clones. For instance, it is not easy to set all the palette RAM registers without causing momentary flicker, and the exact parameters for doing this vary somewhat among EGA clones. However, it's a safe bet that the palette RAM-setting routines in every BIOS are flicker free.

Color-Plane Manipulation

The EGA provides a powerful set of hardware-assist features for manipulating the four display-memory planes. Two features illustrated by the sample program are the ability to control which planes are written to by a CPU write and the ability to copy four bytes—one from each plane—with a single CPU read and a single CPU write.

The Map Mask register (SC register 2) selects which planes are written to by CPU writes. If bit 0 of the Map Mask register is 1, then each byte written by the CPU will be written to EGA memory plane 0, the plane that provides the video data for the least-significant bit of the palette RAM address. If bit 0 of the Map Mask register is 0, then CPU writes will not affect plane 0. Bits 1, 2, and 3 of the Map Mask register similarly control CPU access to planes 1, 2, and 3, respectively. Any of the 16 possible combinations of enabled and disabled planes can be selected. Beware, however, of writing to an area of memory that is not zeroed. Planes that are disabled by the Map Mask register are not altered by CPU writes, and so old and new images can mix on the screen, producing such unwanted color effects as, say, three planes from a written-over image mixing with one plane from a new image. The sample program solves this by ensuring that the memory written to is zeroed. A better way to clear memory is provided by the set/reset capabilities of the EGA, which I'll cover another time.

The sample program writes the image of a colored ball to EGA memory by enabling one plane at a time and writing the image of the ball for that plane. Each image is written to the same EGA addresses; only the destination plane, selected by the Map Mask register, is different. You might think of the ball's image as consisting of four colored overlays, which together make up a multicolored image. The sample program writes a blank image to EGA memory by enabling all planes and writing a block of bytes with value 0; each 0 byte is written to all four EGA planes simultaneously.

The images are written to a nondisplayed portion of EGA memory to take advantage of a useful EGA hardware feature: the ability to copy all four planes at once. As described above, four times as many reads and writes—one per plane—are required to copy a multicolored image into EGA memory as would be needed to draw the same image in the CGA's high-resolution mode, and several OUTs are needed as well. This causes unacceptably slow performance, all the more so because the wait states that occur on accesses to EGA memory make it very desirable to minimize display-memory accesses.

The solution is to take advantage of another EGA write mode: write mode 1, which is selected via bits 0 and 1 of the GC Mode register, GC register 5. (Be careful to set bits 2 through 7 properly for the current mode when setting bits 0 and 1.) By the way, the EGA is normally in write mode 0, the only mode we've discussed until now (I'll discuss write mode 2 in a later installment).

In write mode 1, a single CPU read loads the addressed byte from all four planes into the EGA's four internal latches, and a single CPU write writes the contents of the latches to the four planes. During the write, the byte written by the CPU is irrelevant.

The sample program uses write mode 1 to copy the images that were previously drawn to the high end of EGA memory into a desired area of display memory, all in a single block-copy operation. This is an excellent way to keep the number of reads, writes, and OUTs required to manipulate the EGA's display memory low enough to allow real-time drawing.

The Map Mask register can still mask out planes in write mode 1. All four planes are copied in the sample program, because the Map Mask register is still 0Fh from when the blank image was created.

The animated images appear to move somewhat jerkily, because they are byte-aligned and so must move a minimum of 8 pixels horizontally. This is easily solved by storing rotated versions of all images in EGA memory and then, in each instance, drawing the correct rotation for the pixel alignment at which the image is to be drawn.

Page Flipping

CGA graphics typically flicker or ripple, an unavoidable result of modifying display memory while it is being scanned for video data. The extra display memory of the EGA makes it possible to perform page flipping, which eliminates such problems. The basic premise of page flipping is that one area of display memory is displayed while another is being modified. The modifications never affect an area of memory as it is providing video data, and so no undesirable side effects occur. Once the modification is complete, the modified buffer is selected for display, causing the screen to change in a single frame. The other buffer is then available for modification.

Graphics-mode page flipping is not possible with the CGA, because the CGA's display memory is barely large enough to hold a single screen's bit map (a single page). However, the EGA has 64K per plane, enough to hold two pages and more even in high-resolution mode. (A high-resolution page is 80 × 350 = 28,000 bytes.) For page flipping, two nonoverlapping areas of display memory are needed. The sample program uses two 672-by-384 virtual pages, each 32,256 bytes long, one starting at A000:0000 and the other starting at A000:7E00. Flipping between the pages is as simple as setting the start-address registers to point to one display area or the other.

The timing of the switch between pages is crucial to achieving flicker-free animation. It is critical that the program never modify an area of display memory as that memory is providing video data. This means that the start address should be changed at some time when the frame after which the page flip is to occur, since the start address for a given frame is latched from the start-address registers at the end of the previous frame. The most readily available vertical-display status on the EGA is the vertical-sync-pulse status, available at bit 3 of the Input Status 1 register (addressed at 3BAh/3DAh). A logical approach to page flipping would seem to be to wait for the leading edge of the vertical sync pulse and then to set the start-address registers.

Unfortunately, the vertical-sync bit is not the ideal status to monitor for the end of the frame, since it doesn't begin until part way through the vertical-retrace period, after the start address has been latched into the linear-address-counting circuitry. If the sample program drew to the supposedly undisplayed page while the frame after the start address was being changed to the other page, flicker would occur; at this time, the new start address has not yet taken effect, and so that page is actually still being displayed. To avoid this, the sample program waits twice for the leading edge of the vertical sync pulse—once to be sure about when the starting-address registers are being set and once to allow the page flip to become effective.

Waiting for the sync pulse has the side effect of causing program execution to synchronize to the EGA's frame rate of 60 per second. In a program where all drawing can be done during a single frame time, this synchronization has the useful consequence of causing the program to execute at the same speed on an AT as on a PC.

As mentioned above, the vertical-sync bit is not a perfect status to monitor for the end of a frame. There is a way to detect the true beginning of the EGA's vertical-retrace period, via the vertical interrupt; for a sample implementation, see "Software Sprites for the IBM EGA and CGA," by Michael Abrash and Dan Illowsky, in *PC Tech Journal,* August 1986.

An important point illustrated by the sample program is that while the EGA's bit map is far larger and more versatile than other adapters', it is nonetheless a limited resource and must be used judiciously. The sample program uses EGA memory to store two 672-by-384 virtual pages, leaving only 1024 bytes free to store images. In this case, since the only images needed are a colored ball and a blank block with which to erase it, there is no problem, but many applications require dozens or hundreds of images. The tradeoffs between virtual-page size, page flipping, and image storage must always be kept in mind when designing programs for the EGA.

Just an Introduction

Finally, to see the program in Listing 1.1 run in 640-by-200, 16-color mode, comment out the HIRES_VIDEO_MODE equate. In 640-by-200 mode, the display screen is much smaller vertically relative to the virtual screen than in 640-by-350 mode, and so the smooth panning is far more pronounced.

That pretty well covers the important points of the sample EGA program in Listing 1.1. There are many EGA features we haven't even touched on, but the object of this first installment was to give you a feel for the variety of features available on the EGA, to convey the flexibility and complexity of the EGA's resources, and to point out how different from the CGA the EGA is. Starting with the next chapter, we'll begin to explore the EGA on a feature-by-feature basis.

EGA Clones

There are an amazing number of EGA clones on the market now. Most are built around the Chips and Technologies chip set, but several other chip sets are in use as well. The EGA clones sell for so much less than the IBM version that it's hard to imagine that anyone but the most conservative corporate purchaser would buy the real thing, particularly since all the clones seem to be more than adequately compatible with the IBM EGA.

The clones are not *exactly* like the IBM EGA, however. Some have bugs in the chip-set implementation, others have slightly different board layouts, and all have BIOS ROMs that differ to some extent from IBM's. Some manufacturers have also made a conscious decision to deviate slightly from the IBM standard to build a better board; for example, several manufacturers have provided modes with higher resolution than the EGA can muster.

What this means to the programmer is that EGA code should be tested on several EGA clones before being released. Given the tremendous popularity of the Chips and Technologies EGA-clone chip set, it is not enough to test programs only on the IBM EGA; I suspect that there are more C & T–based EGAs out there than IBM EGAs. In truth, the EGA standard is less standard than, say, the PC standard, because the PC is built with off-the-shelf hardware, not custom VLSI chips, and because the EGA video BIOS is twice as large as the entire PC BIOS. There's no perfect solution to the problem of EGA implementations that differ slightly, but broad testing is a reasonable substitute.

The Macro Assembler

The code I'll be presenting in "On Graphics" will generally be written in assembly language. I think C is a good development environment, but I'm in general agreement with Hal Hardenbergh's assertion that the best code (although not necessarily the easiest to write or the most reliable) is written in assembly language. This is especially true of graphics code for the 8086 family, given segments and the string instructions—and for real-time programming of a complex board like the EGA, there's really no other choice.

Before I'm deluged with protests from C devotees, let me add that the majority of my productive work is done in C. No programmer is immune to the laws of time, and C is simply a faster environment in which to develop, particularly when working on a programming team. I'd like to emphasize that there are many excellent C compilers available for the PC, some of which produce remarkably good code—and all of which are a damn sight more reliable and easier to develop with than the Microsoft Macro Assembler is. In fact, I think MASM is a serious impediment to assembly language programming on a computer that is inherently hard to program in assembly language. My experience with MASM began with version 1.0, compiling a DB that had a DUP factor of 0 into a block of 64 apparently random bytes, and matters have continued in pretty much the same vein ever since. Version 4.0 is much faster and has fewer bugs, but it's far from perfect. For one thing, macros don't always work the way they should, and it can be very difficult just to pin down the source of an error in a nested macro, let alone devise a workaround. For another, the whole structure of the assembly language is, to put it charitably, odd. I'd never seen a strongly typed assembler before MASM, and I hope I never see another one again. I've also never seen another assembler capable of generating a phase error—surely one of the most maddening and least useful error messages ever. I use STRUC and GROUP and OFFSET, and I know a slew of tricks like using LEA or DGROUP:OFFSET to get an accurate offset in a group, but is all this really necessary? In my opinion, MASM is somewhere between a true assembler and a high-level language, with most of the disadvantages of both.

One example, and then I'll get to the point. When a structure element is used in C, the compiler knows which structure definition that element is associated with and consequently has no trouble with elements of different structures that have the same names. For instance, LinkedListBlock.Status and DescriptorBlock.Status can coexist happily in the same module. Not so in assembly language—structure-element names translate into symbols, much as if an EQU had been performed, and the second structure element with a given name produces a redefinition error. As a result, I find myself giving elements names like LLBStatus and DBStatus—a far cry from the power of C structures.

So, what's the point? Well, I'm willing to bet that someone out there knows a way around the STRUC problem I've just described. Perhaps it's not a problem at all and I've simply misunderstood the Macro Assembler manual, or perhaps there's a good workaround. Whether this particular problem is solvable or not, many tricks are being used in similar situations to wring utility out of MASM. Like it or not, MASM is pretty much it for assembly language development for the PC family. True, there are other assemblers, but all my existing assembler code and most of the tools and high-level languages I use are designed to work with MASM, and every time I try to leave MASM I run into incompatibilities that send me running back to the old standard. Since MASM is so important, I'll be writing about the MASM tricks I know, and I'd appreciate it if you'd write in and share your MASM experiences with *PJ*'s readers as well.

Two unsolved MASM puzzles to start things off:

1. I've never figured out how to use STRUC to define negative offsets from BP in a stack frame. C routinely addresses passed parameters at positive offsets from BP and dynamic storage at negative offsets, but since STRUC seems to generate only positive offsets, I've had to put dynamic storage at positive offsets and set BP only after dynamic storage has been allocated. Although this works, it effectively halves the number of bytes that can be addressed with single-byte offsets from BP, potentially increasing code size and execution time.

2. While developing "ROMable" code, I needed to force certain code to be at a certain offset (say offset 2000h) in the final COM file. My thought was to use something like

```
DB     (2000h-$) DUP 0
```

to force the code to assemble at the desired location. Alas, the assembler can handle only constants in this context, and "$" is not a constant. I tried a variety of other approaches, such as ORGing to the offset, but couldn't get the assembler to produce the desired result. I ended up disassembling the file, calculating the needed offset, and hard-wiring it into a DB—which was fine until the next time I changed the code and forgot to adjust the DUP value in the DB. Does anyone know how to force code to assemble at an absolute location?

So. If you know the answers, let us know. If you've got bugs and workarounds of your own, let us know. We MASM developers can use all the help we can get.

Coming Up

Next time, I'll look into the hardware assistance the EGA provides the CPU during display-memory access. There are four latches and four ALUs in those chips, along with some useful masks and comparators; it should be interesting.

See you then.

Listing 1.1

```
; Sample EGA program.
; Animates four balls bouncing around a playfield by using
; page flipping. Playfield is panned smoothly both horizontally
; and vertically.
; Assembled with MASM 4.0, linked with LINK 3.51.
; By Michael Abrash, 11/2/86.
; Updated 6/24/89.
;
stackseg          segment para stack 'STACK'
        db        512 dup(?)
stackseg          ends
;
HIRES_VIDEO_MODE        equ   0          ;define for 640x350 video mode
                                         ; comment out for 640x200 mode
VIDEO_SEGMENT     equ   0a000h           ;display memory segment for
                                         ; true EGA graphics modes
LOGICAL_SCREEN_WIDTH    equ   672/8      ;width in bytes and height in scan
LOGICAL_SCREEN_HEIGHT   equ   384        ; lines of the virtual screen
                                         ; we'll work with
PAGE0             equ   0          ;flag for page 0 when page flipping
PAGE1             equ   1          ;flag for page 1 when page flipping
PAGE0_OFFSET      equ   0          ;start offset of page 0 in EGA memory
PAGE1_OFFSET      equ   LOGICAL_SCREEN_WIDTH * LOGICAL_SCREEN_HEIGHT
                                   ;start offset of page 1 (both pages
                                   ; are 672x384 virtual screens)
BALL_WIDTH        equ   24/8       ;width of ball in display memory bytes
BALL_HEIGHT       equ   24         ;height of ball in scan lines
BLANK_OFFSET      equ   PAGE1_OFFSET * 2        ;start of blank image
                                               ; in EGA memory
BALL_OFFSET       equ   BLANK_OFFSET + (BALL_WIDTH * BALL_HEIGHT)
                                   ;start offset of ball image in EGA memory
NUM_BALLS         equ   4          ;number of balls to animate
;
; EGA register equates.
;
SC_INDEX          equ   3c4h       ;SC index register
MAP_MASK          equ   2          ;SC map mask register
GC_INDEX          equ   3ceh       ;GC index register
GC_MODE           equ   5          ;GC mode register
```

Listing 1.1 continues

Listing 1.1 *continued*

```
CRTC_INDEX         equ    03d4h    ;CRTC index register in color modes
START_ADDRESS_HIGH equ    0ch      ;CRTC start address high byte
START_ADDRESS_LOW  equ    0dh      ;CRTC start address low byte
CRTC_OFFSET        equ    13h      ;CRTC offset register
STATUS_REGISTER_1  equ    03dah    ;EGA status register in color modes
VSYNC_MASK         equ    08h      ;vertical sync bit in status register 1
AC_INDEX           equ    03c0h    ;AC index register
HPELPAN            equ    20h OR 13h    ;AC horizontal pel panning
                                        ; register (bit 5 is 1 to keep
                                        ; palette RAM addressing on)
dseg    segment para common 'DATA'
CurrentPage              db     PAGE1            ;page to draw to
CurrentPageOffset        dw     PAGE1_OFFSET
;
; Four plane's worth of multicolored ball image.
;
BallPlane0Image label   byte             ;blue plane (plane 0) image
        db      000h, 03ch, 000h, 001h, 0ffh, 080h
        db      007h, 0ffh, 0e0h, 00fh, 0ffh, 0f0h
        db      4 * 3 dup(000h)
        db      07fh, 0ffh, 0feh, 0ffh, 0ffh, 0ffh
        db      0ffh, 0ffh, 0ffh, 0ffh, 0ffh, 0ffh
        db      4 * 3 dup(000h)
        db      07fh, 0ffh, 0feh, 03fh, 0ffh, 0fch
        db      03fh, 0ffh, 0fch, 01fh, 0ffh, 0f8h
        db      4 * 3 dup(000h)
BallPlane1Image label   byte             ;green plane (plane 1) image
        db      4 * 3 dup(000h)
        db      01fh, 0ffh, 0f8h, 03fh, 0ffh, 0fch
        db      03fh, 0ffh, 0fch, 07fh, 0ffh, 0feh
        db      07fh, 0ffh, 0feh, 0ffh, 0ffh, 0ffh
        db      0ffh, 0ffh, 0ffh, 0ffh, 0ffh, 0ffh
        db      8 * 3 dup(000h)
        db      00fh, 0ffh, 0f0h, 007h, 0ffh, 0e0h
        db      001h, 0ffh, 080h, 000h, 03ch, 000h
BallPlane2Image label   byte             ;red plane (plane 2) image
        db      12 * 3 dup(000h)
        db      0ffh, 0ffh, 0ffh, 0ffh, 0ffh, 0ffh
        db      0ffh, 0ffh, 0ffh, 07fh, 0ffh, 0feh
        db      07fh, 0ffh, 0feh, 03fh, 0ffh, 0fch
        db      03fh, 0ffh, 0fch, 01fh, 0ffh, 0f8h
        db      00fh, 0ffh, 0f0h, 007h, 0ffh, 0e0h
        db      001h, 0ffh, 080h, 000h, 03ch, 000h
BallPlane3Image label   byte             ;intensity on for all planes,
                                         ; to produce high-intensity colors
                                         ; (plane 3)
        db      000h, 03ch, 000h, 001h, 0ffh, 080h
        db      007h, 0ffh, 0e0h, 00fh, 0ffh, 0f0h
        db      01fh, 0ffh, 0f8h, 03fh, 0ffh, 0fch
        db      03fh, 0ffh, 0fch, 07fh, 0ffh, 0feh
        db      07fh, 0ffh, 0feh, 0ffh, 0ffh, 0ffh
        db      0ffh, 0ffh, 0ffh, 0ffh, 0ffh, 0ffh
        db      0ffh, 0ffh, 0ffh, 0ffh, 0ffh, 0ffh
        db      0ffh, 0ffh, 0ffh, 07fh, 0ffh, 0feh
        db      07fh, 0ffh, 0feh, 03fh, 0ffh, 0fch
        db      03fh, 0ffh, 0fch, 01fh, 0ffh, 0f8h
        db      00fh, 0ffh, 0f0h, 007h, 0ffh, 0e0h
        db      001h, 0ffh, 080h, 000h, 03ch, 000h
```

Listing 1.1 *continues*

Listing 1.1 *continued*

```
;
BallX           dw      15, 50, 40, 70          ;array of ball x coords
BallY           dw      40, 200, 110, 300       ;array of ball y coords
LastBallX       dw      15, 50, 40, 70          ;previous ball x coords
LastBallY       dw      40, 100, 160, 30        ;previous ball y coords
BallXInc        dw      1, 1, 1, 1              ;x move factors for ball
BallYInc        dw      8, 8, 8, 8             ;y move factors for ball
BallRep         dw      1, 1, 1, 1             ;# times to keep moving
                                                ; ball according to
                                                ; current increments
BallControl     dw      Ball0Control, Ball1Control      ;pointers to cur-
                dw      Ball2Control, Ball3Control      ; rent locations
                                                        ; in ball control
                                                        ; strings

BallControlString       dw      Ball0Control, Ball1Control ;pointers to
                        dw      Ball2Control, Ball3Control ; start of
                                                           ; ball control
                                                           ; strings
;
; Ball control strings.
;
Ball0Control    label   word
        dw      10, 1, 4, 10, -1, 4, 10, -1, -4, 10, 1, -4, 0
Ball1Control    label   word
        dw      12, -1, 1, 28, -1, -1, 12, 1, -1, 28, 1, 1, 0
Ball2Control    label   word
        dw      20, 0, -1, 40, 0, 1, 20, 0, -1, 0
Ball3Control    label   word
        dw      8, 1, 0, 52, -1, 0, 44, 1, 0, 0
;
; Panning control string.
;
ifdef HIRES_VIDEO_MODE
PanningControlString    dw      32, 1, 0, 34, 0, 1, 32, -1, 0, 34, 0,
                                        -1, 0
else
PanningControlString    dw      32, 1, 0, 184, 0, 1, 32, -1, 0, 184,
                                        0, -1, 0
endif
PanningControl  dw      PanningControlString    ;pointer to current
                                                ; location in panning
                                                ; control string

PanningRep      dw      1              ;# times to pan according to current
                                       ; panning increments
PanningXInc     dw      1              ;x panning factor
PanningYInc     dw      0              ;y panning factor
HPan            db      0              ;horizontal pel panning setting
PanningStartOffset dw   0              ;start offset adjustment to produce
                                       ; vertical panning & coarse
                                       ; horizontal panning

dseg    ends
;
; Macro to set indexed register P2 of chip with index register
; at P1 to AL.
;
SETREG  macro   P1, P2
        mov     dx,P1
        mov     ah,al
```

Listing 1.1 *continues*

Listing 1.1 *continued*

```
        mov     al,P2
        out     dx,ax
        endm
;
cseg    segment para public 'CODE'
        assume  cs:cseg, ds:dseg
start   proc    near
        mov     ax,dseg
        mov     ds,ax
;
; Select graphics mode.
;
ifdef HIRES_VIDEO_MODE
        mov     ax,010h
else
        mov     ax,0eh
endif
        int     10h
;
; ES always points to EGA memory.
;
        mov     ax,VIDEO_SEGMENT
        mov     es,ax
;
; Draw border around playfield in both pages.
;
        mov     di,PAGE0_OFFSET
        call    DrawBorder      ;page 0 border
        mov     di,PAGE1_OFFSET
        call    DrawBorder      ;page 1 border
;
; Draw all four plane's worth of the ball to undisplayed EGA memory.
;
        mov     al,01h          ;enable plane 0
        SETREG  SC_INDEX, MAP_MASK
        mov     si,offset BallPlane0Image
        mov     di,BALL_OFFSET
        mov     cx,BALL_WIDTH * BALL_HEIGHT
        rep movsb
        mov     al,02h          ;enable plane 1
        SETREG  SC_INDEX, MAP_MASK
        mov     si,offset BallPlane1Image
        mov     di,BALL_OFFSET
        mov     cx,BALL_WIDTH * BALL_HEIGHT
        rep movsb
        mov     al,04h          ;enable plane 2
        SETREG  SC_INDEX, MAP_MASK
        mov     si,offset BallPlane2Image
        mov     di,BALL_OFFSET
        mov     cx,BALL_WIDTH * BALL_HEIGHT
        rep movsb
        mov     al,08h          ;enable plane 3
        SETREG  SC_INDEX, MAP_MASK
        mov     si,offset BallPlane3Image
        mov     di,BALL_OFFSET
        mov     cx,BALL_WIDTH * BALL_HEIGHT
        rep movsb
;
```

Listing 1.1 *continues*

Listing 1.1 *continued*

```
; Draw a blank image the size of the ball to undisplayed EGA memory.
;
        mov     al,0fh                  ;enable all memory planes,
        SETREG  SC_INDEX, MAP_MASK      ; since the blank has to
        mov     di,BLANK_OFFSET         ; erase all planes
        mov     cx,BALL_WIDTH * BALL_HEIGHT
        sub     al,al
        rep stosb
;
; Set EGA to write mode 1, for block copying ball and blank images.
;
        mov     al,1
        SETREG  GC_INDEX, GC_MODE
;
; Set EGA offset register in words to define logical screen width.
;
        mov     al,LOGICAL_SCREEN_WIDTH / 2
        SETREG  CRTC_INDEX, CRTC_OFFSET
;
; Move the balls by erasing each ball, moving it, and
; redrawing it, then switching pages when they're all moved.
;
BallAnimationLoop:
        mov     bx,( NUM_BALLS * 2 ) - 2
EachBallLoop:
;
; Erase old image of ball in this page (at location from one more
; earlier).
;
        mov     si,BLANK_OFFSET ;point to blank image
        mov     cx,[LastBallX+bx]
        mov     dx,[LastBallY+bx]
        call    DrawBall
;
; Set new last ball location.
;
        mov     ax,[BallX+bx]
        mov     [LastballX+bx],ax
        mov     ax,[BallY+bx]
        mov     [LastballY+bx],ax
;
; Change the ball movement values if it's time to do so.
;
        dec     [BallRep+bx]            ;has current repeat factor
                                        ; run out?
        jnz     MoveBall
        mov     si,[BallControl+bx]     ;it's time to change movement
                                        ; values
        lodsw                           ;get new repeat factor from
                                        ; control string
        and     ax,ax                   ;at end of control string?
        jnz     SetNewMove
        mov     si,[BallControlString+bx]       ;reset control string
        lodsw                           ;get new repeat factor
SetNewMove:
        mov     [BallRep+bx],ax         ;set new movement repeat factor
        lodsw                           ;set new x movement increment
        mov     [BallXInc+bx],ax
```

Listing 1.1 *continues*

Listing 1.1 continued

```
        lodsw                              ;set new y movement increment
        mov     [BallYInc+bx],ax
        mov     [BallControl+bx],si        ;save new control string pointer
;
; Move the ball.
;
MoveBall:
        mov     ax,[BallXInc+bx]
        add     [BallX+bx],ax              ;move in x direction
        mov     ax,[BallYInc+bx]
        add     [BallY+bx],ax              ;move in y direction
;
; Draw ball at new location.
;
        mov     si,BALL_OFFSET   ;point to ball's image
        mov     cx,[BallX+bx]
        mov     dx,[BallY+bx]
        call    DrawBall
;
        dec     bx
        dec     bx
        jns     EachBallLoop
;
; Pan and flip displayed page to the one we've been working on, as soon
; as leading edge of vertical sync comes around.
;
        call    WaitVSync
;
; Perform whatever panning's in effect.
;
        call    AdjustPanning
;
; Flip to new page by changing start address.
;
        mov     ax,[CurrentPageOffset]
        add     ax,[PanningStartOffset]
        push    ax
        SETREG  CRTC_INDEX, START_ADDRESS_LOW
        pop     ax
        mov     al,ah
        SETREG  CRTC_INDEX, START_ADDRESS_HIGH
;
; Wait for sync again so the new start address has a chance
; to take effect.
;
        call    WaitVSync
;
; Set horizontal panning now, just as new start address takes effect.
;
        mov     al,[HPan]
        mov     dx,STATUS_REGISTER_1
        in      al,dx                      ;reset AC addressing to index reg
        mov     dx,AC_INDEX                ;note from 1989: word OUTs to the
        mov     al,HPELPAN                 ; AC index and data registers
        out     dx,al                      ; don't work properly on VGAs,
        mov     al,[HPan]                  ; so two byte OUTs are used here
        out     dx,al
;
```

Listing 1.1 continues

Listing 1.1 continued

```
; Flip the page to draw to the undisplayed page.
;
        xor     [CurrentPage],1
        jnz     IsPage1
        mov     [CurrentPageOffset],PAGE0_OFFSET
        jmp     short EndFlipPage
IsPage1:
        mov     [CurrentPageOffset],PAGE1_OFFSET
EndFlipPage:
;
; Exit if a key's been hit.
;
        mov     ah,1
        int     16h
        jnz     Done
        jmp     BallAnimationLoop
;
; Finished, clear key, reset screen mode and exit.
;
Done:
        mov     ah,0      ;clear key
        int     16h
;
        mov     ax,3      ;reset to text mode
        int     10h
;
        mov     ah,4ch    ;exit to DOS
        int     21h
;
start   endp
;
; Routine to draw a ball-sized image to all planes, copying from
; offset SI in EGA memory to offset CX,DX (x,y) in EGA memory in
; the current page.
;
DrawBall        proc    near
        mov     ax,LOGICAL_SCREEN_WIDTH
        mul     dx        ;offset of start of top image scan line
        add     ax,cx     ;offset of upper left of image
        add     ax,[CurrentPageOffset]   ;offset of start of page
        mov     di,ax
        mov     bp,BALL_HEIGHT
        push    ds
        push    es
        pop     ds        ;move from EGA memory to EGA memory
DrawBallLoop:
        push    di
        mov     cx,BALL_WIDTH
        rep movsb         ;draw a scan line of image
        pop     di
        add     di,LOGICAL_SCREEN_WIDTH ;point to next destination
                                        ; scan line
        dec     bp
        jnz     DrawBallLoop
        pop     ds
        ret
DrawBall        endp
;
```

Listing 1.1 continues

Listing 1.1 *continued*

```
; Wait for the leading edge of vertical sync pulse.
;
WaitVSync       proc    near
        mov     dx,STATUS_REGISTER_1
WaitNotVSyncLoop:
        in      al,dx
        and     al,VSYNC_MASK
        jnz     WaitNotVSyncLoop
WaitVSyncLoop:
        in      al,dx
        and     al,VSYNC_MASK
        jz      WaitVSyncLoop
        ret
WaitVSync       endp
;
; Perform horizontal/vertical panning.
;
AdjustPanning   proc    near
        dec     [PanningRep]        ;time to get new panning values?
        jnz     DoPan
        mov     si,[PanningControl]     ;point to current location in
                                        ; panning control string
        lodsw                           ;get panning repeat factor
        and     ax,ax                   ;at end of panning control string?
        jnz     SetnewPanValues
        mov     si,offset PanningControlString  ;reset to start of string
        lodsw                           ;get panning repeat factor
SetNewPanValues:
        mov     [PanningRep],ax         ;set new panning repeat value
        lodsw
        mov     [PanningXInc],ax        ;horizontal panning value
        lodsw
        mov     [PanningYInc],ax        ;vertical panning value
        mov     [PanningControl],si     ;save current location in panning
                                        ; control string
;
; Pan according to panning values.
;
DoPan:
        mov     ax,[PanningXInc]        ;horizontal panning
        and     ax,ax
        js      PanLeft                 ;negative means pan left
        jz      CheckVerticalPan
        mov     al,[HPan]
        inc     al                      ;pan right; if pel pan reaches
        cmp     al,8                    ; 8, it's time to move to the
        jb      SetHPan                 ; next byte with a pel pan of 0
        sub     al,al                   ; and a start offset that's one
        inc     [PanningStartOffset]    ; higher
        jmp     short SetHPan
PanLeft:
        mov     al,[HPan]
        dec     al                      ;pan left; if pel pan reaches -1,
        jns     SetHPan                 ; it's time to move to the next
        mov     al,7                    ; byte with a pel pan of 7 and a
        dec     [PanningStartOffset]    ; start offset that's one lower
SetHPan:
        mov     [HPan],al               ;save new pel pan value
```

Listing 1.1 *continues*

Listing 1.1 *continued*

```
CheckVerticalPan:
        mov     ax,[PanningYInc]         ;vertical panning
        and     ax,ax
        js      PanUp                    ;negative means pan up
        jz      EndPan
        add     [PanningStartOffset],LOGICAL_SCREEN_WIDTH
                                         ;pan down by advancing the start
                                         ; address by a scan line

        jmp     short EndPan
PanUp:
        sub     [PanningStartOffset],LOGICAL_SCREEN_WIDTH
                                         ;pan up by retarding the start
                                         ; address by a scan line

EndPan:
        ret
;
; Draw textured border around playfield that starts at DI.
;
DrawBorder      proc    near
;
; Draw the left border.
;
        push    di
        mov     cx,LOGICAL_SCREEN_HEIGHT / 16
DrawLeftBorderLoop:
        mov     al,0ch          ;select red color for block
        call    DrawBorderBlock
        add     di,LOGICAL_SCREEN_WIDTH * 8
        mov     al,0eh          ;select yellow color for block
        call    DrawBorderBlock
        add     di,LOGICAL_SCREEN_WIDTH * 8
        loop    DrawLeftBorderLoop
        pop     di
;
; Draw the left border.
;
        push    di
        add     di,LOGICAL_SCREEN_WIDTH - 1
        mov     cx,LOGICAL_SCREEN_HEIGHT / 16
DrawRightBorderLoop:
        mov     al,0eh          ;select yellow color for block
        call    DrawBorderBlock
        add     di,LOGICAL_SCREEN_WIDTH * 8
        mov     al,0ch          ;select red color for block
        call    DrawBorderBlock
        add     di,LOGICAL_SCREEN_WIDTH * 8
        loop    DrawRightBorderLoop
        pop     di
;
; Draw the top border.
;
        push    di
        mov     cx,(LOGICAL_SCREEN_WIDTH - 2) / 2
DrawTopBorderLoop:
        inc     di
        mov     al,0eh          ;select yellow color for block
        call    DrawBorderBlock
        inc     di
```

Listing 1.1 *continues*

Listing 1.1 continued

```
        mov     al,0ch          ;select red color for block
        call    DrawBorderBlock
        loop    DrawTopBorderLoop
        pop     di
;
; Draw the bottom border.
;
        add     di,(LOGICAL_SCREEN_HEIGHT - 8) * LOGICAL_SCREEN_WIDTH
        mov     cx,(LOGICAL_SCREEN_WIDTH - 2) / 2
DrawBottomBorderLoop:
        inc     di
        mov     al,0ch           ;select red color for block
        call    DrawBorderBlock
        inc     di
        mov     al,0eh           ;select yellow color for block
        call    DrawBorderBlock
        loop    DrawBottomBorderLoop
        ret
DrawBorder      endp
;
; Draws an 8x8 border block in color in AL at location DI.
; DI preserved.
;
DrawBorderBlock proc    near
        push    di
        SETREG  SC_INDEX, MAP_MASK
        mov     al,0ffh
        rept 8
        stosb
        add     di,LOGICAL_SCREEN_WIDTH - 1
        endm
        pop     di
        ret
DrawBorderBlock endp
AdjustPanning   endp
cseg    ends
        end     start
```

CHAPTER 2

Parallel Processing with the EGA

For me, this is the chapter in which the complexity of the EGA truly hits home. While the first chapter skimmed over a great many EGA features without making any one feature seem too complex, this chapter covers just one feature—the 32-bit processing capabilities of the ALUs—in detail.

The ALUs are just one part of the EGAs data-writing path—a small part of the overall function of the adapter—and yet they require the bulk of an installment and a fairly complex listing all to themselves! The EGA is a complex adapter indeed, too complex to grasp all at once. It must be tackled piece by piece—and the ALUs, which lie smack in the middle of one of the EGA's primary data paths, give us an excellent place to begin.

In this chapter, I also start looking at the graphics marketplace as a whole, in what was intended to be an ongoing feature. Instead, it proved to be only an occasional feature. There was never enough room to discuss all the programming details I wanted to cover and never room for as much code as I would have liked to present—and well-explained, working code has always been the core of "On Graphics."

There are a number of updates to be made to Chapter 2 from the perspective of 1989:

First, TI's 34010 has beaten out Intel's 82786 as the most-used graphics coprocessor, and the IBM 8514/A has entered the fray, with yet-to-be-determined results. As I write this, the only universally accepted standardization at resolutions above 640 by 480 is the 800-by-600

SuperVGA standard, built around stretched VGAs, just as 640-by-480 EEGA standard was built around stretched EGAs. The era of generally available adequate performance through device drivers is still around the corner—although it is closer now than then, what with the increasing use of graphics coprocessors, the debut of Presentation Manager, and the imminent release of Windows 3.0.

Second, regarding the future of PC graphics, I batted about .500. As it turned out, IBM's next graphics standard, the VGA, offered a good deal of EGA compatibility and largely EEGA-compatible 640-by-480 resolution and took the PC world by storm. EGA software did indeed retain its value, as I predicted, but, contrary to my prophesying, IBM showed that it can still set a standard.

Third, I never have figured out how to continue a long macro statement on the next line. If you have the answer, please let me know!

Fourth, I mention Bresenham's line-drawing algorithm in this chapter. For a detailed explanation and implementation, see Chapter 12.

Finally, although I got some interesting responses to my questions about true code performance, I was never able to get fully satisfactory answers. I ultimately resolved the situation by developing my own timing tools and analyzing the components of code performance myself. The timing software can be found in "Measuring Performance" (*Programmer's Journal* 7.4, July/August 1989), and both the software and an exploration of high-performance programming techniques are presented in my book *The Zen of Assembler,* published by Scott, Foresman and Company.

Installment 2: In which we vastly improve performance by learning to handle EGA memory 32 bits at a time.

This installment's title refers to the ability of the powerful EGA chip set to manipulate up to four bytes of display memory—one byte from each of the four planes—at once. The EGA provides four ALUs (arithmetic-logic units) to assist the CPU during display-memory writes, and this hardware is a tremendous resource in the task of manipulating the EGA's massive bit map. The ALUs are actually only one part of the surprisingly complex data-flow architecture of the EGA, but since they're involved in almost all memory-access operations, they're a good place to begin.

There's more to cover, too. Starting with this installment, I'm occasionally going to discuss interesting graphics hardware and software I've come across recently. Since most *PJ* readers are developers, I'm not going to do traditional reviews but, rather, will discuss products' strengths and weaknesses from the perspective of a developer who's deciding what products to support or develop for. In this installment, rather than examining specific products, I'm going to report on the state of PC graphics as observed at Fall COMDEX 1986.

COMDEX

The overriding graphics-related impression from Fall COMDEX 1986 was that the EGA is *the* standard for PC graphics. Virtually no one showed a CGA-level product, and just about all demos were run on EGAs or more-powerful boards. One AT-compatible portable was shown; it had an EGA built into the motherboard. Many more built-in EGAs will surely follow, especially given the one- and two-chip EGA chip sets that are hitting the market. In short, imperfect as it may be, the EGA is the current standard for mass-market PC graphics. (On a related note, inexpensive ATs abounded at COMDEX. The widespread use of ATs will help greatly in overcoming the relatively sluggish performance of the EGA.)

Given that the EGA is today's standard, the big question is, clearly, "What's next?" One answer seems to be what many people are calling the EEGA, which is an EGA with higher-resolution modes than the IBM board—typically 640 by 480, but ranging in some cases to as high as 800 pixels in width and 500 pixels in height. Several EEGA boards were shown at COMDEX, and others have already been announced.

There's nothing revolutionary about the EEGA—it's a natural outgrowth of the development of EGA chip sets that can run faster than IBM's. EEGA hi-res modes are identical to the normal EGA 640-by-350 mode, with 16 of 64 colors available, except that the dot clock speed is higher and the portion of display memory used for video data at any given time is larger. (In 640-by-480 mode, for example, the active bit-map size is over 37K; by contrast, 640-by-350 mode requires less than 28K.)

EEGAs are significant for several reasons: First, they provide enough resolution for emulation of many popular graphics terminals. Second, the market is being flooded with monitors that support the higher resolutions of these boards, such as the NEC MultiSync and Sony MultiScan. Third, 640-by-480 mode provides about a one-to-one aspect ratio (the ratio that helps make Macintosh graphics look so good). Finally, support of EEGAs requires very little new programming, since all the registers and memory addresses that are used in standard EGA programming are used by EEGAs as well; software should become available for them quickly.

EEGAs are hardly a giant step forward, but they are a very practical move toward high-resolution graphics. The bad news is that with a 30-percent larger bit map to manipulate, software running on the EEGA will be slower than software running on the EGA. Among other implications, this makes it imperative that EGA software developers write the highest-performance code possible.

Not all the graphics at COMDEX were EGA-related, though—not by a long shot. There were a number of IBM Professional Graphics Controller (PGC)–compatible systems (in fact, Zenith was demonstrating its 80386-based system with a Turbo PGC, which was interesting, since virtually none of the speed of the graphics was attributable to the 386), there were systems built around both the Intel 82786 and the TI 34010 (which I'm planning to look at soon), and there were proprietary systems with resolutions up to 1K by 1K. Unfortunately, there were no signs of standardization for graphics above the EEGA level. I suppose standardization will have to wait for either the TI or Intel chip to become a mass-market success (or some other chip—it *will* happen eventually). Another possibility is that either or both chips may prove to be powerful enough to support good performance through device drivers, in which case we may (finally!) be near the era of true device independence.

IBM could, of course, set the next graphics standard with its rumored Turbo EGA or with another graphics adapter. However, it doesn't seem to be as easy as it used to be for IBM to set standards: The PGC was hardly an unqualified success, and the EGA became a standard only because third-party manufacturers imitated the technology and brought the price way down. It's not at all clear that if IBM were to come out with a new adapter tomorrow, it would have much impact, particularly if the technology were sufficiently proprietary that other manufacturers couldn't clone it. For the near future, at least, fragmentation seems to be the nature of the high end of the PC graphics market.

On the bright side, many of the high-end display adapters featured EGA compatibility. Whatever direction the graphics market takes in the next few years, it's safe to say that EGA software will retain its value, particularly if that software can support 640-by-480 graphics.

EGA Programming:
ALUs and Latches

I'm going to begin our detailed tour of the EGA at the heart of the flow of data through the EGA: the four ALUs built into the EGA's Graphics

Controller (GC) chips. The ALUs (one for each display-memory plane) are capable of ORing, ANDing, and XORing CPU data and display-memory data together, as well as masking off some or all of the bits in the data from affecting the final result. All the ALUs perform the same logical operation at any given time, but each ALU operates on a different display-memory byte. (Recall that the EGA has four display-memory planes, with one byte in each plane at any given display-memory address. All four display-memory bytes operated on are read from the same address, but each ALU operates on a byte that was read from a different plane and writes the result to that plane.) This arrangement allows four display-memory bytes to be modified by a single CPU write (which must normally be preceded by a single CPU read, as we will see). The benefits are clear: If the CPU had to select each of the four planes in turn via OUTs and perform the four logical operations itself, the performance of EGA software would slow to a crawl.

Figure 2.1 is a simplified depiction of data flow around the ALUs. Each ALU has a matching latch, which holds the byte read from the corresponding plane during the last CPU read from display memory, even if that particular plane wasn't the plane that the CPU actually read last. (Only one byte can normally be read by the CPU with a single display-memory read; the plane supplying the byte is selected by the Read Map register, GC register 4. However, the same address from all four planes is always read when the CPU reads display memory, and those four bytes are held in their respective latches.)

Each ALU logically combines the byte written by the CPU and the byte stored in the matching latch, according to the setting of bits 3 and 4 of the Data Rotate register, GC register 3, (and the Bit Mask register, GC register 8, which I'll cover next time), and then writes the result to display memory. It is *most* important to understand that neither ALU operand comes directly from display memory. The temptation is to think of the ALUs as combining CPU data and the contents of the display memory address being written to, but they actually combine CPU data with the contents of the *last display-memory location read,* which need not be the same location as the one being written to. The most common application of the ALUs is indeed to modify a given display-memory location, but doing so requires a read from that location to load the latches before the write that modifies it. Omission of the read results in a write operation that logically combines CPU data with whatever data happens to be in the latches from the last read, which is normally undesirable.

Occasionally, however, the independence of the latches from the display-memory location being written to can be used to great advantage. The latches can be used to perform four-byte-at-a-time (one byte from each plane) block copying; in this application, the latches are loaded with a read from the source area and written unmodified to the destination area. The latches can be written unmodified in one of two ways: by selecting write mode 1 (for an example of this, see Chapter 1), or via the Bit Mask register.

The latches can also be used to draw fairly complex area-fill patterns, with a different bit pattern used to fill each plane. The mechanism for this is as follows. Generate the desired pattern across all planes at any display memory address; this requires a separate write operation for each plane so that each plane's byte will be unique. Read that memory address to store the pattern in the latches. The contents of the latches can now be

Fig. 2.1   *Simplified data flow around the Arithmetic Logic Units (ALUs) in the graphics controller.*

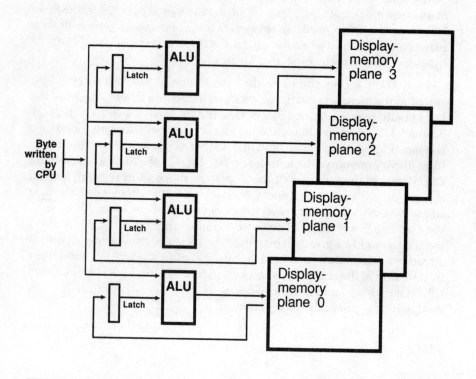

written to memory any number of times by using either write mode 1 or the bit mask, since the latches will not change until a read is performed. If the fill pattern can use the same bit pattern for all planes, filling can be performed more easily by simply writing the pattern to up to four planes at once, using the Map Mask register to control the drawing color. In some applications, the Set/Reset registers are extremely effective for one- and two-color fills.

The sample program in Listing 2.1 [presented at the end of this chapter] fills the screen with horizontal bars and then illustrates the operation of each of the four ALU logical functions by writing four sets of four 80-by-80 boxes—filled with solid, empty, and vertical and horizontal bar patterns and stacked vertically—over that background using each of the ALU logical functions in turn, one function per set of boxes. When observing the output of the sample program, it is important to remember that all four sets of boxes are drawn with *exactly* the same code—only the ALU logical function that is in effect differs from box to box.

You will observe that all graphics in the sample program are done in black and white (by always writing to all planes); this shows the operation of the ALUs most clearly. Selective enabling of planes would produce color effects, in which case the operation of the ALU logical functions would have to be evaluated on a plane-by-plane basis, because only the planes enabled by the Map Mask register at any given time would be affected.

Logical function 0, data unmodified, is the standard mode of operation of the ALUs. In this mode, the CPU data is combined with the latched data by ignoring the latched data entirely. Expressed as a logical function, this could be considered CPU data ANDed with 1 (or ORed with 0). This is the mode to use whenever you want to place CPU data into display memory, replacing the previous contents entirely. It may occur to you that there is no need to latch display memory at all when the data-unmodified function is selected. In the sample program, that is true, but if the bit mask is being used, the latches must be loaded even for the data-unmodified function, as I'll discuss in the next installment.

Logical functions 1 through 3 cause the CPU data to be ANDed, ORed, and XORed, respectively, with latch data, Of these, XOR is the most useful, because exclusive-ORing is a traditional way to perform animation. The uses of the AND and OR logical functions are less obvious. AND can be used to mask a blank area into display memory or to mask off those portions of a form that don't overlap an existing display-memory image. OR could conceivably be used to force an image into display memory over an existing image. To be honest, though, I have yet to come up with a truly valuable application for the OR logical function; if you've got one, write and let me know what it is.

Notes on the ALU/Latch Sample Program

EGA settings such as the logical-function select should be restored to their default condition before the BIOS is called to output text or draw pixels. The EGA BIOS does not guarantee that it will set most EGA registers except on mode sets, and there are so many compatible BIOSes around that the code of IBM's EGA BIOS is not a reliable guide to the interaction between the BIOS and the EGA's registers. For instance, when the BIOS is called to draw text, it's likely that the result will be illegible if the Bit Mask register is not in its default state. Similarly, a mode set should generally be performed before exiting a program that tinkers with EGA settings.

Along the same lines, the sample program does not explicitly set the Map Mask register to ensure that all planes are enabled for writing. The mode set for mode 10h leaves all planes enabled, and so I did not bother to program the Map Mask register—or any other register beside the Data Rotate register, for that matter. However, the profusion of compatible BIOSes means there is some small risk in relying on the BIOS to leave registers set properly. There are only a few clone chip sets, and they all seem to be compatible; so, for the highly safety-conscious, the best course would seem to be to program data-control registers such as the Map Mask and Read Map registers explicitly before relying on their contents.

(On the other hand, any function the BIOS provides explicitly—as part of the interface specification—such as setting the palette RAM, should be used in preference to programming the hardware directly.)

The code that draws each set of boxes in the sample program reads from display memory immediately before writing to display memory. The read operation loads the EGA latches. The value read is irrelevant as far as the sample program is concerned; it is necessary to perform a read in order to load the latches, and there is no way to read without placing a value in a register. This is a bit of a nuisance, since it means that the value of some 8-bit register must be destroyed. Under certain circumstances, a single logical instruction such as XOR or AND can be used to perform both the read to load the latches and the write to modify display memory without affecting any register, but since this generally involves the bit mask or read mode 1 (or both), it'll have to wait until another installment.

All text in the sample program is drawn by EGA BIOS function 13h, **write string**. This function is also present in the AT's BIOS but not in the XT's or PC's, and as a result is rarely used; the function is always available if an EGA is installed, however. Text drawn with this function is relatively slow. If speed is important, a program can draw text directly into display memory much faster in any given display mode. The great virtue of the BIOS **write string** function in the case of the EGA is that it provides an uncomplicated way to get text on the screen reliably in any mode and color and over any background.

The expression used to load DX in the TEXT_UP macro in the sample program may seem strange, but it's a convenient way to save a byte of program code and a few cycles of execution time. In TEXT_UP, DX is loaded with a word value that's composed of two independent immediate byte values. The obvious way to implement this is with

```
mov dl,VALUE1
mov dh,VALUE2
```

which requires four bytes and eight cycles on the 8088. By shifting the value destined for the high byte into the high byte with MASM's shift-left operator, SHL (*100h would work also), and then logically combining the values with MASM's OR operator (or the ADD operator)—all done at assembly time, not run time—both halves of DX can be loaded with a single instruction, as in

```
mov dx,(VALUE2 shl 8) or VALUE1
```

which takes only three bytes and four cycles. As shown, a macro is an ideal place to use this technique: The macro invocation can refer to two separate byte values, making matters easier for the programmer, while the macro itself can combine the values into a single, word-sized constant.

A minor speed tip illustrated in the listing is the use of INC AX and DEC AX in the **DrawVerticalBoxes** subroutine when only AL actually needs to be modified. Word-sized register-increment and -decrement instructions are only one byte long and execute in two cycles on an 8088, while byte-sized register-increment and -decrement instructions are two bytes long and execute in three cycles. Consequently, when speed counts, it is worth using a whole 16-bit register instead of the low 8 bits of that register for INC and DEC—if you don't need the upper 8 bits of the register for any other purpose or if you know that the value in the low byte is such that the high byte won't be affected, and if you don't care that the flags are set on the basis of all 16 bits.

Another speed tip is to use registers to temporarily store all constants in the background-drawing loop. Moving a constant to a 16-bit register takes a three-byte instruction, and adding a constant to a 16-bit register takes a four-byte instruction, while moving and adding 16-bit registers to 16-bit registers require only two-byte instructions. The register–register operations are also at least one cycle faster—and they are probably a good deal faster than that relative to the constant operations because of the prefetch queue. (See my article "More Optimizing For Speed" in *PJ* 4.4, July/August 1986, for an introduction to prefetch queue effects.)

The latches and ALUs are central to high-performance EGA code, because they allow programs to draw across all four memory planes without a series of OUTs and read/write operations. It is not always easy to arrange a program to exploit this power, however, since the ALUs are far more limited than a CPU. In many instances, however, additional hardware in the EGA, including the bit mask, the set/reset features, and the barrel shifter, can assist the ALUs in controlling data. I will begin to examine these features next time.

Puzzles

I've got a couple of unsolved (or, in one case, partially solved) puzzles this month.

First, another MASM problem. When I use macros with several arguments, the text often runs past column 80. The code still assembles properly, but printouts are a mess. Does anyone know how to continue a macro invocation (or a STRUC initialization, for that matter) on the next line?

The second puzzle pops up regularly in coding high-performance graphics drivers: How the heck do you determine just what's the fastest 8088 code for a given purpose? Hand-optimization of assembler code is always an art, but the prefetch queue makes 8088 optimization black magic. Optimizing 80286 code is somewhat less critical, both because the 8088 is far more common right now and because ATs are faster than PCs no matter how 8088-oriented code is; but 80286 optimization is becoming more important, and so that's an issue, too. And, of course, 80386 optimization looms on the horizon.

I ran across a particular optimization puzzle while implementing Bresenham's line-drawing algorithm: how best to rotate a pixel mask (one bit set and the others reset) to the right (moving one pixel to the right), incrementing the screen address by one when the set bit in the pixel mask wraps around from bit 0 to bit 7. The standard code for this instance would be

```
        ror  al,1
        jnc  NO_INC
        inc  di
NO_INC:
```

where AL is the pixel mask (with only one bit set to 1), and DI is the screen address of the byte containing the next pixel to be drawn. However, JNC is executed seven of every eight times the above code is executed, requiring 16 cycles each time, for an average code-execution time for the conditional-increment portion of this code of $[(16 \times 7) + (4 + 2)] / 8 = 14.75$ cycles on the 8088. (The conditional-increment code is JNC NO_INC / INC DI. The ROR AL,1 instruction is not counted because I'm interested only in the *relative* timings of the approaches I'll examine.) On the other hand, the less elegant-looking code

```
             ror  al,1
             jc  DO_INC
CONTINUE_AFTER_INC:
             :
DO_INC:
        inc  di
        jmp  CONTINUE_AFTER_INC
```

where DO_INC is outside the loop the rotate is performed in but within range of a short jump, requires only $[(7 \times 4) + (16 + 2 + 15)] / 8 = 7.6$ cycles to perform the conditional increment, on average. The speed of this code is an artifact of vast difference on the 8088 between a conditional jump taken and one not taken. (Thanks to Dan Illowsky for this unorthodox but effective approach.)

The fastest code, however, is that which eliminates branching entirely, to wit:

```
    ror  al,1
    adc  di,0
```

This code requires exactly four cycles to perform each conditional increment—more than three times faster than the original code. This is an excellent example of the way in which the quirks of the 8088 make it possible to hand-optimize small portions of assembler code to a far greater extent than is true of most processors.

So what's the puzzle? The puzzle is that I still don't know what's *really* the fastest way to perform the above rotate and conditional increment. The performance estimates are based on the execution times Intel publishes, but the published times assume that the prefetch queue isn't empty. For example, since ROR AL,1 / ADC DI,0 constitutes six bytes, since the 8088 prefetch queue is only 4 bytes long, and since 4 cycles are required to fetch each instruction byte, there's no way that particular code fragment could ever execute in only the specified 6 cycles, even if the prefetch queue were full when ROR began executing. If the prefetch queue were empty, the ADC DI,0 instruction alone would require 16 cycles (4 cycles times 4 bytes), a far cry from the 4 cycles assumed above, and, in fact, exactly as long as the nominal time required to make a conditional jump. The time required to jump is unclear as well, because the prefetch queue is emptied by each jump and may take additional time beyond the 16 cycles specified to refill before the instruction branched to can start execution. All the code fragments above are likely to take somewhat longer than specified; just how much longer is the question.

So, here's what I'd like to know (and share with *PJ's* readers). First, what is the precise overhead of branching and flushing the queue? Are additional cycles beyond the published timings required to get enough bytes to begin executing the next instruction?

Second, how long does a conditional jump not taken take to execute? Is the second byte of the instruction even read? If so, is it read while the jump condition is evaluated?

Third, how important, in general, is the prefetch queue in determining performance of 80286/80386 code? The 80286 can fetch twice as many instruction bytes per memory access as the 8088, but it also executes most instructions in many fewer clock cycles and so uses up instruction bytes at a faster rate.

Fourth (and most important), what techniques have *PJ* readers come up with for evaluating the performance of time-critical code? Ideally, Intel would make available all the information about the 8088's microcode required to accurately determine execution times, but I know of no such publication. There are a number of code profilers out there, but most of them measure gross effects by reporting overall time spent in a given routine. When you're trying to wring maximum performance out of assembler code, you must understand where virtually every cycle goes. To do that, each instruction in the innermost time-critical loops has to be examined in the context of normal operation. There's hardware out there that can do this; sadly, such equipment is out of the price range of many developers, especially individuals. On behalf of the underfunded developers of the world, I'd love to hear about a way to do cycle-by-cycle, in-context performance analysis in software.

Who cares about a few cycles here and there? In a time-critical code path, any programmer who cares about turning out a superior product *should* care, and on the PC, virtually all real-time graphics are time critical. Let us know how *you* do it. Make the world of 8088 programming a little better.

Next Time

I'm going to explore a couple of interesting EGA topics in the next article. I'll continue examining data flow around the ALUs, including the bit mask, data rotate, and set/reset capabilities, which are crucial to pixel-aligned graphics and fast color control. I'll also talk about color versus monochrome operation and downward compatibility with the CGA, MDA, and Hercules Graphics Card and provide the usual discussion of interesting hardware or software I've come across.

See you then.

Listing 2.1

```
;
; Program to illustrate operation of ALUs and latches in the EGA's
;   Graphics Data Controller. Draws a variety of patterns against
;   a horizontally striped background, using each of the 4 available
;   logical functions (data unmodified, AND, OR, XOR) in turn to combine
;   the images with the background.
; Assembled with MASM 4.0, linked with LINK 3.51.
; By Michael Abrash, 11/27/86.
; Updated 6/24/89.
;
stackseg        segment para stack 'STACK'
        db      512 dup(?)
stackseg        ends
;
EGA_VIDEO_SEGMENT       equ     0a000h  ;EGA display memory segment
SCREEN_HEIGHT           equ     350
SCREEN_WIDTH_IN_BYTES   equ     80
```

Listing 2.1 continues

Listing 2.1 *continued*

```
DEMO_AREA_HEIGHT            equ      336      ;# of scan lines in area
                                             ; logical function operation
                                             ; is demonstrated in
DEMO_AREA_WIDTH_IN_BYTES equ      40       ;width in bytes of area
                                             ; logical function operation
                                             ; is demonstrated in
VERTICAL_BOX_WIDTH_IN_BYTES equ 10        ;width in bytes of the boxes
                                             ; used to demonstrate the
                                             ; logical functions
;
; EGA register equates.
;
GC_INDEX            equ      3ceh     ;GC index register
GC_ROTATE          equ      3        ;GC data rotate/logical function
                                     ; register index
GC_MODE            equ      5        ;GC mode register index
;
dseg    segment para common 'DATA'
;
; String used to label logical functions.
;
LabelString        label    byte
        db         'UNMODIFIED    AND       OR        XOR    '
LABEL_STRING_LENGTH       equ      $-LabelString
;
; Strings used to label fill patterns.
;
FillPatternFF   db      'Fill Pattern: 0FFh'
FILL_PATTERN_FF_LENGTH  equ      $ - FillPatternFF
FillPattern00   db      'Fill Pattern: 000h'
FILL_PATTERN_00_LENGTH  equ      $ - FillPattern00
FillPatternVert db      'Fill Pattern: Vertical Bar'
FILL_PATTERN_VERT_LENGTH        equ      $ - FillPatternVert
FillPatternHorz db      'Fill Pattern: Horizontal Bar'
FILL_PATTERN_HORZ_LENGTH equ     $ - FillPatternHorz
;
dseg    ends
;
; Macro to set indexed register INDEX of GC chip to SETTING.
;
SETGC   macro    INDEX, SETTING
        mov      dx,GC_INDEX
        mov      ax,(SETTING SHL 8) OR INDEX
        out      dx,ax
        endm
;
;
; Macro to call BIOS write string function to display text string
;   TEXT_STRING, of length TEXT_LENGTH, at location ROW,COLUMN.
;
TEXT_UP macro    TEXT_STRING, TEXT_LENGTH, ROW, COLUMN
        mov      ah,13h                  ;BIOS write string function
        mov      bp,offset TEXT_STRING   ;ES:BP points to string
        mov      cx,TEXT_LENGTH
        mov      dx,(ROW SHL 8) OR COLUMN        ;position
        sub      al,al           ;string is chars only, cursor not moved
        mov      bl,7            ;text attribute is white (light gray)
        int      10h
```

Listing 2.1 *continues*

Listing 2.1 *continued*

```
        endm
;
cseg    segment para public 'CODE'
        assume  cs:cseg, ds:dseg
start   proc    near
        mov     ax,dseg
        mov     ds,ax
;
; Select 640x350 graphics mode.
;
        mov     ax,010h
        int     10h
;
; ES points to EGA memory.
;
        mov     ax,EGA_VIDEO_SEGMENT
        mov     es,ax
;
; Draw background of horizontal bars.
;
        mov     dx,SCREEN_HEIGHT/4
                             ;# of bars to draw (each 4 pixels high)
        sub     di,di        ;start at offset 0 in display memory
        mov     ax,0ffffh    ;fill pattern for light areas of bars
        mov     bx,DEMO_AREA_WIDTH_IN_BYTES / 2 ;length of each bar
        mov     si,SCREEN_WIDTH_IN_BYTES - DEMO_AREA_WIDTH_IN_BYTES
        mov     bp,(SCREEN_WIDTH_IN_BYTES * 3) - DEMO_AREA_WIDTH_IN_BYTES
BackgroundLoop:
        mov     cx,bx        ;length of bar
    rep stosw                ;draw top half of bar
        add     di,si        ;point to start of bottom half of bar
        mov     cx,bx        ;length of bar
    rep stosw                ;draw bottom half of bar
        add     di,bp        ;point to start of top of next bar
        dec     dx
        jnz     BackgroundLoop
;
; Draw four boxes, stacked vertically and filled with a variety of
; fill patterns, using each of the 4 logical functions in turn.
;
        SETGC   GC_ROTATE, 0        ;select data unmodified
                                    ; logical function...
        mov     di,0
        call    DrawVerticalBoxes   ;...and draw boxes

        SETGC   GC_ROTATE, 08h      ;select AND logical function...
        mov     di,10
        call    DrawVerticalBoxes   ;...and draw boxes
;
        SETGC   GC_ROTATE, 10h      ;select OR logical function...
        mov     di,20
        call    DrawVerticalBoxes   ;...and draw boxes
;
        SETGC   GC_ROTATE, 18h      ;select XOR logical function...
        mov     di,30
        call    DrawVerticalBoxes   ;...and draw boxes
;
; Reset the logical function to data unmodified, the default state.
```

Listing 2.1 *continues*

Listing 2.1 continued

```
;
        SETGC    GC_ROTATE, 0
;
; Label the screen.
;
        push    ds
        pop     es       ;strings we'll display are passed to BIOS
                         ; by pointing ES:BP to them
;
; Label the logical functions, using the EGA BIOS's
;  write string function.
;
        TEXT_UP LabelString, LABEL_STRING_LENGTH, 24, 0
;
; Label the fill patterns, using the EGA BIOS's
;  write string function.
;
        TEXT_UP FillPatternFF, FILL_PATTERN_FF_LENGTH, 3, 42
        TEXT_UP FillPattern00, FILL_PATTERN_00_LENGTH, 9, 42
        TEXT_UP FillPatternVert, FILL_PATTERN_VERT_LENGTH, 15, 42
        TEXT_UP FillPatternHorz, FILL_PATTERN_HORZ_LENGTH, 21, 42
;
; Wait until a key's been hit to reset screen mode & exit.
;
WaitForKey:
        mov     ah,1
        int     16h
        jz      WaitForKey
;
; Finished. Clear key, reset screen mode and exit.
;
Done:
        mov     ah,0     ;clear key that we just detected
        int     16h
;
        mov     ax,3     ;reset to text mode
        int     10h
;
        mov     ah,4ch   ;exit to DOS
        int     21h
;
start   endp
;
; Subroutine to draw a set of four boxes, each 80x84 in size, using
;  the currently selected logical function, with the upper left corner
;  at the display memory offset in DI. Each box is filled with a
;  separate pattern. The top box is filled with a 0FFh (solid) pattern,
;  the next box is filled with a 00h (empty) pattern, the next box is
;  filled with a 33h (double-pixel-wide vertical bar) pattern, and the
;  bottom box is filled with a double-pixel-high horizontal bar pattern.
;
; Macro to draw a column of the specified width in bytes, 84 pixels
;  high, filled with the specified fill pattern.
;
DRAW_BOX_QUARTER            macro  FILL, WIDTH
        local   RowLoop, ColumnLoop
        mov     al,FILL                 ;fill pattern
        mov     dx,DEMO_AREA_HEIGHT / 4 ;1/4 of the full box height
```

Listing 2.1 continues

Listing 2.1 continued

```
RowLoop:
        mov     cx,WIDTH
ColumnLoop:
        mov     ah,es:[di]      ;load display memory contents into
                                ; GC latches (we don't actually care
                                ; about value read into AH)
        stosb                   ;write pattern, which is logically
                                ; combined with latch contents for each
                                ; plane and then written to display
                                ; memory

        loop    ColumnLoop
        add     di,SCREEN_WIDTH_IN_BYTES - WIDTH
                                ;point to start of next line down in box

        dec     dx
        jnz     RowLoop
        endm
;
DrawVerticalBoxes       proc    near
        DRAW_BOX_QUARTER        0ffh, VERTICAL_BOX_WIDTH_IN_BYTES
                                        ;first fill pattern: solid fill

        DRAW_BOX_QUARTER        0, VERTICAL_BOX_WIDTH_IN_BYTES
                                        ;second fill pattern: empty fill

        DRAW_BOX_QUARTER        033h, VERTICAL_BOX_WIDTH_IN_BYTES
                                        ;third fill pattern: double-pixel
                                        ; wide vertical bars

        mov     dx,DEMO_AREA_HEIGHT / 4 / 4
                                ;fourth fill pattern: horizontal bars in
                                ; sets of 4 scan lines

        sub     ax,ax
        mov     si,VERTICAL_BOX_WIDTH_IN_BYTES  ;width of fill area
HorzBarLoop:
        dec     ax              ;0ffh fill (faster to do word than
                                ; byte DEC)

        mov     cx,si           ;width to fill
HBLoop1:
        mov     bl,es:[di]      ;load latches (don't care about value)
        stosb                   ;write solid pattern, through ALUs
        loop    HBLoop1
        add     di,SCREEN_WIDTH_IN_BYTES - VERTICAL_BOX_WIDTH_IN_BYTES
        mov     cx,si           ;width to fill
HBLoop2:
        mov     bl,es:[di]      ;load latches
        stosb                   ;write solid pattern, through ALUs
        loop    HBLoop2
        add     di,SCREEN_WIDTH_IN_BYTES - VERTICAL_BOX_WIDTH_IN_BYTES
        inc     ax              ;0 fill (faster to do word than byte INC)
        mov     cx,si           ;width to fill
HBLoop3:
        mov     bl,es:[di]      ;load latches
        stosb                   ;write empty pattern, through ALUs
        loop    HBLoop3
        add     di,SCREEN_WIDTH_IN_BYTES - VERTICAL_BOX_WIDTH_IN_BYTES
        mov     cx,si           ;width to fill
HBLoop4:
        mov     bl,es:[di]      ;load latches
        stosb                   ;write empty pattern, through ALUs
        loop    HBLoop4
        add     di,SCREEN_WIDTH_IN_BYTES - VERTICAL_BOX_WIDTH_IN_BYTES
```

Listing 2.1 continues

Listing 2.1 *continued*

```
        dec     dx
        jnz     HorzBarLoop
;
        ret
DrawVerticalBoxes       endp
cseg    ends
        end     start
```

CHAPTER 3

EGA Data Control

If the last chapter was the one in which it became apparent just how complex the EGA is, then this chapter is the one in which it becomes apparent just how *strange* the EGA is. The EGA's bit mask, barrel shifter, and other hardware-assist features are unique in the microcomputer world and require a new way of thinking about graphics programming altogether.

Still and all, programming the EGA isn't *that* hard, given a solid understanding of the many special features the adapter offers—and such an understanding is exactly what we're building in *Power Graphics Programming,* one piece at a time.

This is also the chapter in which the readers start to answer my questions. As you'll see, they're a knowledgeable crew indeed.

The discussion of advanced EGAs in this chapter is cause for wonderment. Consider the speed with which the leading edge of popular PC-graphics technology of 1987 became the bargain-basement commodity technology of 1989, and wonder where we'll be in another two years!

Installment 3: In which we look deeper into the heart of the beast and find barrel shifters and bit masks.

This month, I'm going to cover a lot of ground. First, I'll discuss the monitors the EGA can support and look into issues of EGA compatibility with other adapters. Next, I'll continue our detailed exploration of the data-management capabilities of the GC chip. Finally, I'll look at three EEGAs.

53

Color, Monochrome, and Compatibility

I've become aware that few people understand exactly what displays EGAs can drive and what adapters EGAs are compatible with. I'm going to do my best to remedy that here. A standard EGA can drive a monochrome display, a color display, or an enhanced-color display. Monochrome operation is simpler, so I'll start with that.

When driving a monochrome display, the EGA supports a text mode that is identical in appearance to that of the Monochrome Display Adapter (MDA), with characters in 9-by-14 boxes. Display memory is at B000:0000, just as with the MDA, and attributes can be (and are set up by the BIOS to be) interpreted in much the same way as with the MDA. There are differences (involving reverse video), but commonly used attributes work in the same way on the EGA as on the MDA.

The EGA is BIOS compatible with the MDA, but the registers of the EGA are only partially compatible. Most importantly, the cursor-location register is MDA compatible. The cursor start and stop scan-line registers are not fully compatible, but they can reliably be set through the BIOS, which is compatible across the MDA, CGA, and EGA. Given the way in which the MDA is normally programmed, the EGA can be considered to be highly MDA compatible. In particular, if registers other than the cursor location aren't set directly, the EGA is generally a good MDA replacement. Since the MDA supports only one mode (mode 7), there is little reason to directly program MDA registers other than the cursor location, and so the EGA can generally be substituted for the MDA.

When configured for monochrome operation, the EGA provides a graphics mode with a resolution of 640 by 350, with attributes of black, white, high-intensity white, and blink. This mode is similar to the 640-by-350 color-graphics mode, except that two planes, rather than four, are used. Unfortunately, the EGA's monochrome-graphics mode is not even remotely compatible with the graphics mode of the Hercules Graphics Card (HGC). It is possible to program an EGA to support the same bit map as the HGC (and someday I'll show how); since, however, the HGC has no BIOS support for mode switches, all software that supports the HGC programs the hardware directly, and because the EGA is not fully register compatible with the HGC, this will not work with the EGA. So, practically speaking, the standard EGA is compatible with the MDA but not with the HGC.

Color EGA operation is more complex. The EGA can be configured to support only 200-scan-line display modes, or it can be configured to support both 200- and 350-scan-line modes. In the configuration switch table for the EGA, there appear to be more choices, but the only important choice is between 200 and 350 scan lines. There is no reason to power up an EGA in 40-column mode, since it has no composite or RF output, and the enhanced-display-emulation setting actually works just like the 200-scan-line, color-display, 80-column setting.

In 200-scan-line operation, the EGA has two new graphics modes (unsupported by the CGA): 320 by 200 in 16 colors and 640 by 200 in 16 colors. In 350-scan-line operation, the EGA has a 640-by-350 16-color-graphics mode; additionally, in 350-scan-line operation, text in 80-by-25 text mode is in an 8-by-14 box, rather than in the coarse, 8-by-8 box of the CGA. High-resolution text is far superior to CGA text, but there is one important limitation: Border colors other than black aren't supported in 350-scan-line modes (owing to tight retrace timings). With that background out of the way, let's look at EGA emulation of the CGA.

In general, the EGA is only a fair Color/Graphics Adapter (CGA) replacement. The EGA supports all the display modes of the CGA as well as all CGA bit maps at B800:0000. The EGA is also BIOS compatible with the CGA, but, unlike the MDA, the CGA's hardware is often programmed directly, and the EGA is not fully register compatible with the CGA. Most notably, the Color Select register, which is used to select among the CGA's palettes and background colors, is not present in the EGA. A BIOS function is provided to set these registers, but it supports only one of the two palette intensities provided by the CGA. Also, border colors in high-resolution modes aren't supported. To write programs that will run on both CGAs and EGAs, all accesses to registers other than the cursor-location and start-address registers must be avoided, again including the cursor start and stop registers. This is possible, but the differences in color capabilities and color-setting techniques between the two adapters mean that a program that would run on both adapters would be limited to two three-color palettes in graphics modes, with a black border only. In short, the EGA can be used to run BIOS-compatible CGA software, but the two boards are really quite different.

Here's a summary of compatibility of the standard EGA with existing display adapters: CGA and MDA programs that do not directly access registers other than the cursor location and start-address registers should run on the EGA. Bit-map compatibility is maintained by the EGA. HGC programs will not run on a standard EGA, although it is possible to program an EGA to support an HGC-format bit map.

Many EGAs have extended CGA or HGC compatibility built in. These boards can create headaches for developers, for many of them are not really hardware compatible with the CGA or HGC. A common method of implementing compatibility is based on generating NMIs (nonmaskable interrupts) on attempted accesses to the CGA's (or HGC's) registers, with the NMI-handling routine forcing the CRT registers to settings that match the setting of the CGA mode register. Software that reprograms the 6845 CRT of the CGA (to get extra rows and columns, for example, or to smooth-scroll) generally will not work on EGAs with NMI-based compatibility.

There are, incidentally, other problems with boards that provide downward compatibility. In particular, it can be difficult to determine what type of adapter a program should be trying to drive. For example, a program that looks for the string "IBM" in the EGA BIOS to see whether an EGA is installed (a common, although ill-advised, method) will attempt to drive an EGA, even if emulation is active and the program should be trying to drive an emulated CGA. One solution to this problem is letting the user select the display type at installation time.

A result is the recommendation for developers to leave registers other than the cursor-location and start-address registers alone and go through the BIOS holds even on CGA- and HGC-compatible EGAs. Bit maps are the same, and so it's all right to go directly to display memory (fortunately, since the BIOS **write dot** and **read dot** functions are so slow as to be virtually useless). It's too bad that the BIOS doesn't provide full support for CGA palettes, though, and that border colors aren't supported in 350-scan-line modes.

Of course, if you're not interested in having your applications run on anything but an EGA (or on anything but a CGA), or if you're willing to write your programs to specifically support a number of display adapters, you can go right to the hardware. I don't mean to say that you shouldn't use fast, nonstandard techniques when you have to—just be aware that as the world of display adapters expands, with CGAs, MDAs, HGCs, EGAs, EEGAs, and new display technologies that provide downward compatibility to varying degrees, it's going to be harder to support them all directly. So . . . where you can afford to, go through the BIOS, and go directly to the hardware when you can't live without it.

There's one other compatibility issue concerning the EGA, and that's what displays the EGA can coexist with. The answer is that an EGA configured for color can be in the same system with an MDA (or an HGC with up to 32K available), while an EGA configured for monochrome can be in the same system with a CGA. This is possible because a color EGA uses registers in the range 3C0–3DC and a monochrome EGA uses registers in the range 3B0–3CF, complementing the address ranges of the MDA and CGA, respectively. Two EGAs, one color and one monochrome, cannot coexist, because both would use registers in the 3CX range. It is possible to jumper an EGA to set its address range to 2XX rather than 3XX, allowing two EGAs to be installed together without conflict; however, no current BIOS supports this alternate address range, and so a good deal of work would be required to use two EGAs together in this fashion.

A Closer Look at the GC

In the last installment, we looked at a simplified model of data flow within the GC chips of the EGA, featuring the latches and ALUs. This month, I'll expand that model to include the barrel shifter and bit mask, leaving only the set/reset capabilities to be explored.

EGA Data Rotation

Figure 3.1 shows an expanded model of GC data flow. First, let's look at the barrel shifter. A barrel shifter is circuitry capable of shifting (or rotating, in the EGA's case) data an arbitrary number of bits in a single cycle. The barrel shifter can rotate incoming CPU data up to seven bits to the right (toward the least-significant bit), with bit 0 wrapping back to bit 7. Thanks to the nature of barrel shifters, this rotation requires no extra processing time over normal, nonrotated EGA operation. The number of bits by which CPU data is shifted is controlled by bits 2–0 of GC register 3, the Data Rotate register, which also contains the ALU function-select bits.

The barrel shifter is powerful, but it sounds more useful than it really is: The GCs can rotate only CPU data, a task that the CPU itself is perfectly capable of performing. Two OUTs (one to set the GC Index register to point to the Data Rotate register and one to set the Data Rotate register) are needed to select a given rotation, and often it's easier or faster simply to have the CPU rotate the data of interest CL times than to set the Data Rotate register. If only the EGA could rotate *latched* data; then there would be all sorts of useful applications for rotation. But, sadly, only CPU data can be rotated.

The drawing of bit-mapped text is one good use of the barrel shifter, and I'll demonstrate that application. In general, though, don't knock yourself out trying to figure out how to work data rotation into your programs—it just isn't all that useful.

The Bit Mask

The EGA has one bit mask, which affects all four memory planes. Figure 3.2 illustrates the operation of one bit of a bit mask on one bit of data for one plane. This circuitry occurs eight times for a given plane—once for each bit of the byte written to display memory by that plane. Briefly, the bit mask determines on a bit-by-bit basis whether the source for each byte written to display memory is the ALU for that plane or the latch for that plane. The bit mask is controlled by GC register 8, the Bit Mask register. If a given bit of the Bit Mask register is 1, then the corresponding bit of data from the ALUs is written to display memory, while if that bit is 0, then the corresponding bit of data from the latches is written to display memory unchanged.

The most common use of the bit mask is to allow updating of selected bits within a display-memory byte. Here's how this works: The display memory location of interest is latched by being read, the bit mask is set to preserve all but the bit or bits to be changed, and the CPU writes to

---

Fig. 3.1 *Simplified data flow through the EGA during write mode 0 display-memory writes.*

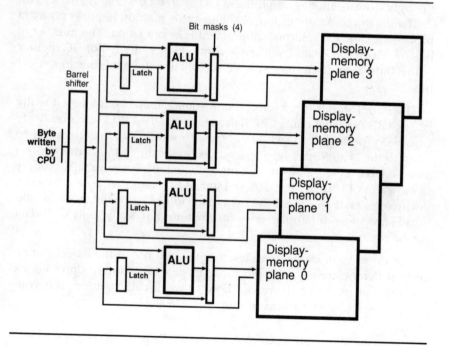

display memory, with the bit mask preserving the indicated latch bits and allowing ALU data through to change the other bits. Remember, though, that it is not possible to alter selected bits in a display-memory byte *directly*. The byte to be altered must first be latched by a CPU read; only then can the bit mask keep selected bits of the latched byte unchanged.

Listing 3.1 [presented at the end of this chapter] shows a program that uses the bit mask and data-rotation capabilities of the GC to draw bit-mapped text at any screen location. (The BIOS draws characters only on character boundaries; in 640-by-350 graphics mode, the default font is drawn on byte boundaries horizontally and every 14 scan lines vertically.) Note that the 8-by-8 BIOS font is used; a pointer to this font is obtained through function 11h of INT 10h.

The bit mask can be used for much more than bit-aligned fonts. For example, the bit mask is useful for fast pixel drawing, such as that performed when drawing lines. At some point in the future, I'll demonstrate such applications.

The example in Listing 3.1 is designed primarily to illustrate the use of the Data Rotate and Bit Mask registers and is not so fast nor complete as

Fig. 3.2   *Operation of one bit of the Bit Mask register on one bit of the data for a single plane.*

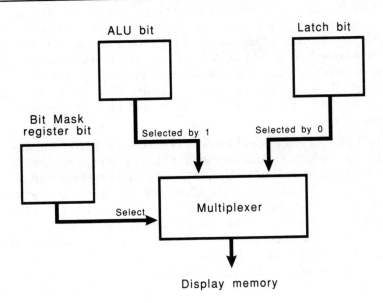

it might be. The case where text is byte aligned, if detected and special cased, could be performed much faster without the use of the Bit Mask or Data Rotate registers and with only one display-memory access per font byte, rather than four. Also, display memory could be both read from and written to with a single instruction, such as XCHG or AND; I'll demonstrate that sort of speedy operation in a later installment.

For another (and more complex) example of drawing bit-mapped text on the EGA, see John Cockerham's article "Pixel Alignment of EGA Fonts," in *PC Tech Journal,* January 1987. I'd like to pass along John's comment about the EGA: "When programming the EGA, *everything* is complex."

He's got a point.

Of Interest

I've gotten the opportunity to try out several EEGAs, with impressive results. If you have a monitor capable of going up to 640 by 480 or higher, you should consider an EEGA, and if you're developing an application that needs higher resolution (What application doesn't?), you should certainly take a long look at supporting one or more EEGAs. As we'll see, all EEGAs are not alike; each of the three I'll look at has unique features.

Before I begin, I'd like to make it clear that what follows is not a "review" in any conventional sense. I'm not trying to cover the boards in every detail, because I'm not trying to help you decide which to buy. By the same token, I'm not trying to blanket the field—you won't find comparison charts of 32 EGAs here. What I *am* trying to do is help you decide whether you should support the special features of these boards, or whether one of them might help you solve special hardware needs. You might think of topics discussed under the "Of Interest" heading as overviews of advanced display technology that I think developers should know about.

The VEGA Deluxe, from Video-7 (550 Sycamore Drive, Milpitas, CA 94035, 408-943-0101), is the follow-up to the extremely popular VEGA, one of the boards that fueled the first great boom in the EGA market. The VEGA Deluxe is built around the Chips & Technologies EGA chip set, which has proven to be highly IBM EGA compatible. The VEGA Deluxe supports resolutions of 640 by 480 and 752 by 410, although the only means of accessing these resolutions in the base package is via Windows drivers. (Late note: Video-7 indicates that other drivers are on the way, and developer's information is available.) The VEGA Deluxe also features full CGA and HGC compatibility. Given Video-7's stature in the EGA market, it would make sense for any developer who is going to support EEGAs to include the VEGA Deluxe.

The EGA 2001/PLUS, from Ahead Systems (1977 O'Toole Ave., Suite B105, San Jose, CA 94131, 408-435-0707), is also built around the C & T chip set. The 2001/PLUS offers full CGA and HGC compatibility and adds a nice touch: HGC compatibility on color monitors. A 640-by-480 mode is supported (I propose this as a minimum requirement for a board to be considered an EEGA), as is 720 by 396, which provides IBM S3G graphics compatibility. Also provided are 80-by-66/45/43/34/25 and 132-by-44/28/25 text modes, which provide IBM 3278/79 MOD 2-5 compatibility as well as compatibility with many popular PC extended-spreadsheet and text-editing modes. The board is a compact, clean half-card—in short, a well-conceived and -executed board that covers a lot of ground, one worth looking at if your requirements exceed the standard EGA.

The EVA 480, from Tseng Laboratories (205 Pheasant Run, Newtown, PA 18940, 215-968-0502), sports a number of extras. Like the other EEGAs, the EVA 480 offers 640-by-480 graphics and complete downward compatibility with the CGA and HGC, as well as 132-by-44/28/25 and 80-by-60/43/25 text and Windows, AutoCAD, and Halo drivers. Because it is built around Tseng Labs' proprietary ET2000-series chip set (which, incidentally, I participated in the design of), the EVA 480 sports two unique extras: a zoomable hardware window and faster memory access.

The EVA 480 features a built-in hardware window (in addition to the standard EGA split screen), which can start and stop on any scan line vertically and on any byte boundary horizontally. This window can display the contents of any area of EGA memory, allowing instant popups, for example. The window area can be zoomed by pixel replication in both directions in graphics modes and horizontally in text mode, by a factor of up to 8 times horizontally and 16 times vertically. This could be very handy for a developer who needs to blow up part or all of the screen quickly.

The EVA 480 also allows the CPU much greater access to display memory than does the standard EGA. The standard EGA allows one CPU access to display memory every four character clocks, while the EVA 480 allows one access every character clock. During highly display-memory-intensive operations, the EVA 480 is noticeably quicker than other EGAs. For example, I ran ATPERF, *PC Tech Journal*'s 286 Performance and Compatibility Suite (see "Out from the Shadow of IBM . . . ," by Steven Armbrust, Ted Forgeron, and Paul Pierce, in *PC Tech Journal,* August 1986) on a 10-MHz AT clone in order to determine how many wait states were being inserted by each of the three EEGAs I've discussed. Both the VEGA Deluxe and the EGA 2001/PLUS performed at the same speed, inserting 18 wait states on average—not surprising, given that they're built around the same chip set. The EVA 480 inserted only 9 wait states, the minimum number of wait states an 8-bit device can cause during a 16-bit access in an AT. For programs that access display memory less frequently, the gain will be less, but the EVA 480 is clearly the faster EGA.

Tseng Labs is the first (but not the only) company to make a higher-performance EGA chip set. Chips and Technologies is coming out with a chip set with all sorts of extensions to the EGA (including more-frequent CPU access to display memory), and other advanced chip sets are on the way.

Don't expect the relatively sluggish performance of the EGA to improve much beyond the EVA 480, though, no matter what chip sets appear. Improving CPU memory access is about all that can be done without losing EGA compatibility, and right now compatibility is essential. Moreover, the higher performance from improved CPU memory access barely balances the performance loss resulting from the greater size of the bit maps in the EEGA's higher-resolution modes.

On Performance

I'm running short on space, so all I'm going to say about performance is that you should read "High-Performance Software Analysis on the IBM PC," by Byron Sheppard (*BYTE*, January 1987). It looks to me like Sheppard's routines provide very good software-based performance analysis. To the extent that I've tried them out, they've worked well and given pretty much the results I'd expect (although I will say that figuring actual jump times on the 286 appears at first cut to be black magic). Thanks to changes induced in the prefetch queue by the timing routines, results aren't necessarily accurate to a cycle, but then there's no way around that with a software solution. On quick examination, it looks to me as if Sheppard's done an excellent job.

Reader Feedback

Tom Heavey provided a solution to my problem of how to generate code that assembles at a specific address (for ROM, in my case). Tom's solution bypasses the Macro Assembler entirely; he suggests using a program called Link and Locate, from Systems and Software, Inc. (714-241-8650), in place of the standard MS-DOS linker, with which it is compatible. According to Tom, Link and Locate adds a locate phase after the link phase, during which you can specify exactly where segments are to go.

Charles Clinton also provided a solution, but one that I can get to work only under certain circumstances. Charles points out that it's acceptable to have two relocatable values in an expression, so long as they combine to generate an absolute. He suggests using

```
db    2000h - ( $ - ProgramStart ) dup (0)
```

where ProgramStart is the offset of the first byte of the program. The assembler does indeed accept this syntax, and as long as ProgramStart is in the same module as the above DB statement, everything's fine. If, however, ProgramStart is in another module, too many bytes are inserted, because "$" is relative to the start of the module, not the start of the final linked program. Perhaps Charles only meant this technique to be used in single-module programs, or perhaps I'm missing something. Charles, can you write and let us know?

John Navas II provided a similar solution. Instead of the start of the program, however, he subtracts the segment name from the location counter. As far as I can tell, this operates exactly like Charles Clinton's approach. John also sent in answers to other MASM problems I've discussed here; his solutions arrived too late to make it into this article, but I'll run them next time.

Thanks to all of you.

Next Time

We've almost completed our tour of GC data flow—only the set/reset features remain. I'll cover these odd but useful features next time. If there's room, I'll begin to strike out into the more specialized read and write modes of the EGA.

See you then.

Listing 3.1

```
;
; Program to illustrate operation of data rotate and bit mask
;   features of Graphics Data Controller. Draws 8x8 character at
;   specified location, using EGA's 8x8 ROM font. Designed
;   for use with modes 0Dh, 0Eh, 0Fh, and 10h.
; Assembled with MASM 4.0, linked with LINK 3.51.
; By Michael Abrash, 2/8/87.
; Updated 6/25/89.

stackseg        segment para stack 'STACK'
        db      512 dup(?)
stackseg        ends
;
EGA_VIDEO_SEGMENT       equ     0a000h  ;EGA display memory segment
SCREEN_WIDTH_IN_BYTES   equ     044ah   ;offset of BIOS variable
FONT_CHARACTER_SIZE     equ     8       ;# bytes in each font char
;
; EGA register equates.
;
GC_INDEX        equ     3ceh    ;GC index register
GC_ROTATE       equ     3       ;GC data rotate/logical function
                                ; register index
GC_BIT_MASK     equ     8       ;GC bit mask register index
;
dseg    segment para common 'DATA'
TEST_TEXT_ROW   equ     69      ;row to display test text at
TEST_TEXT_COL   equ     17      ;column to display test text at
TEST_TEXT_WIDTH equ     8       ;width of a character in pixels
TestString      label   byte
        db      'Hello, world!',0       ;test string to print.
FontPointer     dd      ?               ;font offset
dseg    ends
;
; Macro to set indexed register INDEX of GC chip to SETTING.
;
SETGC   macro   INDEX, SETTING
        mov     dx,GC_INDEX
        mov     ax,(SETTING SHL 8) OR INDEX
        out     dx,ax
        endm
;
cseg    segment para public 'CODE'
        assume  cs:cseg, ds:dseg
start   proc    near
        mov     ax,dseg
        mov     ds,ax
;
; Select 640x350 graphics mode.
;
        mov     ax,010h
        int     10h
;
; Set driver to use the 8x8 font.
;
        call    Select8x8Font
;
; Print the test string.
;
```

Listing 3.1 continues

Listing 3.1 *continued*

```
        mov     si,offset TestString
        mov     bx,TEST_TEXT_ROW
        mov     cx,TEST_TEXT_COL
StringOutLoop:
        lodsb
        and     al,al
        jz      StringOutDone
        call    DrawChar
        add     cx,TEST_TEXT_WIDTH
        jmp     StringOutLoop
StringOutDone:
;
; Reset the data rotate and bit mask registers.
;
        SETGC   GC_ROTATE, 0
        SETGC   GC_BIT_MASK, 0ffh
;
; Exit to DOS. (Still in graphics mode; the MODE CO80 command
; can be used to restore the screen to text mode.)
;
        mov     ah,4ch
        int     21h
Start   endp
;
; Subroutine to draw a text character in a linear graphics mode
;  (0Dh, 0Eh, 0Fh, 010h).
; Font to be used must be pointed to by FontPointer.
;
; Input:
;  AL = character to draw
;  BX = row to draw text character at
;  CX = column to draw text character at
;
;  Forces ALU function to "move".
;
DrawChar        proc    near
        push    ax
        push    bx
        push    cx
        push    dx
        push    si
        push    di
        push    bp
        push    ds
;
; Set DS:SI to point to font and ES to point to display memory.
;
        lds     si,[FontPointer]        ;point to font
        mov     dx,EGA_VIDEO_SEGMENT
        mov     es,dx                   ;point to display memory
;
; Calculate screen address of byte character starts in.
;
        push    ds      ;point to BIOS data segment
        sub     dx,dx
        mov     ds,dx
        xchg    ax,bx
        mov     di,ds:[SCREEN_WIDTH_IN_BYTES]    ;retrieve BIOS
```

Listing 3.1 *continues*

Listing 3.1 *continued*

```
                                      ; screen width
        pop     ds
        mul     di          ;calculate offset of start of row
        push    di          ;set aside screen width
        mov     di,cx       ;set aside the column
        and     cl,0111b ;keep only the column in-byte address
        shr     di,1
        shr     di,1
        shr     di,1        ;divide column by 8 to make a byte address
        add     di,ax       ;and point to byte
;
; Calculate font address of character.
;
        sub     bh,bh
        shl     bx,1        ;assumes 8 bytes per character; use
        shl     bx,1        ; a multiply otherwise
        shl     bx,1        ;offset in font of character
        add     si,bx       ;offset in font segment of character
;
; Set up the GC rotation for the bit alignment of the character
; within each display memory byte.
;
        mov     dx,GC_INDEX
        mov     al,GC_ROTATE
        mov     ah,cl
        out     dx,ax
;
; Set up BH as bit mask for part of character in left byte,
; BL as bit mask for part of character in right byte.
;
        mov     bx,0ff00h
        shr     bx,cl
;
; Draw the character, the part in left byte first, then the part in
; right byte next, using the data rotation to position the character
; across the byte boundary and then using the bit mask to get the
; proper portion of the character into each byte.
;
; Does not check for the case where the character is byte-aligned,
; so no rotation (and hence only one write) is required; special
; code would speed that case considerably.
;
        mov     bp,FONT_CHARACTER_SIZE
        mov     dx,GC_INDEX
        pop     cx          ;get back screen width
        dec     cx
        dec     cx          ; -2 because do two bytes for each char
; Point the GC Index register to the Bit Mask register for the
; duration of the loop.
        mov     al,GC_BIT_MASK
        out     dx,al
        inc     dx          ;point to GC Data register
CharacterLoop:
;
; Set the bit mask for the part of the character in the left byte.
;
        mov     al,bh
        out     dx,al
```

Listing 3.1 *continues*

Listing 3.1 *continued*

```
;
; Get the next character byte & write it to display memory.
; (This draws the part of the character in the left byte.)
;
        mov     al,es:[di]      ;load latches from left byte
        lodsb                   ;get character byte
        stosb                   ;write left part of character byte
;
; Set the bit mask for the part of the character in the right byte.
;
        xchg    ax,bx           ;get right-byte bit mask in AL
                                ; and save the font byte
        out     dx,al           ;set the right-byte bit mask
        xchg    ax,bx           ;put the font byte back in AL
                                ; and the bit masks back in BX
;
; Write the character byte to display memory again.
; (Right part of character.)
;
        mov     ah,es:[di]      ;load latches from right byte
        stosb                   ;write character byte
;
; Point to next line of character in display memory.
;
        add     di,cx
;
        dec     bp
        jnz     CharacterLoop
;
        pop     ds
        pop     bp
        pop     di
        pop     si
        pop     dx
        pop     cx
        pop     bx
        pop     ax
        ret
DrawChar        endp
;
; Set the pointer to the 8x8 font.
;
Select8x8Font   proc    near
        mov     ah,11h  ;EGA BIOS character generator function,
        mov     al,30h  ; return info subfunction
        mov     bh,3    ;get 8x8 font pointer
        int     10h
        mov     word ptr [FontPointer],bp        ;save pointer
        mov     word ptr [FontPointer+2],es
        ret
Select8x8Font   endp
;
cseg    ends
        end     start
```

CHAPTER 4

EGA Set/Reset Capabilities

With this chapter, we complete our understanding of write mode 0. Yes, write mode 0 is indeed complex—after all, it took four installments to explain it!—but it offers capabilities far beyond those of the Color/Graphics Adapter and Hercules Graphics Card. As your comprehension of the EGA grows and jells, you will surely come to realize that the EGA offers tremendous opportunities for inventive programmers. By the same token, you will understand why only skilled, knowledgeable programmers can push the EGA to its potential. "Skilled" is up to you; as for "knowledgeable," that's what *Power Graphics Programming* is all about.

This chapter also features astonishingly insightful reader feedback to the questions I asked in the first chapter. It never ceases to amaze—and delight—me that PC developers are so willing to share their expertise.

Installment 4: In which the final piece of the basic EGA data-path puzzle falls into place.

This month I'll examine a powerful but confusing aspect of the EGA: the set/reset circuitry. I'll also discuss a few odds and ends and print reader responses to some of the questions I've posted in previous installments.

The Set/Reset Circuitry

At long last, we've come to the final aspect of data flow through the Graphics Controller (GC) on write mode 0 writes: the set/reset circuitry. Figure 4.1 shows data flow on a write mode 0 write. The only difference between this figure and the similar figure in the last installment is that on its way to each plane, the rotated CPU data passes through the set/reset circuitry, which may or may not replace the CPU data with set/reset data. Briefly put, the set/reset circuitry enables the programmer to elect to replace the CPU data independently for any or all planes with either 0 or 0FFh.

What is the use of such a feature? Well, the standard way to control color is to set the Map Mask register to enable writes to only those planes that need to be set to produce the desired color. For example, the Map Mask register would be set to 09h to draw in high-intensity blue; here, bits 0 and 3 are set to 1, and so only the blue plane (plane 0) and the intensity plane (plane 3) are written to.

Fig. 4.1   *Data flow through the EGA during write mode 0 display-memory writes.*

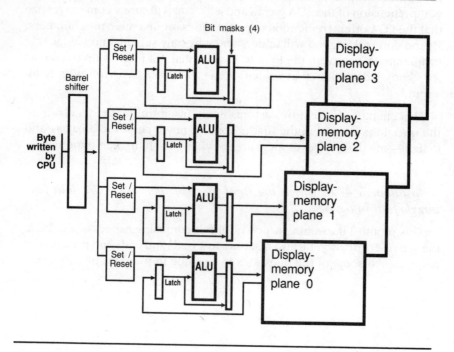

Remember, though, that planes that are disabled by the Map Mask register are not written to or modified in any way. This means that the above approach works only if the memory being written to is zeroed; if, however, the memory already contains nonzero data, that data will remain in the planes disabled by the Map Mask, and the end result will be that some planes contain the data just written and other planes contain old data. In short, color control using the Map Mask does not force all planes to contain the desired color; in particular, it is not possible to force some planes to 0 and other planes to 1 in a single write by way of the Map Mask register.

The program in Listing 4.1 [presented at the end of this chapter] illustrates this problem. A green pattern (plane 1 set to 1, planes 0, 2, and 3 set to 0) is first written to display memory. Display memory is then filled with blue (only plane 0 set to 1), with a Map Mask setting of 01h. Where the blue crosses the green, cyan (planes 0 *and* 1 set to 1) is produced, rather than blue, because the Map Mask register setting of 01h that produces blue leaves the green plane (plane 1) unchanged. In order to generate blue unconditionally, it would be necessary to set the Map Mask register to 0Fh, write 0s to clear memory, and then set the Map Mask register to 01h and fill with blue.

The set/reset circuitry can be used to force some planes to 0 and others to 1 during a single write and so provides an efficient way to set all planes to a desired color. The set/reset circuitry works as follows:

For each of the bits 0 through 3 in the Enable Set/Reset register (Graphics Controller register 1) that is 1, the corresponding bit in the Set/Reset register (GC register 0) is extended to a byte (0 or 0FFh) and replaces the CPU data for the corresponding plane. For each of the bits in the Enable Set/Reset register that is 0, the CPU data is used unchanged for that plane (normal operation). For example, if the Enable Set/Reset register is set to 01h and the Set/Reset register is set to 05h, then the CPU data is replaced for plane 0 only (the blue plane), and the value it is replaced with is 0FFh (bit 0 of the Set/Reset register extended to a byte). Note that in this case, bits 1 through 3 of the Set/Reset register have no effect.

It is important to understand that the set/reset circuitry directly replaces CPU data in Graphics Controller data flow. Refer again to Figure 4.1 to see that the output of the set/reset circuitry passes through (and may be transformed by) the ALU and the bit mask before being written to memory, and even then, the Map Mask register must enable the write. When using set/reset, it is generally desirable to set the Map Mask register to enable all planes the set/reset circuitry is controlling, since those memory planes that are disabled by the Map Mask register cannot be modified, and the purpose of enabling set/reset for a plane is usually to force that plane to be set by the set/reset circuitry.

Listing 4.2 [presented at the end of this chapter] illustrates the use of set/reset to force a specific color to be written. This program is the same as that of Listing 4.1, except that set/reset rather than the Map Mask register is used to control color. The preexisting pattern is completely overwritten this time, because the set/reset circuitry sends bytes of value 0 to planes that must be off as well as bytes of value 0FFh to planes that must be on.

Listing 4.3 [presented at the end of this chapter] illustrates the use of set/reset to control only some, rather than all, planes. Here, the set/reset circuitry forces plane 2 to 1 and planes 0 and 3 to 0. Because bit 1 of the Enable Set/Reset register is 0, however, set/reset does not affect plane 1; the CPU data goes unchanged to the plane-1 ALU. Consequently, the CPU data controls the value written to plane 1. Given the settings of the other three planes, this means that each bit of CPU data that is 1 generates a brown pixel, and each bit that is 0 generates a red pixel. Writing alternating bytes of 07h and 0E0h, then, creates a vertically striped pattern of brown and red.

In Listing 4.3, note that the vertical bars are 10 and 6 pixels wide and do not start on byte boundaries. Although set/reset replaces an entire byte of CPU data for a plane, the combination of set/reset for some planes and CPU data for other planes, as in the example above, can be used to provide pixel-level control.

There is no clearly defined role for the set/reset circuitry, as there is for, say, the bit mask. In many cases, set/reset is largely interchangeable with CPU data. This is particularly true of CPU data written in write mode 2, because write mode 2 operates similarly to the set/reset circuitry. The most powerful use of set/reset, in my experience, is in applications such as the example of Listing 4.3, where it is used to force the value written to certain planes while the CPU data is written to other planes.

Notes on Set/Reset

The set/reset circuitry is not active in write modes 1 or 2. (Write mode 0 was described in the first installment of "On Graphics," while an exploration of write mode 2 is a topic for a future installment.)

Be aware that because set/reset directly replaces CPU data, it does not necessarily have to force an entire display memory byte to 0 or 0FFh, even when set/reset is replacing CPU data for all planes. For example, if the Bit

Mask register is set to 80h, the set/reset circuitry can modify only bit 7 of the destination byte in each plane; the other seven bits will come from the latches for each plane. Similarly, the set/reset value for each plane can be modified by that plane's ALU.

An Update

In an earlier installment, I suggested the use of word OUTs (OUT DX,AX) to set indexed EGA registers. I have since been informed that this does not work on some early models of AT&T personal computers. If your software is likely to run on such a computer, I suggest that you not use word OUTs. One good habit to get into is the use of macros or subroutine calls to set indexed registers. This practice makes it easy to convert from byte OUTs to word OUTs, or vice versa, if needed.

Reference Material

Several readers have asked where they can get information about programming the Color Graphics Adapter and Hercules Graphics Card. The *IBM Technical Reference, Options and Adapters* manual is a reference for the CGA and Monochrome Display Adapter and is also the primary reference for the EGA. The best reference for the CGA, however, is "The IBM Color/Graphics Adapter," by Thomas V. Hoffmann (*PC Tech Journal*, Vol. 1, No. 1, July 1983).

The primary reference for programming the HGC is the manual Hercules supplies with the board. Most companies that supply Hercules-compatible boards also provide programming information.

Reader Feedback

In the last installment, I included responses from several readers explaining how to generate ROMable code at a specific address. This month's reader responses include answers to all three MASM questions I've posed and what surely is the definitive word on the problems of generating code at a specific address.

John Navas II answered all three MASM questions, as follows. The sample program to which he refers is shown in Listing 4.4 [presented at the end of this chapter].

My solutions to your three puzzles range from crude to elegant to simple. I've enclosed a sample program that demonstrates all of them.

(0) You are correct that MASM has only a single symbol space, so that you cannot normally reuse symbols in different STRUCtures. However, if for example you are defining local STRUCtures for small procedures, there is a crude way to reuse symbols. Simply enclose an entire procedure including any local STRUCtures in a MACRO and declare all of the symbols LOCAL. When the macro is expanded, the assembler will generate unique symbols automatically, and there is no danger of referencing the wrong STRUCture. If you reuse the same MACRO name over and over, MASM shouldn't run out of memory. The downside is that the assembly takes longer, the listing is harder to read, and brackets must be used with LOCAL symbols instead of the more logical (.) STRUCture field-name operator (at least under MASM Version 4.0).

(1) Using STRUCtures to define negative offsets from the BP register in a stack frame (typically for local dynamic storage allocation) requires the SIZE of the STRUCture to be subtracted from BP (e.g., [bp-SIZE locs].field1).

The EQU directive can make it all quite elegant. First EQUate a symbol to the SIZE of the STRUCture, adjusted if necessary to an even number. Then EQUate a second symbol to BP minus the first symbol, all enclosed in brackets. Subtract the first symbol from SP to allocate storage. Use the second symbol, followed by the STRUCture field name either separated by the (.) STRUCture field-name operator or enclosed in brackets, to access individual fields (e.g., loc.w1 or loc[field1]).

(2) As you noted, the count for a DUP operator must be a constant expression. Since the location-counter is relocatable, it must be converted to a constant value before it can be used in a DUP count. The simplest way to convert it is to subtract the SEGMENT name. Your example might become:

```
DB    (2000h-($-segname)) DUP ( 0 )
```

Note that the inner parentheses are necessary to force MASM to first perform the necessary conversion, and that parentheses must of course enclose the DUP value.

Thank you, John. I must repeat a comment from the last installment: the last-mentioned solution works only within the first module linked—which makes sense, since the whole point of your solution is to generate an absolute value at assembly time, and relocation takes place at link time.

Charles Clinton wrote, at considerable length, about the problem of putting code or data at an absolute offset, shedding light on the somewhat bewildering operation of MASM and proving both that there's a great deal for a patient and persistent reader to learn from the MASM manual and that there are mysteries that elude even the most patient and persistent reader.

Charles's letter follows. The letter was in the form of a letter to the editor, hence the reference to the author in the third person. Please note that, other than correcting typos, I present it exactly as he wrote it; all editorial comments are his.

The difficulty that Michael Abrash is encountering in attempting to convince MASM to assemble code up to a certain location (*PJ* 5.1, pg. 42) is that MASM has no idea where the code that it is currently assembling is going to end up. The code is assembled into the current program segment, by which MASM means "a collection of instructions and/or data whose address are all relative to the same segment register" (*MASM 4.0 Ref. Man.*, sect. 3.4, pg. 27), and not relative to an absolute memory address or offset.

The solution to the problem involves making the assumption that since we know where the code is going to go, we can talk about absolute memory locations by describing them relative to the code.

The section on arithmetic operators (sect. 5.3.1, pg. 78) says that all arithmetic expressions must either be integers or, in some special cases, "relocatable memory operands." The section on relocatable [memory] operands (sect. 5.2.3, pg. 69) defines them as "any symbol that represents the memory address . . . of an instruction or of data . . . and [has] no explicit value until the program has been linked." Examining the definition of the current location counter (sect. 5.2.4, pg. 69), we see that is has "the same attributes" as a "near label." Flipping around some more, we find the section on symbol declarations (sect. 4.4, pg. 54), which implies that a label generates a symbol. This means that the $ is a relocatable memory operand (if our assumptions have not gone awry).

Going back to the section on arithmetic operators, we find that we can add or subtract a constant from a relocatable memory operand, or we can find the absolute difference between two memory operands in the same [assembler] segment. We can exploit the difference operation to find our location in memory. If we know that a particular label is going to be at a particular location in memory, and we know how to calculate the distance between two labels, we can calculate the location of a second label.

For example, with the problem that Mr. Abrash is presenting we need to determine the location of the end of the assembled code, so that we can zero-fill to the end of the ROM chip. If we define a label at the start of the ROM chip, like this:

```
code        segment   'ROM'
            assume    cs: code
            org       0
rom_start:
            ... code ...
```

We can then calculate how many bytes have been assembled:

```
number_assbld = $ - offset rom_start
```

The number of bytes that need to be filled is the length of the ROM chip (2000h) less the number of bytes assembled:

```
to_fill = 2000h - number_assbld
```

The statement that does the filling is then

```
db    to_fill dup (0)
```

Putting it all together, and simplifying the expressions yields

```
code        segment   'ROM'
            assume    cs: code
            org       0
rom_start:
            ... code ...
            db        2000h - ($ - offset rom_start)
                          dup (0)
code        ends
            end
```

The key to this solution is remembering that MASM will maintain that it does not know in what manner the linker will manipulate the segment being assembled. In fact, in most cases the linker will concatenate many code and data segments, and then concatenate the segments into groups (which are not necessarily contiguous) and classes. This flexibility and power is what gives one the ability to mix multiple languages and memory models in a single program and allow exact specification of the ordering and arrangement of memory. Unfortunately, it has the side effect of making some of the simplest tasks complicated.

The seemingly obvious solution to this problem of using the "at address" combine clause in the segment declaration will not work, as Microsoft's intended use of this was to allow the user to describe existing data areas, and not define them, so they did not make the expression evaluator smart enough to recognize that the current location counter ("$") can sometimes represent a fixed address.

A subtler problem seems to exist in the offset operator. At first glance, it would seem that

```
db    2000h - offset $ dup (0)
```

should produce the desired effect. Although the MASM manual claims that the offset operator returns the number of bytes between the symbol and the beginning of its segment (sect. 5.3.13, pg. 88), a little experimenting shows that this is not entirely true. The .TYPE operand (sect. 5.3.15, pg. 89) reveals some curious things about the way MASM represents numbers. Assembling the following code reveals the problem:

```
code        segment     'ROM'
            assume      cs: code
            org         10
a           =           10
atype       =           .type a
b           =           offset $
btype       =           .type b
code        ends
            end
```

Upon examining the listing, we see:

Name	Type	Value	Attr
A	Number	000A	
ATYPE	Number	0020	
B	Number	000A	CODE
BTYPE	Number	0022	

By the MASM definition of OFFSET, we would expect A and B to have identical values and both be plain numbers. Rather, what we see is that OFFSET is failing to strip off the attribute of 'CODE' from the expression "OFFSET $." Attributes are a little tricky in MASM, as they are not defined in the MASM manual. They are not in the index, and the only mention of attributes that I can find are in sections "Location-Counter Operand" (sect. 5.2.4, pg. 69) and ".TYPE Operator" (sect. 5.3.15, pg. 89), both of which I consider cryptic descriptions at best. There does not seem to be an operator for changing the attribute of an expression, which is what is called for here.

Thank you, Charles, for guiding us far into the murky depths of MASM as pertains to the problem of generating code or data at an absolute offset. As has been my experience with MASM, there is indeed an explanation and a workaround, but it sure seems harder than it need be to perform what should be a straightforward task.

Next Time

We've completed our tour of the EGA's write mode 0 data path, but, important though write mode 0—the workhorse write mode of the EGA—is, we've scarcely begun our exploration of the EGA. We've write mode 2, read modes 0 and 1, the split screen, text mode, and much, much more yet to go. I'm not sure what's coming up in the next installment—I guess we'll just have to wait and see what catches my fancy. As always, I'm open to suggestions.

See you then.

Listing 4.1

```
; Program to illustrate operation of Map Mask register when drawing
;   to memory that already contains data.
; Assembled with MASM 4.0, linked with LINK 3.51.
; By Michael Abrash, 4/26/87.
; Updated 6/25/89.
;
stackseg          segment para stack 'STACK'
        db        512 dup(?)
stackseg          ends
;
EGA_VIDEO_SEGMENT          equ        0a000h  ;EGA display memory segment
;
; EGA register equates.
;
SC_INDEX          equ        3c4h       ;SC index register
SC_MAP_MASK       equ        2          ;SC map mask register
;
; Macro to set indexed register INDEX of SC chip to SETTING.
;
SETSC   macro     INDEX, SETTING
        mov       dx,SC_INDEX
        mov       al,INDEX
        out       dx,al
        inc       dx
        mov       al,SETTING
        out       dx,al
        dec       dx
        endm
;
cseg    segment para public 'CODE'
        assume    cs:cseg
start   proc      near
;
; Select 640x350 graphics mode.
;
        mov       ax,010h
        int       10h
;
        mov       ax,EGA_VIDEO_SEGMENT
        mov       es,ax                       ;point to video memory
;
; Draw 18 10-scan-line high horizontal bars in green, 10 scan lines apart.
;
        SETSC     SC_MAP_MASK,02h             ;map mask setting enables only
                                              ; plane 1, the green plane
        sub       di,di            ;start at beginning of video memory
        mov       al,0ffh
        mov       bp,18            ;# bars to draw
HorzBarLoop:
        mov       cx,80*10         ;# bytes per horizontal bar
        rep stosb                  ;draw bar
        add       di,80*10         ;point to start of next bar
        dec       bp
        jnz       HorzBarLoop
;
; Fill screen with blue, using Map Mask register to enable writes
; to plane 0, the blue plane, only.
;
```

Listing 4.1 continues

Listing 4.1 *continued*

```
        SETSC   SC_MAP_MASK,01h          ;map mask setting enables only
                                         ; plane 0, the blue plane
        sub     di,di
        mov     cx,80*350                ;# bytes per screen
        mov     al,0ffh
        rep stosb                        ;perform fill (affects only
                                         ; plane 0, the blue plane)
;
; Exit to DOS. (Still in graphics mode; the MODE CO80 command
; can be used to restore the screen to text mode.)
;
        mov     ah,4ch
        int     21h
start   endp
cseg    ends
        end     start
```

Listing 4.2

```
; Program to illustrate operation of set/reset circuitry to force
;   setting to 0 of memory that already contains data.
; Assembled with MASM 4.0, linked with LINK 3.51.
; By Michael Abrash, 4/26/87.
; Updated 6/25/89.
;
stackseg          segment para stack 'STACK'
        db        512 dup(?)
stackseg          ends
;
EGA_VIDEO_SEGMENT         equ     0a000h  ;EGA display memory segment
;
; EGA register equates.
;
SC_INDEX          equ     3c4h    ;SC index register
SC_MAP_MASK       equ     2       ;SC map mask register
GC_INDEX          equ     3ceh    ;GC index register
GC_SET_RESET      equ     0       ;GC set/reset register
GC_ENABLE_SET_RESET equ 1         ;GC enable set/reset register
;
; Macro to set indexed register INDEX of SC chip to SETTING.
;
SETSC   macro   INDEX, SETTING
        mov     dx,SC_INDEX
        mov     al,INDEX
        out     dx,al
        inc     dx
        mov     al,SETTING
        out     dx,al
        dec     dx
        endm
;
; Macro to set indexed register INDEX of GC chip to SETTING.
;
SETGC   macro   INDEX, SETTING
```

Listing 4.2 *continues*

Listing 4.2 continued

```
        mov     dx,GC_INDEX
        mov     al,INDEX
        out     dx,al
        inc     dx
        mov     al,SETTING
        out     dx,al
        dec     dx
        endm
;
cseg    segment para public 'CODE'
        assume  cs:cseg
start   proc    near
;
; Select 640x350 graphics mode.
;
        mov     ax,010h
        int     10h
;
        mov     ax,EGA_VIDEO_SEGMENT
        mov     es,ax                   ;point to video memory
;
; Draw 18 10-scan-line high horizontal bars in green, 10 scan lines apart.
;
        SETSC   SC_MAP_MASK,02h         ;map mask setting enables only
                                        ; plane 1, the green plane
        sub     di,di           ;start at beginning of video memory
        mov     al,0ffh
        mov     bp,18           ;# bars to draw
HorzBarLoop:
        mov     cx,80*10        ;# bytes per horizontal bar
        rep stosb               ;draw bar
        add     di,80*10        ;point to start of next bar
        dec     bp
        jnz     HorzBarLoop
;
; Fill screen with blue, using set/reset to force plane 0 to 1s and all
; other plane to 0s.
;
        SETSC   SC_MAP_MASK,0fh         ;must set map mask to enable all
                                        ; planes, so set/reset values can
                                        ; be written to memory
        SETGC   GC_ENABLE_SET_RESET,0fh ;CPU data to all planes will be
                                        ; replaced by set/reset value
        SETGC   GC_SET_RESET,01h        ;set/reset value is 0ffh for
                                        ; plane 0 (the blue plane)
                                        ; and 0 for other planes
        sub     di,di
        mov     cx,80*350               ;# bytes per screen
        mov     al,0ffh                 ;since set/reset is enabled for
                                        ; all planes, the CPU data is
                                        ; ignored--only the act of
                                        ; writing is important
        rep stosb                       ;perform fill (affects all planes)
;
; Turn off set/reset.
;
        SETGC   GC_ENABLE_SET_RESET,0
;
```

Listing 4.2 continues

Listing 4.2 *continued*

```
; Exit to DOS. (Still in graphics mode; the MODE CO80 command
; can be used to restore the screen to text mode.)
;
        mov     ah,4ch
        int     21h
start   endp
cseg    ends
        end     start
```

Listing 4.3

```
; Program to illustrate operation of set/reset circuitry in conjunction
;  with CPU data to perform two-color modification of memory that
;  already contains data.
; Assembled with MASM 4.0, linked with LINK 3.51.
; By Michael Abrash, 4/26/87.
; Updated 6/25/89.
;
stackseg        segment para stack 'STACK'
        db      512 dup(?)
stackseg        ends
;
EGA_VIDEO_SEGMENT       equ     0a000h  ;EGA display memory segment
;
; EGA register equates.
;
SC_INDEX        equ     3c4h    ;SC index register
SC_MAP_MASK     equ     2       ;SC map mask register
GC_INDEX        equ     3ceh    ;GC index register
GC_SET_RESET    equ     0       ;GC set/reset register
GC_ENABLE_SET_RESET equ 1       ;GC enable set/reset register
;
; Macro to set indexed register INDEX of SC chip to SETTING.
;
SETSC   macro   INDEX, SETTING
        mov     dx,SC_INDEX
        mov     al,INDEX
        out     dx,al
        inc     dx
        mov     al,SETTING
        out     dx,al
        dec     dx
        endm
;
; Macro to set indexed register INDEX of GC chip to SETTING.
;
SETGC   macro   INDEX, SETTING
        mov     dx,GC_INDEX
        mov     al,INDEX
        out     dx,al
        inc     dx
        mov     al,SETTING
        out     dx,al
        dec     dx
```

Listing 4.3 *continues*

Listing 4.3 continued

```
        endm
;
cseg    segment para public 'CODE'
        assume  cs:cseg
start   proc    near
;
; Select 640x350 graphics mode.
;
        mov     ax,010h
        int     10h
;
        mov     ax,EGA_VIDEO_SEGMENT
        mov     es,ax                   ;point to video memory
;
; Draw 18 10-scan-line high horizontal bars in green, 10 scan lines apart.
;
        SETSC   SC_MAP_MASK,02h         ;map mask setting enables only
                                        ; plane 1, the green plane
        sub     di,di           ;start at beginning of video memory
        mov     al,0ffh
        mov     bp,18           ;# bars to draw
HorzBarLoop:
        mov     cx,80*10        ;# bytes per horizontal bar
        rep stosb               ;draw bar
        add     di,80*10        ;point to start of next bar
        dec     bp
        jnz     HorzBarLoop
;
; Fill screen with alternating bars of red and brown, using CPU data
; to set plane 1 and set/reset to set planes 0, 2, & 3.
;
        SETSC   SC_MAP_MASK,0fh         ;must set map mask to enable all
                                        ; planes, so set/reset values can
                                        ; be written to planes 0, 2, & 3
                                        ; and CPU data can be written to
                                        ; plane 1 (the green plane)
        SETGC   GC_ENABLE_SET_RESET,0dh ;CPU data to planes 0, 2, & 3
                                        ; will be replaced by set/reset
                                        ; value
        SETGC   GC_SET_RESET,04h        ;set/reset value is 0ffh for
                                        ; plane 2 (the red plane) and
                                        ; 0 for other planes
        sub     di,di
        mov     cx,80*350/2             ;# words per screen
        mov     ax,07e0h                ;CPU data controls only plane 1;
                                        ; set/reset controls other planes
        rep stosw                       ;perform fill (affects all planes)
;
; Turn off set/reset.
;
        SETGC   GC_ENABLE_SET_RESET,0
;
; Exit to DOS. (Still in graphics mode; the MODE C080 command
; can be used to restore the screen to text mode.)
;
        mov     ah,4ch
        int     21h
start   endp
```

Listing 4.3 continues

Listing 4.3 *continued*

```
cseg    ends
        end     start
```

Listing 4.4

```
; By John Navas.
;
cseg    SEGMENT
        ASSUME  cs:cseg
mproc   MACRO                               ; for local names
        LOCAL   locs,field1,field2,loc1,loc
locs    STRUC                               ; local storage on stack
field1  DW      ?
field2  DW      ?
locs    ENDS
loc1    EQU     SIZE locs + 1 AND -2    ; even length
loc     EQU     [bp-loc1]               ; negative offset from bp
sub     PROC
        push    bp                      ; save old bp
        mov     bp,sp                   ; setup new bp
        sub     sp,loc1                 ; allocate local storage
        mov     loc[field1],1           ; access local storage
        mov     loc[field2],2
        mov     sp,bp                   ; deallocate storage
        pop     bp                      ; restore old bp
        ret                             ; return to caller
sub     ENDP
        ENDM                            ; mproc may be reused
        mproc                           ; expand local names
        DB      2000h - ( $ - cseg ) DUP( 0 )
        call    sub                     ; forced by DB to 2000h
cseg    ENDS
        END
```

5

Write Mode 3
of the VGA

I n April 1987, the long-rumored VGA arrived. As expected, the VGA
replaced the EGA as the PC graphics standard (and in fact did so in
record time); oddly enough, however, the VGA *increased* the value of
good EGA programming at the same time. How so? Well, while the VGA
is clearly a superset of the EGA, it is nonetheless compatible with most
EGA programming techniques, and even offers a completely
EGA-compatible programming model in its highest-resolution mode. In
other words, solid EGA programming techniques didn't go out of style
when the VGA came on the scene. Quite the opposite: Those
programming techniques were just coming into their prime, for IBM chose
to put the VGA on the motherboards of its new PS/2 computers, thereby
ensuring that the VGA would be a standard to be reckoned with.

Happily, "On Graphics" encountered the VGA and continued on with
nary a glitch; just about everything I'd covered before this chapter applied
as well as it ever had and was now guaranteed to be relevant for years to
come. Better yet, the VGA was (and is) clearly superior to the EGA, and
so the new standard meant that we had yet more features to explore.

In this chapter, I predicted that the VGA would take off even faster than
the EGA did. Prophetic words indeed—in fact, they turned out to be a bit
understated, if anything.

I asked in this installment if anyone had come up with uses for write mode 3 other than the one I described. I have since learned of two other uses for write mode 3: line drawing and transparent one-color drawing. I'm sure there are other good applications for write mode 3, and I'm still interested in hearing about them.

Installment 5: In which the VGA arrives, and we find that—Hallelujah!—all we've learned about the EGA still applies, but many new wonders lie ahead.

Well, the VGA is here, and it's a dandy, with 256-color capability (selected from a palette of 256K colors, no less), higher resolution, square pixels, readable registers (finally!), lots of new BIOS functions, better text, relatively good performance, and more. The VGA represents a whole new level of video capability, providing all the basics needed for decent business graphics for the first time in standard IBM graphics. The VGA provides reasonable backward compatibility with the CGA, the MDA, and, most importantly, the EGA. In short, the first video circuitry IBM has ever built into a motherboard is good—about as good as it could be given the lack of a built-in graphics processor and the constraints of backward compatibility.

For *PJ* readers, of course, the concern is how the VGA will affect their software-development efforts. The answer is: a great deal. All IBM PS/2 Micro Channel computers (including models 50, 60, and 80) have the VGA built in; the PC/XT/AT version of the VGA, the remarkably unimaginatively named "Display Adapter," is priced at a fairly reasonable $595; and third-party video companies are scrambling to be the first to clone the VGA. Between the benefits of the VGA and IBM's commitment to the new standard, the VGA should take off even faster than the EGA did.

So, readers, support the VGA in your development efforts—it's the hottest thing around right now. Besides, if you want your software to run on any of the more powerful PS/2 computers, it *has* to run on the VGA, although the BIOS does a good job of masking the differences between the VGA and earlier adapters for older applications.

I'm not going to do a review/evaluation of the VGA—you'll have plenty of opportunities to read such articles in other magazines, and my theory is that *PJ* readers want practical tips and working code. With that in mind, I'm going to note a few points about identifying and programming the VGA and then revisit an old application in order to illuminate an unusual VGA programming feature, write mode 3.

Notes on Programming the VGA

The first point about the VGA is that while it's certainly different from earlier adapters, most old software should run on it. CGA and MDA software should run on the VGA to about the extent to which they run on the EGA, which is to say that the VGA is BIOS-level compatible with the CGA and MDA.

Most EGA software should also run on the VGA, as long as the BIOS is used whenever possible. While the VGA's hardware is actually a good bit different from the EGA's, IBM managed to retain in the VGA the BIOS–register interface through which reasonably well-behaved application programs access the EGA. This doesn't mean that programs that load all the registers directly—or, indeed, touch more registers than they absolutely must—will run; most VGA registers are, in fact, not EGA compatible.

On balance, though, the VGA's compatibility with the EGA is quite good; with an exception or two that I'll note shortly, everything about the EGA that we've covered in "On Graphics" applies equally well to the VGA. The rule of thumb is this: When in doubt, refer to the EGA and VGA technical reference material and make sure that the registers you're accessing are functionally the same on both adapters.

VGA Reference Material

Which brings me to my next point: IBM's hardware reference material on the VGA can be found in the Technical Reference manuals for the Micro Channel computers, including the *Model 50 and 60 Technical Reference* and the *Model 80 Technical Reference*. The Display Adapter technical reference material is available as a separately purchased supplement, the *Display Adapter Technical Reference* (part number S68X-2251-0). Oddly enough, the register descriptions in the *Display Adapter Technical Reference* and in the technical references for the PS/2 computers are not identical, although they seem to describe the same registers. It may be worth your while to buy both the *Display Adapter Technical Reference* and one of the PS/2 computer technical references in order to have two descriptions of some registers.

The *Display Adapter Technical Reference* includes a specification of the interface to the Display Adapter BIOS (which appears to be functionally pretty much the same as the VGA BIOS) as well as a register-level description of the Display Adapter. The technical references for the PS/2 computers do not contain any BIOS interface information; if you don't have the *Display Adapter Technical Reference*, you can get a specification of the entire IBM BIOS interface (including all video BIOS functions), by purchasing IBM's *BIOS Interface Technical Reference* manual (part number S68X-2260-00).

Differences between the VGA and the Display Adapter

IBM notes a few significant differences between the Display Adapter and the VGA. (Incidentally, VGA stands for Video Graphics Array, which describes the chip on the Micro Channel motherboard. As far as I can determine, the same chip is on the Display Adapter—at least it has the same part number and does the same things—but it's easiest to refer to the motherboard video circuitry as the VGA and the PC/XT/AT plug-in board as the Display Adapter.) I'll discuss these differences, which include vertical interrupt capability and monochrome text attributes, next.

Although the VGA offers EGA-compatible vertical interrupt support, IBM's documentation states that the Display Adapter cannot generate a vertical interrupt at all. The reasoning behind this difference isn't clear, but I've tested the Display Adapter myself, and the vertical interrupt is indeed not available.

On page 4-5 of the *Display Adapter Technical Reference*, there is a note to the effect that "the Personal System/2 Display Adapter displays a reverse video intensified character as white on white." It's not clear exactly what the problem is from that quote, and so I did some experimentation. As far as I can tell, when the Display Adapter is in mode 7, characters for which either the foreground or background attribute is 8 are displayed as white on white, and are consequently not readable. The VGA, on the other hand, does display such text correctly. I'm not sure why this problem occurs or what a workaround might be; does anyone out there have any suggestions?

By the way, the VGA is capable of driving either a color or a monochrome monitor automatically. (The monitors must be analog monitors compatible with IBM's PS/2 monitors, the 8503, 8512, 8513, and 8514.) There are no switches—the VGA identifies the monitor through the video connector. Color summing to gray scales is performed when driving a monochrome monitor. What's more, in PS/2 computers, programs can select *any* mode—color or monochrome—directly through INT 10h, function 0. For example, a program can go from mode 3 (color text) to mode 7 (monochrome text) simply by performing

```
mov ax,7
int 10h
```

It is no longer necessary to fiddle with the equipment flag in order to switch between color and monochrome modes (in fact, the VGA BIOS automatically changes the equipment flag as needed on mode sets), and the VGA by itself can emulate any of the CGA, MDA, or EGA adapters at the BIOS—but not hardware—level at any time. However, the VGA can only do this serially; it can't emulate both a color adapter and a monochrome adapter at once, because it is in truth only a single adapter.

The Display Adapter can also drive either a monochrome or a color monitor and also features switchless installation. However, switching between color and monochrome operation still requires changing the equipment flag; unlike the VGA, the Display Adapter is constrained by the possible presence of other adapters in the system. Overall, IBM seems to have done a good job of designing the BIOS and the VGA in such a way that, in most cases, application programs will run just as they would on earlier adapters.

An important note about programming the VGA: Don't use word OUTs to the Attribute Controller at port 3C0h. The EGA addresses the Attribute Controller at both 3C0h and 3C1h, so word OUTs to the Attribute Controller work despite its strange toggling nature. (See Chapter 1 for a description of programming the Attribute Controller.) The VGA addresses the Attribute Controller at 3C0h only, meaning that the high byte of a value written to the VGA's Attribute Controller by a word OUT goes into the bit bucket. However, word OUTs to the Sequencer, the CRT Controller, and the Graphics Controller seem to work fine on the VGA.

All VGA registers are readable, which makes it possible to save the video context (for example, in a TSR program that takes over the screen). While the VGA maintains the EGA's toggling Attribute Controller port operation on writes, it implements Attribute Controller reads in a sensible fashion. The Attribute Controller Index register is always readable at 3C0h, and the Attribute Controller Data register is always readable at 3C1h. Sadly, the need for EGA compatibility prevented IBM from making Attribute Controller writes operate equally sensibly.

There is one aspect of the VGA state that can't be read out, and which consequently can't be saved on a context switch, and that's the state of the Attribute Controller index/data toggle. As a result, it seems advisable to disable interrupts while programming Attribute Controller registers, lest an interrupt come along and trigger a TSR that accesses the Attribute Controller. Better yet, use BIOS functions to program Attribute Controller registers whenever possible. The palette RAM registers (Attribute Controller registers 0 through 0Fh) can be written (and read) through the BIOS, and those are usually the only Attribute Controller registers that application programs change.

Identifying the VGA

IBM has added a couple of functions to the VGA BIOS (and to the Model 30 BIOS as well) that make it much easier to identify installed adapters and their capabilities. Both are accessed through the standard INT 10h video interrupt.

Function 1Ah returns a display combination code indicating the type of the currently active display adapter and the alternate display adapter, if any. Function 1Ah isn't supported by earlier adapters, and so the first test is whether function 1Ah is supported by the installed adapter. If, on return from a function 1Ah call, register AL is set to 1Ah, then function 1Ah is supported. If the function is supported, then BL returns the active display code, and BH returns the alternate display code. Function 1Ah can also be used to change the active and alternate display adapters.

Function 1Bh returns a buffer containing functionality/state information. This information includes the current display mode, the width of the screen, the display buffer size, other BIOS variables, the display combination code, the number of colors supported by the current mode, and font information. Best of all, it includes information about the video modes supported by the active adapter. I haven't had a chance to dig into the functionality/state information yet, but it looks like a gold mine of information. If this function had been available back in the heyday of the MDA and CGA, the world of PC graphics would be a lot less confusing today.

Write Mode 3

The MDA offered only text mode, and so it was easy to program. The CGA had a couple of graphics modes, and while the bit-map organization in these modes was a bit complex, at least the bit map was directly addressed as one linear block of memory. The EGA added the complications of three write modes and two read modes, all operating across four planes. The VGA supports all the modes of the earlier adapters and adds one new write mode, write mode 3, to the list.

Write mode 3 is strange indeed, and its use is not immediately obvious. In write mode 3, set/reset is automatically enabled for all four planes (the Enable Set/Reset register is ignored). The CPU data byte is rotated and then ANDed with the contents of the Bit Mask register, and the result of this operation is used as the contents of the Bit Mask register alone would normally be used. (If this is Greek to you, I suggest you reread chapters 1 through 4. There's no way to understand write mode 3 without understanding write mode 0 first.)

That's what write mode 3 does—but what is it for? I'm not certain what IBM had in mind, but the best applications for write mode 3 I've been able to think of to date have to do with bit-mapped text applications. Write mode 3 seems reasonably well suited to drawing large quantities of graphics-mode text quickly without wiping out the background in the process.

Listing 5.1 [presented at the end of this chapter] is a modification of the code presented in Chapter 3, which used the data-rotate and bit-mask features of the EGA to draw bit-mapped text in write mode 0. Listing 5.1 uses write mode 3 to draw bit-mapped text and, in the process, gains the important benefit of preserving the background into which the text is being drawn. Whereas the code in Listing 3.1 drew the entire character box for each character, with font-pattern bits of value 0 causing a black box to appear around each character, the code in Listing 5.1 affects display memory only when font-pattern bits of value 1 are drawn. As a result, the characters appear to be painted *into* the background rather than *over* it. Another advantage of the code in Listing 5.1 is that the characters can be drawn in any of the 16 available colors.

The key to understanding Listing 5.1 lies in understanding the effect of ANDing the rotated CPU data with the contents of the Bit Mask register. The CPU data is the pattern for the character to be drawn, with bits equal to 1 indicating where character pixels are to appear. The Data Rotate register is set to rotate the CPU data to pixel-align it, since without rotation, characters could be drawn only on byte boundaries. At the same time, the Bit Mask register is set to allow the CPU to modify only the portion of the display-memory byte accessed that the pixel-aligned character falls in; other characters or graphics data won't be wiped out.

The result of ANDing the rotated CPU data byte and the contents of the Bit Mask register is a bit mask that allows only the bits equal to 1 in the original character pattern, rotated and masked to provide pixel alignment, to be modified by the CPU; all other bits come straight from the latches. The latches should have previously been loaded from the target address, and so the effect of the ultimate bit-mask pattern is to allow the CPU to modify only those pixels in display memory that correspond to the bits equal to 1 in that part of the pixel-aligned character that falls in the currently addressed byte. The color of the pixels drawn is determined by the contents of the Set/Reset register.

Whew. It sounds complex, but given an understanding of what the VGA's data rotate, set/reset, and bit-mask features do, it's not that bad. One good way to make sense of it is to refer to the original text-drawing program in Chapter 3 to see how Listing 5.1 differs from that program.

It's worth noting that the text generated by Listing 5.1 could have been drawn without write mode 3, and at relatively little performance cost; with a bit of thought, write mode 0 could have been used instead. Instead of letting write mode 3 rotate each font byte and AND it with the contents of the Bit Mask register, the CPU could simply have rotated each font byte directly, ANDed it with the value destined for the Bit Mask register, and then set the Bit Mask register to the resulting value. Additionally, enable set/reset could simply be forced on for all planes, emulating the way in which write mode 3 generates pixel color. While this arrangement would require additional bit manipulation by the CPU and would have required CPU rotation, which is slower than rotation performed by the VGA's barrel shifter, it would save setting the Data Rotate register and might well turn out to run at about the same speed as the write mode 3 implementation.

Write mode 3 is particularly useful for the drawing of large blocks of text. For example, suppose that we were to draw a line of 8-dot-wide bit-mapped text 40 characters long. It would be possible to set up the bit mask and data rotation as appropriate for the left portions of the bit-aligned characters in the line (the portions of the characters to the left of the byte boundaries) and draw only the left portions of all 40 characters in write mode 3. Then the bit mask could be set up for the right portions of the characters, and the right portions of all 40 characters could be drawn. The VGA's barrel shifter would perform all rotations at no performance cost, and the only OUTs required would be those few needed to set the bit mask twice and the data rotation once and those needed to select the drawing color and write mode 3.

The above technique could well outperform single-character bit-mapped text drivers such as the one in Listing 5.1 by a significant margin. Listing 5.2 [presented at the end of this chapter] illustrates one implementation of such an approach. Incidentally, note the use of the 8-by-14 ROM font in Listing 5.2, rather than the 8-by-8 ROM font used in Listing 5.1. There is also an 8-by-16 font stored in ROM, along with the tables used to modify the 8-by-14 and 8-by-16 ROM fonts into 9-by-14 and 9-by-16 fonts.

It's very possible that there's a better application for write mode 3 than the sort of bit-mapped text handling I've discussed. If you think of such an application, please write and let *PJ*'s readers know about it.

Preserving Reserved Bits

Note that the code in Listing 5.1 uses the readable register feature of the VGA to preserve reserved bits and bits other than those being modified. The EGA has no readable registers, and so on the EGA it is necessary to set all bits in a given register whenever that register is modified. The VGA makes it possible to change only those bits of immediate interest, and this procedure is highly recommended, since IBM (or clone manufacturers) may well use some of those reserved bits in the future.

In Conclusion

The VGA is a complex, powerful, fascinating video standard. There's a heck of a lot to learn, and knowledge is the key to high-performance VGA programs. One area I'll try to cover soon is 256-color mode, another is the ability to select colors from a set of 256K, and yet another is text mode font handling. And then there's the new two-color high-resolution mode, the pel panning compatibility feature, the high-bandwidth blanking bit, the . . .

Yes indeed, there's a lot to cover next time.

See you then.

Listing 5.1

```
; Program to illustrate operation of write mode 3 of the VGA.
;   Draws 8x8 characters at arbitrary locations without disturbing
;   the background, using VGA's 8x8 ROM font.  Designed
;   for use with modes 0Dh, 0Eh, 0Fh, 10h, and 12h.
; Runs only on VGAs (in Models 50 & up and IBM Display Adapter
;   and 100% compatibles).
; Assembled with MASM 4.0, linked with LINK 3.51.
; By Michael Abrash, 9/1/87.
; Updated 6/25/89.
;
stackseg        segment para stack 'STACK'
        db          512 dup(?)
stackseg        ends
;
VGA_VIDEO_SEGMENT       equ     0a000h  ;VGA display memory segment
SCREEN_WIDTH_IN_BYTES   equ     044ah   ;offset of BIOS variable
FONT_CHARACTER_SIZE     equ     8       ;# bytes in each font char
;
; VGA register equates.
;
SC_INDEX              equ     3c4h    ;SC index register
SC_MAP_MASK          equ     2       ;SC map mask register index
GC_INDEX             equ     3ceh    ;GC index register
GC_SET_RESET         equ     0       ;GC set/reset register index
GC_ENABLE_SET_RESET equ 1            ;GC enable set/reset register index
GC_ROTATE            equ     3       ;GC data rotate/logical function
                                     ; register index
GC_MODE              equ     5       ;GC Mode register
GC_BIT_MASK          equ     8       ;GC bit mask register index
;
dseg    segment para common 'DATA'
TEST_TEXT_ROW    equ     69      ;row to display test text at
TEST_TEXT_COL    equ     17      ;column to display test text at
TEST_TEXT_WIDTH  equ     8       ;width of a character in pixels
TestString       label   byte
        db          'Hello, world!',0       ;test string to print.
FontPointer      dd      ?               ;font offset
dseg    ends
;
cseg    segment para public 'CODE'
        assume  cs:cseg, ds:dseg
start   proc    near
        mov     ax,dseg
        mov     ds,ax
;
; Select 640x480 graphics mode.
;
        mov     ax,012h
        int     10h
;
; Set the screen to all blue, using the readability of VGA registers
; to preserve reserved bits.
;
        mov     dx,GC_INDEX
        mov     al,GC_SET_RESET
        out     dx,al
        inc     dx
        in      al,dx
```

Listing 5.1 *continues*

Listing 5.1 continued

```
            and     al,0f0h
            or      al,1                ;blue plane only set, others reset
            out     dx,al
            dec     dx
            mov     al,GC_ENABLE_SET_RESET
            out     dx,al
            inc     dx
            in      al,dx
            and     al,0f0h
            or      al,0fh              ;enable set/reset for all planes
            out     dx,al
            mov     dx,VGA_VIDEO_SEGMENT
            mov     es,dx               ;point to display memory
            mov     di,0
            mov     cx,8000h            ;fill all 32k words
            mov     ax,0ffffh           ;because of set/reset, the value
                                        ; written actually doesn't matter
            rep stosw                   ;fill with blue
;
; Set driver to use the 8x8 font.
;
            call    Select8x8Font
;
; Print the test string, cycling through colors.
;
            mov     si,offset TestString
            mov     bx,TEST_TEXT_ROW
            mov     cx,TEST_TEXT_COL
            mov     ah,0                ;start with color 0
StringOutLoop:
            lodsb
            and     al,al
            jz      StringOutDone
            push    ax                  ;preserve color
            call    DrawChar
            pop     ax                  ;restore color
            inc     ah                  ;next color
            and     ah,0fh              ;colors range from 0 to 15
            add     cx,TEST_TEXT_WIDTH
            jmp     StringOutLoop
StringOutDone:
;
; Wait for a key, then set to text mode & end.
;
            mov     ah,1
            int     21h         ;wait for a key
            mov     ax,3
            int     10h         ;restore text mode
;
; Exit to DOS.
;
            mov     ah,4ch
            int     21h
Start   endp
;
; Subroutine to draw a text character in a linear graphics mode
;   (0Dh, 0Eh, 0Fh, 010h, 012h). Background around the pixels that
;   make up the character is preserved.
```

Listing 5.1 continues

Listing 5.1 *continued*

```
; Font used should be pointed to by FontPointer.
;
; Input:
;   AL = character to draw
;   AH = color to draw character in (0-15)
;   BX = row to draw text character at
;   CX = column to draw text character at
;
;   Forces ALU function to "move".
;   Forces write mode 3.
;
DrawChar        proc    near
        push    ax
        push    bx
        push    cx
        push    dx
        push    si
        push    di
        push    bp
        push    ds

        push    ax      ;preserve character to draw in AL
;
; Set up set/reset to produce character color, using the readability
; of VGA register to preserve the setting of reserved bits 7-4.
;
        mov     dx,GC_INDEX
        mov     al,GC_SET_RESET
        out     dx,al
        inc     dx
        in      al,dx
        and     al,0f0h
        and     ah,0fh
        or      al,ah
        out     dx,al
;
; Select write mode 3, using the readability of VGA registers
; to leave bits other than the write mode bits unchanged.
;
        mov     dx,GC_INDEX
        mov     al,GC_MODE
        out     dx,al
        inc     dx
        in      al,dx
        or      al,3
        out     dx,al
;
; Set DS:SI to point to font and ES to point to display memory.
;
        lds     si,[FontPointer]        ;point to font
        mov     dx,VGA_VIDEO_SEGMENT
        mov     es,dx                   ;point to display memory
;
; Calculate screen address of byte character starts in.
;
        pop     ax      ;get back character to draw in AL

        push    ds      ;point to BIOS data segment
```

Listing 5.1 *continues*

Listing 5.1 continued

```
        sub     dx,dx
        mov     ds,dx
        xchg    ax,bx
        mov     di,ds:[SCREEN_WIDTH_IN_BYTES]   ;retrieve BIOS
                                                ; screen width

        pop     ds
        mul     di      ;calculate offset of start of row
        push    di      ;set aside screen width
        mov     di,cx   ;set aside the column
        and     cl,0111b ;keep only the column in-byte address
        shr     di,1
        shr     di,1
        shr     di,1    ;divide column by 8 to make a byte address
        add     di,ax   ;and point to byte
;
; Calculate font address of character.
;
        sub     bh,bh
        shl     bx,1    ;assumes 8 bytes per character; use
        shl     bx,1    ; a multiply otherwise
        shl     bx,1    ;offset in font of character
        add     si,bx   ;offset in font segment of character
;
; Set up the GC rotation. In write mode 3, this is the rotation
; of CPU data before it is ANDed with the Bit Mask register to
; form the bit mask. Force the ALU function to "move". Uses the
; readability of VGA registers to leave reserved bits unchanged.
;
        mov     dx,GC_INDEX
        mov     al,GC_ROTATE
        out     dx,al
        inc     dx
        in      al,dx
        and     al,0e0h
        or      al,cl
        out     dx,al
;
; Set up BH as bit mask for part of character in left byte,
; BL as bit mask for part of character in right byte.
;
        mov     bx,0ff00h
        shr     bx,cl
;
; Draw the character, the part in left byte first, then the part in
; right byte next, using the data rotation to position the character
; across the byte boundary and then using write mode 3 to combine the
; character data with the bit mask to allow the set/reset value (the
; character color) through only for the proper portion (where the
; font bits for the character are 1) of the character for each byte.
; Wherever the font bits for the character are 0, the background
; color is preserved.
;
; Does not check for the case where the character is byte-aligned,
; so no rotation (and hence only one write) is required; special
; code would speed that case considerably.
;
        mov     bp,FONT_CHARACTER_SIZE
        mov     dx,GC_INDEX
```

Listing 5.1 continues

Listing 5.1 *continued*

```
        pop     cx      ;get back screen width
        dec     cx
        dec     cx      ;-2 because do two bytes for each char
; Point the GC Index register to the Bit Mask register for the
; duration of the loop.
        mov     al,GC_BIT_MASK
        out     dx,al
        inc     dx      ;point to GC Data register
CharacterLoop:
;
; Set the bit mask for the part of the character in the left byte.
;
        mov     al,bh
        out     dx,al
;
; Get the next character byte & write it to display memory.
; (This draws the part of the character in the left byte.)
;
        mov     al,es:[di]      ;load latches from left byte
        lodsb                   ;get character byte
        stosb                   ;write left part of character byte
;
; Set the bit mask for the part of the character in the right byte.
;
        xchg    ax,bx           ;get right-byte bit mask in AL
                                ; and save the font byte
        out     dx,al           ;set the right-byte bit mask
        xchg    ax,bx           ;put the font byte back in AL
                                ; and the bit masks back in BX
;
; Write the character byte to display memory again.
; (Right part of character.)
;
        mov     ah,es:[di]      ;load latches from right byte
        stosb                   ;write character byte
;
; Point to next line of character in display memory.
;
        add     di,cx
;
        dec     bp
        jnz     CharacterLoop
;
        pop     ds
        pop     bp
        pop     di
        pop     si
        pop     dx
        pop     cx
        pop     bx
        pop     ax
        ret
DrawChar        endp
;
; Set the pointer to the 8x8 font.
;
Select8x8Font   proc    near
        mov     ah,11h  ;EGA BIOS character generator function,
```

Listing 5.1 *continues*

Listing 5.1 *continued*

```
        mov     al,30h   ; return info subfunction
        mov     bh,3     ;get 8x8 font pointer
        int     10h
        mov     word ptr [FontPointer],bp        ;save pointer
        mov     word ptr [FontPointer+2],es
        ret
Select8x8Font   endp
;
cseg    ends
        end     start
```

Listing 5.2

```
; Program to illustrate high-speed text-drawing operation of
;  write mode 3 of the VGA.
;  Draws a string of 8x14 characters starting at any location
;  without disturbing the background, using VGA's 8x14 ROM font.
;  Designed for use with modes 0Dh, 0Eh, 0Fh, 10h, and 12h.
; Runs only on VGAs (in Models 50 & up and IBM Display Adapter
;  and 100% compatibles).
; Assembled with MASM 4.0, linked with LINK 3.51.
; By Michael Abrash, 9/1/87.
; Updated 6/25/89.
;
stackseg        segment para stack 'STACK'
        db      512 dup(?)
stackseg        ends
;
VGA_VIDEO_SEGMENT       equ     0a000h  ;VGA display memory segment
SCREEN_WIDTH_IN_BYTES   equ     044ah   ;offset of BIOS variable
FONT_CHARACTER_SIZE     equ     14      ;# bytes in each font char
;
; VGA register equates.
;
SC_INDEX        equ     3c4h    ;SC index register
SC_MAP_MASK     equ     2       ;SC map mask register index
GC_INDEX        equ     3ceh    ;GC index register
GC_SET_RESET    equ     0       ;GC set/reset register index
GC_ENABLE_SET_RESET equ 1       ;GC enable set/reset register index
GC_ROTATE       equ     3       ;GC data rotate/logical function
                                ; register index
GC_MODE         equ     5       ;GC Mode register
GC_BIT_MASK     equ     8       ;GC bit mask register index
;
dseg    segment para common 'DATA'
TEST_TEXT_ROW   equ     69      ;row to display test text at
TEST_TEXT_COL   equ     17      ;column to display test text at
TEST_TEXT_COLOR equ     0fh     ;high intensity white
TestString      label   byte
        db      'Hello, world!',0       ;test string to print.
FontPointer     dd      ?               ;font offset
dseg    ends
;
cseg    segment para public 'CODE'
```

Listing 5.2 *continues*

Listing 5.2 *continued*

```
        assume  cs:cseg, ds:dseg
start   proc    near
        mov     ax,dseg
        mov     ds,ax
;
; Select 640x480 graphics mode.
;
        mov     ax,012h
        int     10h
;
; Set the screen to all blue, using the readability of VGA registers
; to preserve reserved bits.
;
        mov     dx,GC_INDEX
        mov     al,GC_SET_RESET
        out     dx,al
        inc     dx
        in      al,dx
        and     al,0f0h
        or      al,1            ;blue plane only set, others reset
        out     dx,al
        dec     dx
        mov     al,GC_ENABLE_SET_RESET
        out     dx,al
        inc     dx
        in      al,dx
        and     al,0f0h
        or      al,0fh          ;enable set/reset for all planes
        out     dx,al
        mov     dx,VGA_VIDEO_SEGMENT
        mov     es,dx           ;point to display memory
        mov     di,0
        mov     cx,8000h        ;fill all 32k words
        mov     ax,0ffffh       ;because of set/reset, the value
                                ; written actually doesn't matter
        rep stosw               ;fill with blue
;
; Set driver to use the 8x14 font.
;
        call    Select8x14Font
;
; Print the test string.
;
        mov     si,offset TestString
        mov     bx,TEST_TEXT_ROW
        mov     cx,TEST_TEXT_COL
        mov     ah,TEST_TEXT_COLOR
        call    DrawString
;
; Wait for a key, then set to text mode & end.
;
        mov     ah,1
        int     21h             ;wait for a key
        mov     ax,3
        int     10h             ;restore text mode
;
; Exit to DOS.
;
```

Listing 5.2 *continues*

Listing 5.2 *continued*

```
        mov     ah,4ch
        int     21h
Start   endp
;
; Subroutine to draw a text string left-to-right in a linear
;  graphics mode (0Dh, 0Eh, 0Fh, 010h, 012h) with 8-dot-wide
;  characters. Background around the pixels that make up the
;  characters is preserved.
; Font used should be pointed to by FontPointer.
;
; Input:
;  AH = color to draw string in
;  BX = row to draw string on
;  CX = column to start string at
;  DS:SI = string to draw
;
;  Forces ALU function to "move".
;  Forces write mode 3.
;
DrawString      proc    near
        push    ax
        push    bx
        push    cx
        push    dx
        push    si
        push    di
        push    bp
        push    ds
;
; Set up set/reset to produce the desired character color, using
; the readability of VGA register to preserve the setting of
; reserved bits 7-4.
;
        mov     dx,GC_INDEX
        mov     al,GC_SET_RESET
        out     dx,al
        inc     dx
        in      al,dx
        and     al,0f0h
        and     ah,0fh
        or      al,ah
        out     dx,al
;
; Select write mode 3, using the readability of VGA registers
; to leave bits other than the write mode bits unchanged.
;
        mov     dx,GC_INDEX
        mov     al,GC_MODE
        out     dx,al
        inc     dx
        in      al,dx
        or      al,3
        out     dx,al
        mov     dx,VGA_VIDEO_SEGMENT
        mov     es,dx                       ;point to display memory
;
; Calculate screen address of byte character starts in.
;
```

Listing 5.2 *continues*

Listing 5.2 *continued*

```
        push    ds      ;point to BIOS data segment
        sub     dx,dx
        mov     ds,dx
        mov     di,ds:[SCREEN_WIDTH_IN_BYTES]   ;retrieve BIOS
                                               ; screen width
        pop     ds
        mov     ax,bx   ;row
        mul     di      ;calculate offset of start of row
        push    di      ;set aside screen width
        mov     di,cx   ;set aside the column
        and     cl,0111b ;keep only the column in-byte address
        shr     di,1
        shr     di,1
        shr     di,1    ;divide column by 8 to make a byte address
        add     di,ax   ;and point to byte
;
; Set up the GC rotation. In write mode 3, this is the rotation
; of CPU data before it is ANDed with the Bit Mask register to
; form the bit mask. Force the ALU function to "move". Uses the
; readability of VGA registers to leave reserved bits unchanged.
;
        mov     dx,GC_INDEX
        mov     al,GC_ROTATE
        out     dx,al
        inc     dx
        in      al,dx
        and     al,0e0h
        or      al,cl
        out     dx,al
;
; Set up BH as bit mask for part of character in left byte,
; BL as bit mask for part of character in right byte.
;
        mov     bx,0ff00h
        shr     bx,cl
;
; Draw all characters, all left-byte portions first, followed by all
; right-byte portions. Uses the VGA's barrel shifter to position
; characters across byte boundaries and then uses write mode 3 to
; combine character data and left/right byte masks to allow the
; set/reset value (the character color) through only for the proper
; portion (where the font bits for the character are 1) of the
; character for each byte.
; Wherever the font bits for the character are 0, the background
; color is preserved.
;
; Does not check for the case where the character is byte-aligned,
; so no rotation (and hence only one write) is required; special
; code would speed that case considerably.
;
; First, draw the left portion of each character in the string.
;
        pop     cx      ;get back screen width
        push    si
        push    di
        push    bx
;
; Set the bit mask for the left half of the character.
```

Listing 5.2 *continues*

Listing 5.2 *continued*

```
;
        mov     dx,GC_INDEX
        mov     al,GC_BIT_MASK
        mov     ah,bh
        out     dx,ax
LeftHalfLoop:
        lodsb
        and     al,al
        jz      LeftHalfLoopDone
        call    CharacterUp
        inc     di        ;point to next character location
        jmp     LeftHalfLoop
LeftHalfLoopDone:
        pop     bx
        pop     di
        pop     si
;
; Draw the right portion of each character in the string.
;
        inc     di        ;right portion of each character is across
                          ; byte boundary
;
; Set the bit mask for the right half of the character.
;
        mov     dx,GC_INDEX
        mov     al,GC_BIT_MASK
        mov     ah,bl
        out     dx,ax
RightHalfLoop:
        lodsb
        and     al,al
        jz      RightHalfLoopDone
        call    CharacterUp
        inc     di        ;point to next character location
        jmp     RightHalfLoop
RightHalfLoopDone:
;
        pop     ds
        pop     bp
        pop     di
        pop     si
        pop     dx
        pop     cx
        pop     bx
        pop     ax
        ret
DrawString      endp
;
; Draw a character.
;
; Input:
;   AL = character
;   CX = screen width
;   ES:DI = address to draw character at
;
CharacterUp     proc    near
        push    cx
        push    si
```

Listing 5.2 *continues*

Listing 5.2 continued

```
        push    di
        push    ds
;
; Set DS:SI to point to font and ES to point to display memory.
;
        lds     si,[FontPointer]        ;point to font
;
; Calculate font address of character.
;
        mov     bl,14   ;14 bytes per character
        mul     bl
        add     si,ax   ;offset in font segment of character

        mov     bp,FONT_CHARACTER_SIZE
        dec     cx      ;-1 because one byte per char
CharacterLoop:
        lodsb                   ;get character byte
        mov     ah,es:[di]      ;load latches
        stosb                   ;write character byte
;
; Point to next line of character in display memory.
;
        add     di,cx
;
        dec     bp
        jnz     CharacterLoop
;
        pop     ds
        pop     di
        pop     si
        pop     cx
        ret
CharacterUp     endp
;
; Set the pointer to the 8x14 font.
;
Select8x14Font  proc    near
        mov     ah,11h  ;VGA BIOS character generator function,
        mov     al,30h  ; return info subfunction
        mov     bh,2    ;get 8x14 font pointer
        int     10h
        mov     word ptr [FontPointer],bp       ;save pointer
        mov     word ptr [FontPointer+2],es
        ret
Select8x14Font  endp
;
cseg    ends
        end     start
```

CHAPTER 6

Yet Another Write Mode

I n Chapter 6, after a year's worth of "On Graphics" installments, we're *still* covering write modes! Is there no end to the intricacies of the EGA and VGA?

Actually, this chapter completes our exploration of write modes. Admittedly, the write modes *are* many and complex . . . but they're also remarkably powerful and flexible. And now that you've acquired a thorough understanding of the write modes, you can put them to good use in creating graphics software. As we've seen in the first five chapters of *Power Graphics Programming,* each EGA/VGA feature has its uses; EGA/VGA programming is a matter of understanding those uses and selecting the right mix of features for each particular task.

I'd like to make two updates to installment 6. First, *Turbo Technix,* the Borland magazine, closed its doors before my article on the VGA made it into print. The article remains unpublished to this day, and so I'm sorry to say that there's nowhere you can look it up. So it goes.

Second, the description in this chapter of how to switch from graphics mode to text mode and back without losing the contents of the graphics screen works fine for standard EGAs and VGAs. However, some EGAs and VGAs that offer special text modes or attributes may use plane 3—which IBM EGAs and VGAs leave untouched in text mode—to store text information, in the process destroying a part of the graphics screen that is not saved by Listing 6.3 [presented at the end of this chapter]. The result could be incorrect intensity information that produces a band of corrupted pixels across the top of the display on the return to graphics mode in Listing 6.3.

I've modified Listing 6.3 to address this potential problem. If you want to save the first 8K of plane 3 as well as the first 8K of plane 2, set the SAVE_PLANE_3 equate in Listing 6.3 to 1. Of course, an extra 8K of storage space is required to hold the contents of plane 3 while the display is in text mode; so, you may not want to use this option unless you actually encounter the plane-3 problem in the real world. Still, it's safest to save those extra 8K bytes . . .

As is usually the case for video programming in the diverse world of EGA/VGA clones, testing across a broad spectrum of third-party adapters is the safest course.

Installment 6: In which we venture ever deeper into unknown waters, encountering yet another of those damnable write modes.

In the last installment of "On Graphics," we learned about the markedly peculiar write mode 3 of the VGA, after having spent four installments learning the ins and outs of the EGA's write mode 0, touching on write mode 1 as well in the first installment. Happily, it turns out that the VGA supports all the write modes (write modes 0, 1, and 2) of the EGA and supports the same read modes as the EGA as well. Which leaves two burning questions: What is write mode 2, and how the heck do you *read* VGA (and EGA) memory?

Write mode 2 is a bit unusual but not really hard to understand, particularly for those of you who followed my description of set/reset in Chapter 4. Reading VGA memory, on the other hand, can be stranger than you would ever imagine.

Let's start with the easy stuff, write mode 2. If there's room, I'll start in on reading VGA memory, but I suspect that will have to wait until next time.

Write Mode 2

Remember how set/reset worked? Good, because that's pretty much how write mode 2 works. (You *don't* remember? Well, I'll provide a brief refresher.

Recall that the set/reset circuitry for each of the four planes affects the byte written by the CPU in one of three ways: by replacing the CPU byte with 0, by replacing it with 0FFh, or by leaving it unchanged. The nature of the transformation for each plane is controlled by two bits. The enable set/reset bit for a given plane selects whether the CPU byte is replaced or not, and the set/reset bit for that plane selects the value with which each bit of the CPU byte is replaced if the enable set/reset bit is 1. The net effect of set/reset is to independently force any, none, or all planes to either all 1s or all 0s on CPU writes. As we discussed a few articles back, this is a convenient way to force a specific color to appear no matter what color the pixels being overwritten are. Set/reset also allows the CPU to control the contents of some planes while the set/reset circuitry controls the contents of other planes.

Write mode 2 is basically a set/reset–type mode with enable set/reset always on for all planes and with the set/reset data coming directly from the byte written by the CPU. To put it another way, the lower four bits written by the CPU are written across the four planes, thereby becoming a color value. To put it yet another way, bit 0 of the CPU byte is expanded to a byte and sent to the plane-0 ALU (if bit 0 is 0, a 0 byte is the CPU-side input to the plane-0 ALU, while if bit 0 is 1, a 0FFh byte is the CPU-side input); likewise, bit 1 of the CPU byte is expanded to a byte for plane 1, bit 2 is expanded for plane 2, and bit 3 is expanded for plane 3.

Those of you who have been following this series probably understand write mode 2 at this point; I suspect that the rest of you could use some additional explanation of an admittedly nonobvious mode. Let's follow the CPU byte through write mode 2, step by step.

Figure 6.1 shows the write mode 2 data path. The CPU byte comes into the VGA (or EGA) and is split into four separate bits, one for each plane. Bits 7–4 of the CPU byte vanish into the bit bucket, never to be heard from again. Speculation long held that those four unused bits indicated that IBM would someday come out with an 8-plane EGA that supported 256 colors. When IBM did finally come out with a 256-color mode (mode 13h of the VGA), it turned out not to be planar at all, and the upper nibble of the CPU byte remains unused in write mode 2 to this day.

The bit of the CPU byte sent to each plane is expanded to a 0 or 0FFh byte, depending on whether the bit is 0 or 1, respectively. The byte for each plane then becomes the CPU-side input to the respective plane's ALU. From this point on, the write mode 2 data path is identical to the write mode 0 data path. As I discussed in earlier chapters, the latch byte for each plane is the other ALU input, and the ALU either ANDs, ORs, or XORs the two bytes together or simply passes the CPU-side byte through. The byte generated by each plane's ALU then goes through the bit-mask circuitry, which selects on a bit-by-bit basis between the ALU byte and the latch byte. Finally, the byte from the bit-mask circuitry for each plane is written to that plane if the corresponding bit in the Map Mask register is set to 1.

It's worth noting the two differences between write mode 2 and write mode 0, the standard write mode of the VGA. First, rotation of the CPU data byte does not take place in write mode 2. Second, the Set/Reset and Enable Set/Reset registers have no effect in write mode 2.

Now that we understand the mechanics of write mode 2, we can step back and get a feel for what it might be useful for. View bits 3–0 of the CPU byte as a single pixel in one of 16 colors. Next, imagine that nibble

---

Fig. 6.1   *Data flow through the VGA in write mode 2.*

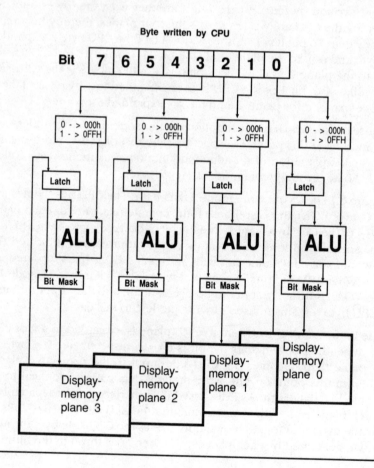

turned sideways and written across the four planes, one bit to a plane. Finally, expand each of the bits to a byte, as shown in Figure 6.2, so that eight pixels are drawn in the color selected by bits 3–0 of the CPU byte. Within the constraints of the VGA's data paths, that's exactly what write mode 2 does.

By "the constraints of the VGA's data paths," I mean the ALUs, the bit mask, and the map mask. As Figure 6.1 indicates, the ALUs can modify the color written by the CPU, the map mask can prevent the CPU from altering selected planes, and the bit mask can prevent the CPU from altering selected bits of the byte written to. (Actually, the bit mask simply substitutes latch bits for ALU bits, but since the latches are normally loaded from the destination display-memory byte, the net effect of the bit mask is usually to preserve bits of the destination byte.) These are not really constraints at all, of course, but, rather, features of the VGA; I simply want

Fig. 6.2   *In write mode 2, the lower four bits of the byte written by the CPU are written as a color across the four planes, with each bit expanded to a byte.*

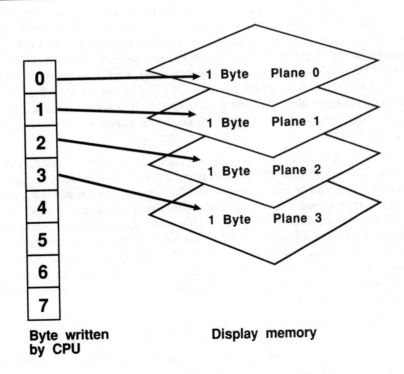

Byte written
by CPU

Display memory

to make it clear that the use of write mode 2 to set eight pixels to a given color is a rather simple special case among the many possible ways in which write mode 2 can be used.

Write mode 2 is selected by setting bits 1 and 0 of the Graphics Mode register (indexed Graphics Controller register 5) to 1 and 0, respectively. Since VGA registers are readable, the correct way to select write mode 2 on the VGA is to read the Graphics Mode register, mask off bits 1 and 0, OR in 00000010b (02h), and write the result back to the Graphics Mode register, thereby leaving the other bits in the register undisturbed. Unfortunately, EGA registers are emphatically *not* readable, making it difficult to take advantage of the VGA's readable registers without separate EGA and VGA drivers.

Copying Chunky Bit Maps to VGA Memory Using Write Mode 2

Let's take a look at two examples of write mode 2 in action. Listing 6.1 [presented at the end of this chapter] shows a program that uses write mode 2 to copy a graphics image in "chunky format" to the VGA. In chunky format, adjacent bits in a single byte make up each pixel: Mode 4 of the CGA, EGA, and VGA is a two-bit-per-pixel chunky mode, and mode 13h of the VGA is an eight-bit-per-pixel chunky mode. Chunky format is convenient, since all the information about each pixel is contained in a single byte; consequently, chunky format is often used to store bit maps in system memory.

Unfortunately, VGA memory is organized as a planar, rather than chunky, bit map in modes 0Dh through 12h, with the bits that make up each pixel spread across four planes. The conversion from chunky to planar format in write mode 0 is quite a nuisance, requiring a good deal of bit manipulation. In write mode 2, however, the conversion becomes a snap, as shown in Listing 6.1. Once the VGA is placed in write mode 2, the lower four bits (the lower nibble) of the CPU byte (a single, four-bit chunky pixel) become eight planar pixels, all the same color. As discussed in Chapter 3, the bit mask makes it possible to narrow the effect of a CPU write down to a single pixel.

Given the above, conversion of a chunky four-bit-per-pixel bit map to the VGA's planar format in write mode 2 is trivial. First, the Bit Mask register is set to allow only the VGA display-memory bits corresponding to the leftmost chunky pixel of the two stored in the first chunky bit-map byte to be modified. Next, the destination byte in display memory is read in order to load the latches. Then, a byte containing two chunky pixels is read from the chunky bit map in system memory, and the byte is rotated four bits to the right to get the leftmost chunky pixel in position. This rotated byte is written to the destination byte; since write mode 2 is active, each bit of the chunky pixel goes to its respective plane, and since the Bit Mask register is set up to allow only one bit in each plane to be modified, a single pixel in the color of the chunky pixel is written to VGA memory.

The above process is then repeated for the rightmost chunky pixel, if necessary, and repeated again for as many pixels as are in the image.

"That's an interesting application of write mode 2," you may well say, "but is it really useful?" While the ability to convert chunky bit maps into VGA bit maps does have its uses, Listing 6.1 is intended primarily to illustrate the mechanics of write mode 2. In fact, I've heard of a considerably faster (and truly ingenious) way to write chunky pixel bit maps to EGA memory using write mode 2, read mode 1, and the graphics-position registers; sadly, since the VGA lacks graphics-position registers, the faster conversion technique works only on the EGA, and so it is no longer really useful.

Drawing Color-Patterned Lines Using Write Mode 2

A more serviceable use of write mode 2 is shown in Listing 6.2 [presented at the end of this chapter]. The program shown in Listing 6.2 draws multicolored horizontal, vertical, and diagonal lines, basing the color patterns on passed color tables. Write mode 2 is ideal because in this application, color can vary from one pixel to the next, and in write mode 2 all that's required to set pixel color is a change of the lower nibble of the byte written by the CPU. Set/reset could be used to achieve the same result, but an index/data pair of OUTs would be required to set the Set/Reset register to each new color. Similarly, the Map Mask register could be used in write mode 0 to set pixel color, but in this case, not only would an index/data pair of OUTs be required, but also there would be no guarantee that data already in display memory wouldn't interfere with the color of the pixel being drawn, since the Map Mask register allows drawing only to selected planes.

Listing 6.2 is hardly a comprehensive line-drawing program, since it draws only a few special line cases. And although it is reasonably fast, it is far from the fastest possible code to handle those cases, given that it goes through a dot-plot routine and draws horizontal lines a pixel, rather than a byte, at a time. Write mode 2 would, however, serve just as well in a full-blown line-drawing routine. For any type of patterned line drawing on the VGA, or indeed for any type of patterned drawing at all, the basic principle remains the same: Use the Bit Mask to select the pixel (or pixels) to be altered, and use the CPU byte in write mode 2 to select the color in which the pixel is to be drawn.

When to Use Write Mode 2 and When to Use Set/Reset

As indicated above, write mode 2 and set/reset are functionally interchangeable. Write mode 2 lends itself to more efficient implementations when the drawing color changes frequently, as in Listing 6.2.

Set/reset tends to be superior when many pixels in succession are drawn in the same color. With set/reset enabled for all planes, the Set/Reset register provides the color data; as a result, the CPU is free to draw whatever byte value it wishes. For example, the CPU can execute an OR instruction to display memory when set/reset is enabled for all planes, thus both loading the latches and writing the color value with a single instruction, secure in the knowledge that the value it writes is ignored in favor of the set/reset color.

Set/reset is also the mode of choice whenever it is necessary to force the bytes written to some planes to fixed values while allowing the CPU byte to modify other planes. This is the mode of operation when set/reset is enabled for some but not all planes.

Mode 13h—320 by 200 with 256 Colors

I've been asked several times recently about the programming model for mode 13h, the VGA's 320-by-200 256-color mode. Frankly, there's just not much to it. Mode 13h offers the simplest programming model in the history of PC graphics: a linear bit map at A000:0000, consisting of 64,000 bytes each controlling one pixel. The byte at offset 0 controls the upper left pixel on the screen, the byte at offset 13Fh controls the upper right pixel on the screen, the byte at offset 140h controls the second pixel down at the left of the screen, and the byte at offset 63,999 controls the lower right pixel on the screen. That's all there is to it; it's so simple that I'm not going to waste your time with a demo program. If you do desire a demo program for mode 13h (and modes 11h and 12h as well), a forthcoming issue of *Turbo Technix,* the Borland magazine (possibly Volume 1, Number 4, but that's currently up in the air) will provide just that in the form of "The VGA Standard," by yours truly.

Flipping Pages from Text to Graphics and Back

In the past week or so I've gotten both a phone call and a letter on an interesting EGA/VGA topic; I didn't remember the name of the caller, but the question is unusual enough that both probably came from the same person. At any rate, the letter came from Phil Coleman, of La Jolla, who writes:

> Suppose I have the EGA in mode $10 (color 640-by-350 graphics). I would like to preserve some or all of the image while I temporarily switch to text mode 3 to give my user a "Help" screen. Naturally, memory is scarce, so I'd rather not make a copy of the video buffer at $A000 to "remember" the image while I digress to the Help text. The EGA BIOS says that the screen memory will not be cleared on a mode set if bit 7 of AL is set. Yet if I try that, it is clear that writing text into the $B800 buffer trashes much more than the 4K bytes of a text page; when I switch back to mode $10, "ghosts" appear in the form of bands of colored dots. (When in text mode, I do make a copy of the 4K buffer at $B800 before showing the help; and I restore the 4K before switching back to mode $10.) Is there a way to preserve the graphics image (or at least >24K of it) while I switch to text mode?

> A corollary to this question is: Where does the 64/128/256K of EGA memory "hide" when the EGA is in text mode? Some I guess is used to store character sets, but what happens to the rest? Or rather, how can I protect it?

Those are good questions. Alas, answering them in full would require considerable explanation, and while I intend to do that someday, now is not the time. However, the issue of how to go to text mode and back without losing the graphics image is worth discussing briefly.

Phil is indeed correct in his observation that setting bit 7 of AL instructs the BIOS not to clear display memory on mode sets, and he is also correct in surmising that a font is loaded when going to text mode. The normal mode 10h bit map occupies the first 28,000 bytes of each of the VGA's four planes. The normal mode 3 character/attribute memory map resides in the first 4000 bytes of planes 0 and 1 (the blue and green planes in mode 10h). The standard font in mode 3 is stored in the first 8K of plane 2 (the red plane in mode 10h). Neither mode 3 nor any other text mode makes use of plane 3; if necessary, plane 3 could be used as scratch memory in text mode.

Consequently, you can certainly get away with saving a total of just under 16K bytes—the first 4000 bytes of planes 0 and 1 and the first 8K bytes of plane 2—when going from mode 10h to mode 3, to be restored on returning to mode 10h.

That's hardly all there is to the matter of going from text to graphics and back without bit-map corruption, though. One interesting point is that the mode 10h bit map can be relocated to A000:8000 simply by doing a mode set to mode 10h and setting the start address (programmed at CRT Controller registers 0Ch and 0Dh) to 8000h. You can then access display memory starting at A800:0000 instead of the normal A000:0000, with the resultant display exactly like that of normal mode 10h. (There are BIOS issues, since the BIOS doesn't automatically access display memory at the new start address, but if your program does all its drawing directly without the help of the BIOS, that's no problem.)

At any rate, once the mode 10h bit map is relocated to A800:0000, flipping to text mode and back becomes painless. The memory used by mode 3 doesn't overlap the relocated mode 10h bit map at all, and so all you need do is set bit 7 of AL on mode sets.

Another interesting point about flipping from graphics to text and back is that the standard mode 3 character/attribute map doesn't actually take up every byte of the first 4000 bytes of planes 0 and 1. The standard mode 3 character/attribute map actually takes up only every even byte of the first 4000 in each plane; the odd bytes are left untouched. This means that only about 12K bytes actually have to be saved when going to text mode. The code in Listing 6.3 [presented at the end of this chapter] flips from graphics mode to text mode and back, saving only those 12K bytes that actually have to be saved. This code saves and restores the first 8K of plane 2 (the font area) while in graphics mode but saves and restores the 4000 bytes used for the character/attribute map in text mode, since the characters and attributes, which are actually every other byte of planes 0 and 1, respectively, appear to be contiguous bytes in memory in text mode and so are easily saved as a single block.

Explaining why only every other byte of planes 0 and 1 is used in text mode and why characters and attributes appear to be contiguous bytes when they are actually in different planes is a large part of the explanation I haven't room to go into now. One bit of fallout from this, however, is that if you flip to text mode and preserve the graphics bit map using the mechanism illustrated in Listing 6.3, you shouldn't write to any text page other than page 0 (that is, don't write to any offset in display memory above 3999 in text mode) or alter the Page Select bit in the Miscellaneous Output register (3C2h) while in text mode.

To allow unfettered access to text pages, it would be necessary to save the first 32K of each of planes 0 and 1. (On the other hand, this would allow up to 16 text screens to be stored simultaneously, with any one displayable instantly—a topic for yet another installment.) Moreover, if any fonts other than the default font are loaded, the portion of plane 2 those particular fonts are loaded into would have to be saved, up to a maximum of all 64K of plane 2. In the worst case, a full 128K would have to be saved to preserve all the memory potentially used by text mode.

As I said, Phil Coleman's question is a complex one, and I've only touched on the intriguing possibilities arising from the various configurations of display memory in VGA graphics and text modes. Someday I'll return to it, but for now we've still got the basics of the remarkably complex VGA to cover.

Until Next Time

As I suspected, we didn't get around to learning how to read VGA memory. That's probably just as well, since that leaves the whole next installment in which to cover that fairly esoteric subject. If there are any other EGA or VGA topics you'd like to see covered, write to me in care of *PJ* or drop me a line on MCI mail (username MABRASH), and I'll try to get to it soon.

See you next time.

Listing 6.1

```
; Program to illustrate one use of write mode 2 of the VGA and EGA by
; animating the image of an "A" drawn by copying it from a chunky
; bit-map in system memory to a planar bit-map in VGA or EGA memory.
;
; Assembled with MASM 5.0, linked with MS-LINK 3.60.
;
; By Michael Abrash 11/8/87
;
stackseg          segment para stack 'STACK'
        db        512 dup(0)
stackseg          ends

SCREEN_WIDTH_IN_BYTES   equ     80
DISPLAY_MEMORY_SEGMENT  equ     0a000h
SC_INDEX          equ     3c4h     ;Sequence Controller Index register
MAP_MASK          equ     2        ;index of Map Mask register
GC_INDEX          equ     03ceh    ;Graphics Controller Index reg
GRAPHICS_MODE     equ     5        ;index of Graphics Mode reg
BIT_MASK          equ     8        ;index of Bit Mask reg

Data    segment para common 'DATA'
;
; Current location of "A" as it is animated across the screen.
;
CurrentX          dw      ?
CurrentY          dw      ?
RemainingLength   dw      ?
;
; Chunky bit-map image of a yellow "A" on a bright blue background
;
AImage            label   byte
                  dw      13, 13                ;width, height in pixels
                  db      000h, 000h, 000h, 000h, 000h, 000h, 000h
                  db      009h, 099h, 099h, 099h, 099h, 099h, 000h
                  db      009h, 099h, 099h, 099h, 099h, 099h, 000h
                  db      009h, 099h, 099h, 0e9h, 099h, 099h, 000h
                  db      009h, 099h, 09eh, 0eeh, 099h, 099h, 000h
                  db      009h, 099h, 0eeh, 09eh, 0e9h, 099h, 000h
                  db      009h, 09eh, 0e9h, 099h, 0eeh, 099h, 000h
                  db      009h, 09eh, 0eeh, 0eeh, 0eeh, 099h, 000h
                  db      009h, 09eh, 0e9h, 099h, 0eeh, 099h, 000h
                  db      009h, 09eh, 0e9h, 099h, 0eeh, 099h, 000h
                  db      009h, 099h, 099h, 099h, 099h, 099h, 000h
                  db      009h, 099h, 099h, 099h, 099h, 099h, 000h
                  db      000h, 000h, 000h, 000h, 000h, 000h, 000h
Data    ends

Code    segmentpara public 'CODE'
        assume    cs:Code, ds:Data
Start   proc      near
        mov       ax,Data
        mov       ds,ax
        mov       ax,10h
        int       10h                  ;select video mode 10h (640x350)
;
; Prepare for animation.
;
        mov       [CurrentX],0
```

Listing 6.1 continues

Listing 6.1 continued

```
        mov     [CurrentY],200
        mov     [RemainingLength],600    ;move 600 times
;
; Animate, repeating RemainingLength times. It's unnecessary to erase
; the old image, since the one pixel of blank fringe around the image
; erases the part of the old image not overlapped by the new image.
;
AnimationLoop:
        mov     bx,[CurrentX]
        mov     cx,[CurrentY]
        mov     si,offset AImage
        call    DrawFromChunkyBitmap    ;draw the "A" image
        inc     [CurrentX]              ;move one pixel to the right
        dec     [RemainingLength]
        jnz     AnimationLoop
;
; Wait for a key before returning to text mode and ending.
;
        mov     ah,01h
        int     21h
        mov     ax,03h
        int     10h
        mov     ah,4ch
        int     21h
Start   endp
;
; Draw an image stored in a chunky-bit map into planar VGA/EGA memory
; at the specified location.
;
; Input:
;       BX = X screen location at which to draw the upper left corner
;               of the image
;       CX = Y screen location at which to draw the upper left corner
;               of the image
;       DS:SI = pointer to chunky image to draw, as follows:
;               word at 0: width of image, in pixels
;               word at 2: height of image, in pixels
;               byte at 4: msb/lsb = first & second chunky pixels,
;                       repeating for the remainder of the scan line
;                       of the image, then for all scan lines. Images
;                       with odd widths have an unused null nibble
;                       padding each scan line out to a byte width
;
; AX, BX, CX, DX, SI, DI, ES destroyed.
;
DrawFromChunkyBitmap    proc    near
        cld
;
; Select write mode 2.
;
        mov     dx,GC_INDEX
        mov     al,GRAPHICS_MODE
        out     dx,al
        inc     dx
        mov     al,02h
        out     dx,al
;
; Enable writes to all 4 planes.
```

Listing 6.1 continues

Listing 6.1 *continued*

```
;
        mov     dx,SC_INDEX
        mov     al,MAP_MASK
        out     dx,al
        inc     dx
        mov     al,0fh
        out     dx,al
;
; Point ES:DI to the display memory byte in which the first pixel
; of the image goes, with AH set up as the bit mask to access that
; pixel within the addressed byte.
;
        mov     ax,SCREEN_WIDTH_IN_BYTES
        mul     cx                      ;offset of start of top scan line
        mov     di,ax
        mov     cl,bl
        and     cl,111b
        mov     ah,80h                  ;set AH to the bit mask for the
        shr     ah,cl                   ; initial pixel
        shr     bx,1
        shr     bx,1
        shr     bx,1                    ;X in bytes
        add     di,bx                   ;offset of upper left byte of image
        mov     bx,DISPLAY_MEMORY_SEGMENT
        mov     es,bx                   ;ES:DI points to the byte at which the
                                        ; upper left of the image goes
;
; Get the width and height of the image.
;
        mov     cx,[si]                 ;get the width
        inc     si
        inc     si
        mov     bx,[si]                 ;get the height
        inc     si
        inc     si
        mov     dx,GC_INDEX
        mov     al,BIT_MASK
        out     dx,al                   ;leave the GC Index register pointing
        inc     dx                      ; to the Bit Mask register
RowLoop:

        push    ax                      ;preserve the left column's bit mask
        push    cx                      ;preserve the width
        push    di                      ;preserve the destination offset

ColumnLoop:
        mov     al,ah
        out     dx,al                   ;set the bit mask to draw this pixel
        mov     al,es:[di]              ;load the latches
        mov     al,[si]                 ;get the next two chunky pixels
        shr     al,1
        shr     al,1
        shr     al,1
        shr     al,1                    ;move the first pixel into the lsb
        stosb                           ;draw the first pixel
        ror     ah,1                    ;move mask to next pixel position
        jc      CheckMorePixels         ;is next pixel in the adjacent byte?
        dec     di                      ;no
```

Listing 6.1 *continues*

Listing 6.1 *continued*

```
CheckMorePixels:
        dec     cx              ;see if there are any more pixels
                                ; across in image
        jz      AdvanceToNextScanLine
        mov     al,ah
        out     dx,al           ;set the bit mask to draw this pixel
        mov     al,es:[di]      ;load the latches
        lodsb                   ;get the same two chunky pixels again
                                ; and advance pointer to the next
                                ; two pixels
        stosb                   ;draw the second of the two pixels
        ror     ah,1            ;move mask to next pixel position
        jc      CheckMorePixels2 ;is next pixel in the adjacent byte?
        dec     di              ;no

CheckMorePixels2:
        loop    ColumnLoop      ;see if there are any more pixels
                                ; across in the image
        jmp     short CheckMoreScanLines

AdvanceToNextScanLine:
        inc     si              ;advance to the start of the next
                                ; scan line in the image

CheckMoreScanLines:
        pop     di              ;get back the destination offset
        pop     cx              ;get back the width
        pop     ax              ;get back the left column's bit mask
        add     di,SCREEN_WIDTH_IN_BYTES
                                ;point to the start of the next scan
                                ; line of the image
        dec     bx              ;see if there are any more scan lines
        jnz     RowLoop         ; in the image
        ret
DrawFromChunkyBitmap    endp
Code    ends
        end     Start
```

Listing 6.2

```
; Program to illustrate one use of write mode 2 of the VGA and EGA by
; drawing lines in color patterns.
;
; Assembled with MASM 5.0, linked with MS-LINK 3.60.
;
; By Michael Abrash 11/8/87
; Updated 6/27/89.
;
stackseg        segment para stack 'STACK'
        db      512 dup(0)
stackseg        ends

SCREEN_WIDTH_IN_BYTES   equ     80
```

Listing 6.2 *continues*

Listing 6.2 *continued*

```
GRAPHICS_SEGMENT equ      0a000h   ;mode 10 bit-map segment
SC_INDEX         equ      3c4h     ;Sequence Controller Index register
MAP_MASK         equ      2        ;index of Map Mask register
GC_INDEX         equ      03ceh    ;Graphics Controller Index reg
GRAPHICS_MODE    equ      5        ;index of Graphics Mode reg
BIT_MASK         equ      8        ;index of Bit Mask reg

Data     segment para common 'DATA'
Pattern0         db       16
                 db       0, 1, 2, 3, 4, 5, 6, 7, 8
                 db       9, 10, 11, 12, 13, 14, 15
Pattern1         db       6
                 db       2, 2, 2, 10, 10, 10
Pattern2         db       8
                 db       15, 15, 15, 0, 0, 15, 0, 0
Pattern3         db       9
                 db       1, 1, 1, 2, 2, 2, 4, 4, 4
Data     ends

Code     segment para public 'CODE'
         assume  cs:Code, ds:Data
Start    proc    near
         mov     ax,Data
         mov     ds,ax
         mov     ax,10h
         int     10h                  ;select video mode 10h (640x350)
;
; Draw 8 radial lines in upper left quadrant in pattern 0.
;
         mov     bx,0
         mov     cx,0
         mov     si,offset Pattern0
         call    QuadrantUp
;
; Draw 8 radial lines in upper right quadrant in pattern 1.
;
         mov     bx,320
         mov     cx,0
         mov     si,offset Pattern1
         call    QuadrantUp
;
; Draw 8 radial lines in lower left quadrant in pattern 2.
;
         mov     bx,0
         mov     cx,175
         mov     si,offset Pattern2
         call    QuadrantUp
;
; Draw 8 radial lines in lower right quadrant in pattern 3.
;
         mov     bx,320
         mov     cx,175
         mov     si,offset Pattern3
         call    QuadrantUp
;
; Wait for a key before returning to text mode and ending.
;
         mov     ah,01h
```

Listing 6.2 *continues*

Listing 6.2 continued

```
        int     21h
        mov     ax,03h
        int     10h
        mov     ah,4ch
        int     21h
;
; Draws 8 radial lines with specified pattern in specified mode 10h
; quadrant.
;
; Input:
;       BX = X coordinate of upper left corner of quadrant
;       CX = Y coordinate of upper left corner of quadrant
;       SI = pointer to pattern, in following form:
;               Byte 0: Length of pattern
;               Byte 1: Start of pattern, one color per byte
;
; AX, BX, CX, DX destroyed
;
QuadrantUp      proc    near
        add     bx,160
        add     cx,87            ;point to the center of the quadrant
        mov     ax,0
        mov     dx,160
        call    LineUp           ;draw horizontal line to right edge
        mov     ax,1
        mov     dx,88
        call    LineUp           ;draw diagonal line to upper right
        mov     ax,2
        mov     dx,88
        call    LineUp           ;draw vertical line to top edge
        mov     ax,3
        mov     dx,88
        call    LineUp           ;draw diagonal line to upper left
        mov     ax,4
        mov     dx,161
        call    LineUp           ;draw horizontal line to left edge
        mov     ax,5
        mov     dx,88
        call    LineUp           ;draw diagonal line to lower left
        mov     ax,6
        mov     dx,88
        call    LineUp           ;draw vertical line to bottom edge
        mov     ax,7
        mov     dx,88
        call    LineUp           ;draw diagonal line to bottom right
        ret
QuadrantUp      endp
;
; Draws a horizontal, vertical, or diagonal line (one of the eight
; possible radial lines) of the specified length from the specified
; starting point.
;
; Input:
;       AX = line direction, as follows:
;               3 2 1
;               4 * 0
;               5 6 7
;       BX = X coordinate of starting point
```

Listing 6.2 continues

Listing 6.2 continued

```
;       CX = Y coordinate of starting point
;       DX = length of line (number of pixels drawn)
;
; All registers preserved.
;
; Table of vectors to routines for each of the 8 possible lines.
;
LineUpVectors   label   word
        dw      LineUp0, LineUp1, LineUp2, LineUp3
        dw      LineUp4, LineUp5, LineUp6, LineUp7

;
; Macro to draw horizontal, vertical, or diagonal line.
;
; Input:
;       XParm = 1 to draw right, -1 to draw left, 0 to not move horz.
;       YParm = 1 to draw down, -1 to draw up, 0 to not move vert.
;       BX = X start location
;       CX = Y start location
;       DX = number of pixels to draw
;       DS:SI = line pattern
;
MLineUp macro   XParm, YParm
        local   LineUpLoop, CheckMoreLine
        mov     di,si           ;set aside start offset of pattern
        lodsb                   ;get length of pattern
        mov     ah,al

LineUpLoop:
        lodsb                   ;get color of this pixel...
        call    DotUpInColor    ;...and draw it
if XParm EQ 1
        inc     bx
endif
if XParm EQ -1
        dec     bx
endif
if YParm EQ 1
        inc     cx
endif
if YParm EQ -1
        dec     cx
endif
        dec     ah              ;at end of pattern?
        jnz     CheckMoreLine
        mov     si,di           ;get back start of pattern
        lodsb
        mov     ah,al           ;reset pattern count

CheckMoreLine:
        dec     dx
        jnz     LineUpLoop
        jmp     LineUpEnd
        endm

LineUp  proc    near
        push    ax
        push    bx
```

Listing 6.2 continues

Listing 6.2 continued

```
        push    cx
        push    dx
        push    si
        push    di
        push    es

        mov     di,ax

        mov     ax,GRAPHICS_SEGMENT
        mov     es,ax

        push    dx                      ;save line length
;
; Enable writes to all planes.
;
        mov     dx,SC_INDEX
        mov     al,MAP_MASK
        out     dx,al
        inc     dx
        mov     al,0fh
        out     dx,al
;
; Select write mode 2.
;
        mov     dx,GC_INDEX
        mov     al,GRAPHICS_MODE
        out     dx,al
        inc     dx
        mov     al,02h
        out     dx,al
;
; Vector to proper routine.
;
        pop     dx                      ;get back line length

        shl     di,1
        jmp     cs:[LineUpVectors+di]
;
; Horizontal line to right.
;
LineUp0:
        MLineUp 1, 0
;
; Diagonal line to upper right.
;
LineUp1:
        MLineUp 1, -1
;
; Vertical line to top.
;
LineUp2:
        MLineUp 0, -1
;
; Diagonal line to upper left.
;
LineUp3:
        MLineUp -1, -1
;
```

Listing 6.2 continues

Listing 6.2 *continued*

```
; Horizontal line to left.
;
LineUp4:
        MLineUp -1, 0
;
; Diagonal line to bottom left.
;
LineUp5:
        MLineUp -1, 1
;
; Vertical line to bottom.
;
LineUp6:
        MLineUp 0, 1
;
; Diagonal line to bottom right.
;
LineUp7:
        MLineUp 1, 1

LineUpEnd:
        pop     es
        pop     di
        pop     si
        pop     dx
        pop     cx
        pop     bx
        pop     ax
        ret
LineUp  endp
;
; Draws a dot in the specified color at the specified location.
; Assumes that the VGA is in write mode 2 with writes to all planes
; enabled and that ES points to display memory.
;
; Input:
;       AL = dot color
;       BX = X coordinate of dot
;       CX = Y coordinate of dot
;       ES = display memory segment
;
; All registers preserved.
;
DotUpInColor    proc    near
        push    bx
        push    cx
        push    dx
        push    di
;
; Point ES:DI to the display memory byte in which the pixel goes, with
; the bit mask set up to access that pixel within the addressed byte.
;
        push    ax                      ;preserve dot color
        mov     ax,SCREEN_WIDTH_IN_BYTES
        mul     cx                      ;offset of start of row pixel is in
        mov     di,ax
        mov     cl,bl
        and     cl,111b
```

Listing 6.2 *continues*

Listing 6.2 *continued*

```
        mov     dx,GC_INDEX
        mov     al,BIT_MASK
        out     dx,al
        inc     dx
        mov     al,80h
        shr     al,cl
        out     dx,al           ;set the bit mask for the pixel
        shr     bx,1
        shr     bx,1
        shr     bx,1            ;X in bytes
        add     di,bx           ;offset of byte pixel is in
        mov     al,es:[di]      ;load latches
        pop     ax              ;get back dot color
        stosb                   ;write dot in desired color

        pop     di
        pop     dx
        pop     cx
        pop     bx
        ret
DotUpInColor    endp
Start   endp
Code    ends
        end     Start
```

Listing 6.3

```
; Program to illustrate flipping from bit-mapped graphics mode to
; text mode and back without losing any of the graphics mode
; bit map.
;
; Assembled with MASM 5.0, linked with MS-LINK 3.60.
;
; By Michael Abrash 11/8/87
; Updated 6/27/89.
;
stackseg        segment para stack 'STACK'
        db      512 dup(0)
stackseg        ends

SAVE_PLANE_3    equ     0       ;set to 1 to save the first 8K of
                                ; plane 3, used to handle EGAs and
                                ; VGAs that store text info in
                                ; plane 3. IBM EGAs and VGAs don't
                                ; use plane 3.
                                ; Set to 0 not to save the first
                                ; 8K of plane 3

GRAPHICS_SEGMENT equ    0a000h  ;mode 10 bit-map segment
TEXT_SEGMENT    equ     0b800h  ;mode 3 bit-map segment
SC_INDEX        equ     3c4h    ;Sequence Controller Index register
MAP_MASK        equ     2       ;index of Map Mask register
GC_INDEX        equ     3ceh    ;Graphics Controller Index register
READ_MAP        equ     4       ;index of Read Map register
```

Listing 6.3 continues

Listing 6.3 continued

```
Data      segment para common 'DATA'

GStrikeAnyKeyMsg0      label   byte
          db      0dh, 0ah, 'Graphics mode', 0dh, 0ah
          db      'Strike any key to continue...', 0dh, 0ah, '$'

GStrikeAnyKeyMsg1      label   byte
          db      0dh, 0ah, 'Graphics mode again', 0dh, 0ah
          db      'Strike any key to continue...', 0dh, 0ah, '$'

TStrikeAnyKeyMsg       label   byte
          db      0dh, 0ah, 'Text mode', 0dh, 0ah
          db      'Strike any key to continue...', 0dh, 0ah, '$'

Plane2Save    db      2000h dup (?)     ;save area for plane 2 data
                                        ; where font gets loaded
if SAVE_PLANE_3
Plane3Save    db      2000h dup (?)     ;save area for plane 3 data
endif
CharAttSave   db      4000 dup (?)      ;save area for memory wiped
                                        ; out by character/attribute
                                        ; data in text mode
Data      ends

Code      segment para public 'CODE'
          assume  cs:Code, ds:Data
Start     proc    near
          mov     ax,10h
          int     10h             ;select video mode 10h (640x350)
;
; Fill the graphics bit-map with a colored pattern.
;
          cld
          mov     ax,GRAPHICS_SEGMENT
          mov     es,ax
          mov     ah,3            ;initial fill pattern
          mov     cx,4            ;four planes to fill
          mov     dx,SC_INDEX
          mov     al,MAP_MASK
          out     dx,al           ;leave the SC Index pointing to the
                                  ; Map Mask register
          inc     dx

FillBitMap:
          mov     al,10h
          shr     al,cl           ;generate map mask for this plane
          out     dx,al           ;set map mask for this plane
          sub     di,di           ;start at offset 0
          mov     al,ah           ;get the fill pattern
          push    cx              ;preserve plane count
          mov     cx,8000h        ;fill 32K words
          rep stosw               ;do fill for this plane
          pop     cx              ;get back plane count
          shl     ah,1
          shl     ah,1
          loop    FillBitMap
;
```

Listing 6.3 continues

Listing 6.3 *continued*

```
; Put up "strike any key" message.
;
        mov     ax,Data
        mov     ds,ax
        mov     dx,offset GStrikeAnyKeyMsg0
        mov     ah,9
        int     21h
;
; Wait for a key.
;
        mov     ah,01h
        int     21h
;
; Save the 8K of plane 2 that will be used by the font.
;
        mov     dx,GC_INDEX
        mov     al,READ_MAP
        out     dx,al
        inc     dx
        mov     al,2
        out     dx,al           ;set up to read from plane 2
        mov     ax,Data
        mov     es,ax
        mov     ax,GRAPHICS_SEGMENT
        mov     ds,ax
        sub     si,si
        mov     di,offset Plane2Save
        mov     cx,2000h/2       ;save 8K (length of default font)
        rep movsw
if SAVE_PLANE_3
;
; Save the 8K of plane 3 that is used by some BIOSes in text mode.
;
        mov     dx,GC_INDEX
        mov     al,READ_MAP
        out     dx,al
        inc     dx
        mov     al,3
        out     dx,al           ;set up to read from plane 3
        mov     ax,Data
        mov     es,ax
        mov     ax,GRAPHICS_SEGMENT
        mov     ds,ax
        sub     si,si
        mov     di,offset Plane3Save
        mov     cx,2000h/2       ;save 8K (length of default font)
        rep movsw
endif
;
; Go to text mode without clearing display memory.
;
        mov     ax,083h
        int     10h
;
; Save the text mode bit-map.
;
        mov     ax,Data
        mov     es,ax
```

Listing 6.3 *continues*

Listing 6.3 *continued*

```
        mov     ax,TEXT_SEGMENT
        mov     ds,ax
        sub     si,si
        mov     di,offset CharAttSave
        mov     cx,4000/2       ;length of one text screen in words
        rep movsw
;
; Fill the text mode screen with dots and put up "strike any key"
; message.
;
        mov     ax,TEXT_SEGMENT
        mov     es,ax
        sub     di,di
        mov     al,'.'          ;fill character
        mov     ah,7            ;fill attribute
        mov     cx,4000/2       ;length of one text screen in words
        rep stosw
        mov     ax,Data
        mov     ds,ax
        mov     dx,offset TStrikeAnyKeyMsg
        mov     ah,9
        int     21h
;
; Wait for a key.
;
        mov     ah,01h
        int     21h
;
; Restore the text mode screen to the state it was in on entering
; text mode.
;
        mov     ax,Data
        mov     ds,ax
        mov     ax,TEXT_SEGMENT
        mov     es,ax
        mov     si,offset CharAttSave
        sub     di,di
        mov     cx,4000/2       ;length of one text screen in words
        rep movsw
;
; Return to mode 10h without clearing display memory.
;
        mov     ax,90h
        int     10h
;
; Restore the portion of plane 2 that was wiped out by the font.
;
        mov     dx,SC_INDEX
        mov     al,MAP_MASK
        out     dx,al
        inc     dx
        mov     al,4
        out     dx,al           ;set up to write to plane 2
        mov     ax,Data
        mov     ds,ax
        mov     ax,GRAPHICS_SEGMENT
        mov     es,ax
        mov     si,offset Plane2Save
```

Listing 6.3 *continues*

Listing 6.3 continued

```
        sub     di,di
        mov     cx,2000h/2      ;restore 8K (length of default font)
        rep movsw
if SAVE_PLANE_3
;
; Restore the portion of plane 3 that is used by some BIOSes in
; text mode.
;
        mov     dx,SC_INDEX
        mov     al,MAP_MASK
        out     dx,al
        inc     dx
        mov     al,8
        out     dx,al           ;set up to write to plane 3
        mov     ax,Data
        mov     ds,ax
        mov     ax,GRAPHICS_SEGMENT
        mov     es,ax
        mov     si,offset Plane3Save
        sub     di,di
        mov     cx,2000h/2      ;restore 8K (length of default font)
        rep movsw
endif
;
; Put up "strike any key" message.
;
        mov     ax,Data
        mov     ds,ax
        mov     dx,offset GStrikeAnyKeyMsg1
        mov     ah,9
        int     21h
;
; Wait for a key before returning to text mode and ending.
;
        mov     ah,01h
        int     21h
        mov     ax,03h
        int     10h
        mov     ah,4ch
        int     21h
Start   endp
Code    ends
        end     Start
```

Reading VGA Memory

This installment marks the completion of our exploration of the data paths to and from display memory in the EGA and VGA. Is that the end of the trail, then?

Hardly!

Learning the EGA/VGA data paths is a beginning, not an end. That knowledge, and the understanding of the EGA/VGA that goes with it, gives us a strong foundation, from which we can branch out to more sophisticated and esoteric topics such as line drawing, 256-color modes, text pages, and the like.

In other words, now that we've learned our lessons well, we get to do the *really* fun stuff.

This installment offers one wonderful example of the sort of power programming that becomes possible once we have a thorough understanding of the VGA. By using write mode 3 *and* read mode 1 simultaneously, Listing 7.3 [presented at the end of this chapter] is able to draw individual pixels with just one instruction, in a fashion that I doubt the designers of the VGA ever intended. Try doing *that* without knowing the VGA inside and out!

By the end of this installment, you *will* know the VGA inside and out, at least as far as read and write paths go. It's been a long journey to this point, but you'll soon see that the journey was a rewarding one as well. Believe me, the view from here is worth the trip.

Installment 7: In which we learn to read VGA memory and encounter the strange but useful Color Compare register.

Well, it's taken six installments of "On Graphics," but we've finally covered all four write modes of the VGA. Now it's time to tackle the VGA's two read modes. While the read modes aren't so complex as the write modes, they're nothing to sneeze at. In particular, read mode 1 (also known as color compare mode) is rather unusual and not particularly intuitive.

You may well ask, isn't *anything* about programming the VGA straightforward? Well . . . no. But then, clearing up the mysteries of VGA programming is what these articles are all about.

So, let's get started.

Read Mode 0

Read mode 0 is actually relatively uncomplicated, given that you understand the four-plane nature of the VGA, as explained over the first six installments of "On Graphics." Read mode 0, the read mode counterpart of write mode 0, lets you read from one (and only one) plane of VGA memory at any one time.

Read mode 0 is selected by setting bit 3 of the Graphics Mode register (Graphics Controller register 5) to 0. When read mode 0 is active, the plane that supplies the data when the CPU reads VGA memory is the plane selected by bits 1 and 0 of the Read Map register (Graphics Controller register 4). When the Read Map register is set to 0, CPU reads come from plane 0, the plane that normally contains blue pixel data. When the Read Map register is set to 1, CPU reads come from plane 1, the green plane; when the Read Map register is 2, CPU reads come from plane 2, the red plane; and when the Read Map register is 3, CPU reads come from plane 3, the intensity plane.

That all seems simple enough: In read mode 0, the Read Map register acts as a selector among the four planes, determining which one of the planes will supply the value returned to the CPU. There is a slight complication, however, in that the value written to the Read Map register in order to read from a given plane is not the same as the value written to the Map Mask register (Sequence Controller register 2) in order to write to that plane.

Why is that? Well, in read mode 0, only one plane can be read at a time; so, there are only four possible settings of the Read Map register: 0, 1, 2, or 3, to select reads from plane 0, 1, 2, or 3. In write mode 0, in contrast (in fact, in any write mode), any or all planes may be written to at once, since the byte written by the CPU can "fan out" to multiple planes. Consequently, there are, not 4, but 16 possible settings of the Map Mask register. The setting of the Map Mask register to write only to plane 0 is 1; to write only to plane 1, 2; to write only to plane 2, 4; and to write only to plane 3, the setting is 8.

As you can see, the settings of the Read Map and Map Mask registers for accessing a given plane don't match. The code in Listing 7.1 [presented at the end of this chapter] illustrates this. Listing 7.1 simply copies a 16-color image from system memory to VGA memory, one plane at a time, and then animates by repeatedly copying the image back to system memory, again one plane at a time, clearing the old image, and copying the image to a new location in VGA memory. Note the differing settings of the Read Map and Map Mask registers in Listing 7.1.

By the way, the code in Listing 7.1 is intended only to illustrate read mode 0, and is, in general, a poor way to perform animation, since it's slow and tends to flicker. In a future issue of *PJ*, I'll take a look at VGA animation techniques.

A you might expect, neither the read mode nor the setting of the Read Map register affects CPU *writes* to VGA memory in any way.

An important point regarding reading VGA memory involves the VGA's latches. (Remember that each of the four latches stores a byte for one plane; on CPU writes, the latches can provide some or all of the data written to display memory, allowing fast scrolling and efficient pixel masking.) Whenever the CPU reads a given address in VGA memory, each of the four latches is loaded with the contents of the byte at the specified address in the plane associated with the latch. Even though the CPU receives data from only one plane in read mode 0, all four planes are always read, and the values read are stored in the latches. This is true in read mode 1, as well. In short, whenever the CPU reads VGA memory in any read mode, all four planes are read and all four latches are loaded.

Finally, before we go on to read mode 1, I'd like to note that the EGA supports slightly different versions of read mode 0 and read mode 1. The EGA's read modes are compatible with the VGA's read modes as long as you don't set bit 2 of the EGA's Read Map register to 1 and as long as you don't touch the EGA's Graphics Position registers (at ports 3CCh and 3CAh).

Read Mode 1

Read mode 0 is the workhorse read mode of the VGA, but it's got an annoying limitation: Whenever you want to determine the color of a given pixel in read mode 0, you have to perform four VGA memory reads, one for each plane, and then interpret the four bytes you've read as eight 16-color pixels. That's a lot of programming. The code is also likely to run slowly—all the more so because the VGA takes an average of 1.1 microseconds to complete each memory read, and read mode 0 requires four reads to read the four planes. (One and one-tenth microseconds may not sound like much, but on an 8-MHz AT, it's 9 clock cycles, and on a 20-MHz Compaq 80386 machine, it's 22 clock cycles!)

Read mode 1, or color compare mode, provides special hardware assistance for determining whether a pixel is a given color. With a single read-mode-1 read, you can determine whether any or all of eight pixels are a specific color, and you can even specify any or all planes as "don't care" planes in the pixel color comparison.

Read mode 1 is selected by setting bit 3 of the Graphics Mode register (Graphics Controller register 5) to 1. In its simplest form, read mode 1 compares the cross-plane value of each of the eight pixels at a given address to the color value in bits 3–0 of the Color Compare register (Graphics Controller register 2) and returns a 1 to the CPU in the bit position of each pixel that matches the color in the Color Compare register and a 0 for each pixel that does not match.

That's certainly interesting, but what's read mode 1 good for? One obvious application is in implementing flood-fill algorithms, since read mode 1 makes it easy to tell when a given byte contains a pixel of a boundary color. Another application is in detecting on-screen object collisions, as illustrated by the code in Listing 7.2 [presented at the end of this chapter].

Still and all, there aren't all that many uses for basic color compare operation. There is, however, a genuinely odd application of read mode 1 that's worth knowing about; in order to understand that, we must first look at the "don't care" aspect of color compare operation.

As described above, during read-mode-1 reads, the color stored in the Color Compare register is compared to each of the 8 pixels at a given address in VGA memory. But—and it's a big *but*—any plane for which the corresponding bit in the Color Don't Care register is a 0 is always considered a color compare match, regardless of the values of that plane's bits and of the corresponding bit in the Color Compare register.

Let's look at this another way. A given pixel is controlled by four bits, one in each plane. Normally (when the Color Don't Care register is 0Fh), the color in the Color Compare register is compared to the four bits of each pixel; bit 0 of the Color Compare register is compared to the plane 0 bit of each pixel, bit 1 of the Color Compare register is compared to the plane 1 bit of each pixel, and so on. That is, when the lower four bits of the Color Don't Care register are all set to 1, then all four bits of a given pixel must match the Color Compare register in order for a read-mode-1 read to return a 1 for that pixel to the CPU.

However, if any bit of the Color Don't Care register is 0, then the corresponding bit of each pixel is unconditionally considered to match the corresponding bit of the Color Compare register. You might think of the Color Don't Care register as selecting exactly which planes should matter in a given read-mode-1 read. At the extreme, if all bits of the Color Don't Care register are 0, then read-mode-1 reads will always return 0FFh, since all planes are considered to match all bits of all pixels.

Now, we're all prone to using tools the "right" way—that is, in the way in which they were intended to be used. By that token, the Color Don't Care register is clearly intended to mask one or more planes out of a color comparison, and in that capacity, it has limited use. However, the Color Don't Care register becomes far more interesting in the "extreme" case described above, where all planes become "don't care" planes.

Why? Well, as I've said, when all planes are "don't care" planes, read-mode-1 reads always return 0FFh. Now, when you AND any value with 0FFh, the value remains unchanged, and that can be awfully handy when you're using the bit mask to modify selected pixels in VGA memory. Recall that you must always read VGA memory to load the latches before writing to VGA memory when you're using the bit mask. Traditionally, two separate instructions—a read followed by a write—are used to perform this task. The code in Listing 7.2 uses this approach. Suppose, though, that you've set the VGA to read mode 1, with the Color Don't Care register set to 0 (meaning all reads of VGA memory will return 0FFh). Under these circumstances, you can use a single AND instruction to both read and write VGA memory, since ANDing any value with 0FFh leaves that value unchanged.

Listing 7.3 [presented at the end of this chapter] illustrates an efficient use of write mode 3 in conjunction with read mode 1 and a Color Don't Care register setting of 0. The mask in AL is passed directly to the VGA's bit mask (that's how write mode 3 works—see Chapter 5 for details). Because the VGA always returns 0FFh, the single AND instruction loads the latches, leaves AL unchanged, and writes the value in AL to the VGA, where it is used to generate the bit mask. This is faster, more compact, and more register efficient than using separate instructions to read and write.

By the way, I commented in Chapter 5 that I hadn't come across any particularly noteworthy applications for write mode 3. That's true no longer—Listing 7.3 shows how write mode 3 can make for excellent dot-drawing and line-drawing code.

I hope I've given you a good feel for what color compare mode is and what it might be used for. Color compare mode isn't particularly easy to understand, but it's not that complicated in actual operation, and it's certainly useful at times. Take some time to study the sample code and perform a few experiments of your own, and you may well find some useful applications for color compare mode in your graphics code.

A final note: The Read Map register has no effect in read mode 1, and the Color Compare and Color Don't Care registers have no effect either in read mode 0 or when writing to VGA memory.

Using Local Labels in REPT Blocks

I'm going to round out this installment with some odds and ends that have accumulated while I've been covering read and write modes. First, a truly annoying MASM 5.0 bug (at least, I think it's a bug): How the heck can I use local variables in REPT blocks? On page 223 of the MASM 5.0 manual I find the statement, "Macro operators, symbols declared with the LOCAL directive, and the EXITM directive can be used in repeat blocks."

Well, sure, the LOCAL directive can be used in a REPT block, and symbols declared with LOCAL can be used in repeat blocks—however, those symbols can't be used more than once in a given repeat block, which kind of defeats the purpose of using local symbols. I've also tried embedding REPT blocks inside macros and declaring symbols local in the macro, both inside and outside the REPT block, but that didn't work either. Listing 7.4 [presented at the end of this chapter] shows some of the approaches I've tried without success.

In the past, *PJ* readers have always come up with innovative solutions to the MASM problems I've encountered. Any help with this one would be appreciated and would, of course, be shared with *PJ*'s readers.

Slow VGA Mode 13h Mode Sets

I've gotten reader feedback to the effect that mode 13h mode sets on IBM's VGA are extremely slow, to the point of interfering with code that performs frequent mode sets without clearing display memory (by way of setting bit 7 of AL high when invoking INT 10h, function 0). I haven't noticed this myself, but then I haven't done much work with mode 13h. Does anyone out there know more about this problem, and, if so, do you have a workaround?

Reference Material

My primary reason for starting the "On Graphics" column was the then near-total absence of useful reference material on graphics adapters. That situation is now much eased by the appearance of Richard Wilton's excellent book, *Programmer's Guide to PC & PS/2 Video Systems*, from Microsoft Press. I haven't read the entire book (sorry about that, but after all, I do already know much of the subject matter); however, the chapters I have read are accurate, readable, and come with large quantities of sample code. The book covers all current graphics standards, including CGA, EGA, VGA, and Hercules, and does a good job of it. Simply put, *Programmer's Guide to PC & PS/2 Video Systems* is far and away the best PC graphics reference I've seen to date.

There is one flaw with Wilton's book, however, although I very much doubt it's the author's doing: The listings are typeset in pale green and are virtually invisible without good lighting. It's a shame that so much useful code should be so hard to read.

Video Image Capture

David P. Holberton wrote me with an interesting question about the image-capture capabilities of the EGA and VGA: Can the EGA or VGA easily be modified to allow video images to be captured directly into EGA/VGA display memory?

I surely didn't know the answer—hardware is not my field—but I asked several hardware engineers, and they were unanimous in expressing the opinion that any such change would require major surgery to the EGA or VGA board. (They were also unanimous in expressing the opinion that while *they* could make such a change, they didn't recommend it for other people.) The feature connectors at the top of the EGA and Display Adapter boards (which are not identical, by the way) are useless for this purpose, since they provide no path to display memory. In short, the answer seems to be "no." However, David's question was sparked by a paragraph from page 640 of Nelson Johnson's book *Advanced Graphics in C*, so perhaps there's something we're missing here. Possibly the modification involved the EGA's memory-expansion connector; however, that would be of limited use, since very few EGA clones have memory-expansion connectors. In any case, contributions on this topic are welcome.

In Conclusion

Gee, we're actually done with the basics of accessing VGA memory! Fortunately, that still leaves a slew of interesting VGA topics, such as multiple font support, multiple text pages, 43- and 50-line text, smooth panning and scrolling, the split screen, the vertical interrupt, and color selection. Not to mention actual applications, including my personal favorite, animation. Frankly, I don't know just what I'll cover next time—tune in and find out.

See you then.

Listing 7.1

```
; Program to illustrate the use of the Read Map register in read mode 0.
; Animates by copying a 16-color image from VGA memory to system memory,
; one plane at a time, then copying the image back to a new location
; in VGA memory.
;
; By Michael Abrash 4/2/88
;
stackseg        segment word stack 'STACK'
        db      512 dup (?)
stackseg        ends
;
data    segment word 'DATA'
IMAGE_WIDTH     EQU     4           ; in bytes
IMAGE_HEIGHT    EQU     32          ; in pixels
LEFT_BOUND      EQU     10          ; in bytes
RIGHT_BOUND     EQU     66          ; in bytes
VGA_SEGMENT     EQU     0a000h
SCREEN_WIDTH    EQU     80          ; in bytes
SC_INDEX        EQU     3c4h        ; Sequence Controller Index register
GC_INDEX        EQU     3ceh        ; Graphics Controller Index register
MAP_MASK        EQU     2           ; Map Mask register index in SC
READ_MAP        EQU     4           ; Read Map register index in GC
;
; Base pattern for 16-color image.
;
PatternPlane0   label   byte
        db      32 dup (0ffh,0ffh,0,0)
```

Listing 7.1 *continues*

***Listing* 7.1** *continued*

```
PatternPlane1   label    byte
        db       32 dup (0ffh,0,0ffh,0)
PatternPlane2   label    byte
        db       32 dup (0f0h,0f0h,0f0h,0f0h)
PatternPlane3   label    byte
        db       32 dup (0cch,0cch,0cch,0cch)
;
; Temporary storage for 16-color image during animation.
;
ImagePlane0     db       32*4 dup (?)
ImagePlane1     db       32*4 dup (?)
ImagePlane2     db       32*4 dup (?)
ImagePlane3     db       32*4 dup (?)
;
; Current image location & direction.
;
ImageX          dw       40        ;in bytes
ImageY          dw       100       ;in pixels
ImageXDirection dw       1         ;in bytes
data    ends
;
code    segment word 'CODE'
        assume  cs:code,ds:data
Start   proc    near
        cld
        mov     ax,data
        mov     ds,ax
;
; Select graphics mode 10h.
;
        mov     ax,10h
        int     10h
;
; Draw the initial image.
;
        mov     si,offset PatternPlane0
        call    DrawImage
;
; Loop to animate by copying the image from VGA memory to system memory,
; erasing the image, and copying the image from system memory to a new
; location in VGA memory. Ends when a key is hit.
;
AnimateLoop:
;
; Copy the image from VGA memory to system memory.
;
        mov     di,offset ImagePlane0
        call    GetImage
;
; Clear the image from VGA memory.
;
        call    EraseImage
;
; Advance the image X coordinate, reversing direction if either edge
; of the screen has been reached.
;
        mov     ax,[ImageX]
        cmp     ax,LEFT_BOUND
```

***Listing* 7.1** *continues*

Listing 7.1 *continued*

```
        jz      ReverseDirection
        cmp     ax,RIGHT_BOUND
        jnz     SetNewX
ReverseDirection:
        neg     [ImageXDirection]
SetNewX:
        add     ax,[ImageXDirection]
        mov     [ImageX],ax
;
; Draw the image by copying it from system memory to VGA memory.
;
        mov     si,offset ImagePlane0
        call    DrawImage
;
; Slow things down a bit for visibility.
;
        mov     cx,1000h
DelayLoop:
        loop    DelayLoop
;
; See if a key has been hit, ending the program.
;
        mov     ah,1
        int     16h
        jz      AnimateLoop
;
; Clear the key, return to text mode, and return to DOS.
;
        sub     ah,ah
        int     16h
        mov     ax,3
        int     10h
        mov     ah,4ch
        int     21h
Start   endp
;
; Draws the image at offset DS:SI to the current image location in
; VGA memory.
;
DrawImage       proc    near
        mov     ax,VGA_SEGMENT
        mov     es,ax
        call    GetImageOffset  ;ES:DI is the destination address for the
                                ; image in VGA memory
        mov     dx,SC_INDEX
        mov     al,1            ;do plane 0 first
DrawImagePlaneLoop:
        push    di              ;image is drawn at the same offset in
                                ; each plane
        push    ax              ;preserve plane select
        mov     al,MAP_MASK     ;Map Mask index
        out     dx,al           ;point SC Index to the Map Mask register
        pop     ax              ;get back plane select
        inc     dx              ;point to SC index register
        out     dx,al           ;set up the Map Mask to allow writes to
                                ; the plane of interest
        dec     dx              ;point back to SC Data register
        mov     bx,IMAGE_HEIGHT ;# of scan lines in image
```

Listing 7.1 *continues*

Listing 7.1 continued

```
DrawImageLoop:
        mov     cx,IMAGE_WIDTH  ;# of bytes across image
        rep     movsb
        add     di,SCREEN_WIDTH-IMAGE_WIDTH
                                ;point to next scan line of image
        dec     bx              ;any more scan lines?
        jnz     DrawImageLoop
        pop     di              ;get back image start offset in VGA memory
        shl     al,1            ;Map Mask setting for next plane
        cmp     al,10h          ;have we done all four planes?
        jnz     DrawImagePlaneLoop
        ret
DrawImage       endp
;
; Copies the image from its current location in VGA memory into the
; buffer at DS:DI.
;
GetImage        proc    near
        mov     si,di   ;move destination offset into SI
        call    GetImageOffset  ;DI is offset of image in VGA memory
        xchg    si,di   ;SI is offset of image, DI is destination offset
        push    ds
        pop     es      ;ES:DI is destination
        mov     ax,VGA_SEGMENT
        mov     ds,ax   ;DS:SI is source
;
        mov     dx,GC_INDEX
        sub     al,al           ;do plane 0 first
GetImagePlaneLoop:
        push    si              ;image comes from same offset in
                                ; each plane
        push    ax              ;preserve plane select
        mov     al,READ_MAP     ;Read Map index
        out     dx,al           ;point GC Index to Read Map register
        pop     ax              ;get back plane select
        inc     dx              ;point to GC Index register
        out     dx,al           ;set up the Read Map to select reads from
                                ; the plane of interest
        dec     dx              ;point back to GC data register
        mov     bx,IMAGE_HEIGHT ;# of scan lines in image
GetImageLoop:
        mov     cx,IMAGE_WIDTH  ;# of bytes across image
        rep     movsb
        add     si,SCREEN_WIDTH-IMAGE_WIDTH
                                ;point to next scan line of image
        dec     bx              ;any more scan lines?
        jnz     GetImageLoop
        pop     si              ;get back image start offset
        inc     al              ;Read Map setting for next plane
        cmp     al,4            ;have we done all four planes?
        jnz     GetImagePlaneLoop
        push    es
        pop     ds              ;restore original DS
        ret
GetImage        endp
;
; Erases the image at its current location.
;
```

Listing 7.1 continues

Listing 7.1 *continued*

```
EraseImage       proc    near
        mov      dx,SC_INDEX
        mov      al,MAP_MASK
        out      dx,al    ;point SC Index to the Map Mask register
        inc      dx       ;point to SC Data register
        mov      al,0fh
        out      dx,al    ;set up the Map Mask to allow writes to go to
                          ; all 4 planes
        mov      ax,VGA_SEGMENT
        mov      es,ax
        call     GetImageOffset  ;ES:DI points to the start address
                                 ; of the image
        sub      al,al    ;erase with zeros
        mov      bx,IMAGE_HEIGHT;# of scan lines in image
EraseImageLoop:
        mov      cx,IMAGE_WIDTH  ;# of bytes across image
        rep      stosb
        add      di,SCREEN_WIDTH-IMAGE_WIDTH
                                 ;point to next scan line of image
        dec      bx               ;any more scan lines?
        jnz      EraseImageLoop
        ret
EraseImage       endp
;
; Returns the current offset of the image in the VGA segment in DI.
;
GetImageOffset   proc    near
        mov      ax,SCREEN_WIDTH
        mul      [ImageY]
        add      ax,[ImageX]
        mov      di,ax
        ret
GetImageOffset   endp
code    ends
        end      Start
```

Listing 7.2

```
; Program to illustrate use of read mode 1 (color compare mode)
; to detect collisions in display memory. Draws a yellow line on a
; blue background, then draws a perpendicular green line until the
; yellow line is reached.
;
; By Michael Abrash 4/2/88
;
stackseg         segment word stack 'STACK'
        db       512 dup (?)
stackseg         ends
;
VGA_SEGMENT        EQU    0a000h
SCREEN_WIDTH       EQU    80       ;in bytes
GC_INDEX           EQU    3ceh     ;Graphics Controller Index register
SET_RESET          EQU    0        ;Set/Reset register index in GC
ENABLE_SET_RESET   EQU    1        ;Enable Set/Reset register index in GC
```

Listing 7.2 *continues*

Listing 7.2 continued

```
COLOR_COMPARE    EQU     2        ;Color Compare register index in GC
GRAPHICS_MODE    EQU     5        ;Graphics Mode register index in GC
BIT_MASK         EQU     8        ;Bit Mask register index in GC
;
code    segment word 'CODE'
        assume  cs:code
Start   proc    near
        cld
;
; Select graphics mode 10h.
;
        mov     ax,10h
        int     10h
;
; Fill the screen with blue.
;
        mov     al,1             ;blue is color 1
        call    SelectSetResetColor ;set to draw in blue
        mov     ax,VGA_SEGMENT
        mov     es,ax
        sub     di,di
        mov     cx,7000h
        rep     stosb            ;the value written actually doesn't
                                 ; matter, since set/reset is providing
                                 ; the data written to display memory
;
; Draw a vertical yellow line.
;
        mov     al,14            ;yellow is color 14
        call    SelectSetResetColor ;set to draw in yellow
        mov     dx,GC_INDEX
        mov     al,BIT_MASK
        out     dx,al            ;point GC Index to Bit Mask
        inc     dx               ;point to GC Data
        mov     al,10h
        out     dx,al            ;set Bit Mask to 10h
        mov     di,40            ;start in the middle of the top line
        mov     cx,350           ;do full height of screen
VLineLoop:
        mov     al,es:[di]       ;load the latches
        stosb                    ;write next pixel of yellow line
                                 ; (set/reset provides the data written
                                 ; to display memory, and AL is actually
                                 ; ignored)
        add     di,SCREEN_WIDTH-1 ;point to the next scan line
        loop    VLineLoop
;
; Select write mode 0 and read mode 1.
;
        mov     dx,GC_INDEX
        mov     al,GRAPHICS_MODE
        out     dx,al            ;point GC Index to Graphics Mode register
        inc     dx               ;point to GC Data
        mov     al,00001000b     ;bit 3=1 is read mode 1, bits 1 & 0=00
                                 ; is write mode 0
        out     dx,al            ;set Graphics Mode to read mode 1,
                                 ; write mode 0
;
```

Listing 7.2 continues

Listing 7.2 *continued*

```
; Draw a horizontal green line, one pixel at a time, from left
; to right until color compare reports a yellow pixel is encountered.
;
; Draw in green.
;
        mov     al,2                ;green is color 2
        call    SelectSetResetColor ;set to draw in green
;
; Set color compare to look for yellow.
;
        mov     dx,GC_INDEX
        mov     al,COLOR_COMPARE
        out     dx,al               ;point GC Index to Color Compare register
        inc     dx                  ;point to GC Data
        mov     al,14               ;we're looking for yellow, color 14
        out     dx,al               ;set color compare to look for yellow
        dec     dx                  ;point to GC Index
;
; Set up for quick access to Bit Mask register.
;
        mov     al,BIT_MASK
        out     dx,al               ;point GC Index to Bit Mask register
        inc     dx                  ;point to GC Data
;
; Set initial pixel mask and display memory offset.
;
        mov     al,80h              ;initial pixel mask
        mov     di,100*SCREEN_WIDTH
                                    ;start at left edge of scan line 100
HLineLoop:
        mov     ah,es:[di]          ;do a read mode 1 (color compare) read.
                                    ; This also loads the latches.
        and     ah,al               ;is the pixel of current interest yellow?
        jnz     WaitKeyAndDone      ;yes--we've reached the yellow line, so
                                    ; we're done
        out     dx,al               ;set the Bit Mask register so that we
                                    ; modify only the pixel of interest
        mov     es:[di],al          ;draw the pixel. The value written is
                                    ; irrelevant, since set/reset is providing
                                    ; the data written to display memory
        ror     al,1                ;shift pixel mask to the next pixel
        adc     di,0                ;advance the display memory offset if
                                    ; the pixel mask wrapped
        jmp     HLineLoop
;
; Wait for a key to be pressed to end, then return to text mode and
; return to DOS.
;
WaitKeyAndDone:
WaitKeyLoop:
        mov     ah,1
        int     16h
        jz      WaitKeyLoop
        sub     ah,ah
        int     16h         ;clear the key
        mov     ax,3
        int     10h         ;return to text mode
        mov     ah,4ch
```

Listing 7.2 *continues*

Listing 7.2 *continued*

```
        int     21h      ;done
Start   endp
;
; Enables set/reset for all planes, and sets the set/reset color
; to AL.
;
SelectSetResetColor     proc     near
        mov     dx,GC_INDEX
        push    ax                ;preserve color
        mov     al,SET_RESET
        out     dx,al             ;point GC Index to Set/Reset register
        inc     dx                ;point to GC Data
        pop     ax                ;get back color
        out     dx,al             ;set Set/Reset register to selected color
        dec     dx                ;point to GC Index
        mov     al,ENABLE_SET_RESET
        out     dx,al             ;point GC Index to Enable Set/Reset
                                  ; register
        inc     dx                ;point to GC Data
        mov     al,0fh
        out     dx,al             ;enable set/reset for all planes
        ret
SelectSetResetColor     endp
code    ends
        end     Start
```

Listing 7.3

```
; Program that draws a diagonal line to illustrate the use of a
; Color Don't Care register setting of 0FFh to support fast
; read-modify-write operations to VGA memory in write mode 3 by
; drawing a diagonal line.
;
; Note: Works on VGAs only.
;
; By Michael Abrash 4/2/88
; Updated 6/27/89.
;
stackseg        segment word stack 'STACK'
        db      512 dup (?)
stackseg        ends
;
VGA_SEGMENT      EQU    0a000h
SCREEN_WIDTH     EQU    80        ;in bytes
GC_INDEX         EQU    3ceh      ;Graphics Controller Index register
SET_RESET        EQU    0         ;Set/Reset register index in GC
GRAPHICS_MODE    EQU    5         ;Graphics Mode register index in GC
COLOR_DONT_CARE  EQU    7         ;Color Don't Care register index in GC
;
code    segment word 'CODE'
        assume  cs:code
Start   proc    near
;
; Select graphics mode 12h.
```

Listing 7.3 continues

Listing 7.3 *continued*

```
;
        mov     ax,12h
        int     10h
;
; Select write mode 3 and read mode 1.
;
        mov     dx,GC_INDEX
        mov     al,GRAPHICS_MODE
        out     dx,al
        inc     dx
        in      al,dx           ;VGA registers are readable, bless them!
        or      al,00001011b    ;bit 3=1 selects read mode 1, and
                                ; bits 1 & 0=11 selects write mode 3
        jmp     $+2             ;delay between IN and OUT to same port
        out     dx,al
        dec     dx
;
; Set up set/reset to always draw in white. It's not necessary to
; enable set/reset, which is always enabled in write mode 3.
;
        mov     al,SET_RESET
        out     dx,al
        inc     dx
        mov     al,0fh
        out     dx,al
        dec     dx
;
; Set Color Don't Care to 0, so reads of VGA memory always return 0FFh.
;
        mov     al,COLOR_DONT_CARE
        out     dx,al
        inc     dx
        sub     al,al
        out     dx,al
;
; Set up the initial memory pointer and pixel mask.
;
        mov     ax,VGA_SEGMENT
        mov     ds,ax
        sub     bx,bx
        mov     al,80h
;
; Draw 400 points on a diagonal line sloping down and to the right.
;
        mov     cx,400
DrawDiagonalLoop:
        and     [bx],al ;reads display memory, loading the latches,
                        ; then writes AL to the VGA. AL becomes the
                        ; bit mask, and set/reset provides the
                        ; actual data written
        add     bx,SCREEN_WIDTH
                        ; point to the next scan line
        ror     al,1    ;move the pixel mask one pixel to the right
        adc     bx,0    ;advance to the next byte if the pixel mask
                        ; wrapped
        loop    DrawDiagonalLoop
;
; Wait for a key to be pressed to end, then return to text mode and
```

Listing 7.3 *continued*

Listing 7.3 continues

```
; return to DOS.
;
WaitKeyLoop:
        mov     ah,1
        int     16h
        jz      WaitKeyLoop
        sub     ah,ah
        int     16h     ;clear the key
        mov     ax,3
        int     10h     ;return to text mode
        mov     ah,4ch
        int     21h     ;done
Start   endp
code    ends
        end     Start
```

Listing 7.4

```
; Sample code to illustrate various approaches to generating local
; symbols within REPT loops that don't seem to work with MASM 5.0.
;
        dosseg
        .model  small
        .code

mac1    macro
        rept    10
        local   testlabel
        jmp     testlabel
testlabel:
        endm
        endm

mac2    macro
        local   testlabel
        rept    10
        jmp     testlabel
testlabel:
        endm
        endm

start:
        mac1

        mac2

        rept    10
        local   testlabel
        jmp     testlabel
testlabel:
        endm

        end     start
```

CHAPTER 8

VGA Text Paging

The "On Graphics" column spends most of its time discussing—no surprise here—graphics. In this installment, however, we switch over to text mode to explore the 32 pages of text that the EGA and VGA can handle at once. In truth, the text capabilities of the EGA and VGA are remarkable, what with soft fonts, smooth scrolling, split screen, and more.

Yes, I know it seems a bit silly to discuss text mode in a column entitled "On Graphics." Perhaps I should have named the column "On Video," but that has less of a ring to it—and besides, it was too late to change.

This chapter may well start you thinking that the official modes and documented programming techniques of the EGA and VGA are actually just a few special cases out of the millions of possibilities for mixing and matching features in these complex adapters—and you would be absolutely right. The EGA and VGA are like those three-part flip-and-match books that kids play with, where you can put a dog's head on a cat's body with a chicken's feet—or any such combination you desire. In the case of the EGA and VGA, however, instead of dogs' heads and chickens' feet, you get to select the read mode, write mode, data rotation, ALU logical function, bit mask, latch contents, map mask, display mode, displayed page, panning/scrolling settings, and more.

Although it may not be apparent right now, most of the features of the EGA and VGA are actually independent of one another. For example, you could, if you wished, use the bit mask in text mode. Why you'd *want* to do such a thing is another story, but it does drive home the point that the features of the EGA and VGA are yours to mix and match as you please.

The more you work with the EGA and VGA, the more you'll realize that these are no normal graphics adapters. Both broad knowledge about the adapters *and* active creativity are absolutely essential to producing good code for any mode, be it graphics or text. Given that knowledge and creativity, the potential of these adapters is wondrous.

Installment 8: In which we explore the text-paging capabilities of the VGA and find 8 extra pages by moving display memory, and 16 more pages hiding in the Page bit, for an amazing total of 32 text pages.

Now that we've covered all the read and write modes of the VGA, we'll have to cast about for a new graphics topic. We won't have to cast too far, though, given the power and complexity of the VGA; the real problem is selecting among the many possibilities. Andrew Chalk, of Magna Carta Software, suggested that I discuss the VGA's text-paging capabilities; that sounds like a good idea to me, and so that's what we'll look at in this installment.

A Quick Overview of Text Paging

Text paging is the technique of storing information for two or more screens of text simultaneously in separate areas of display memory and then flipping between those screens virtually instantaneously by changing the portion of display memory that the CRT controller (CRTC) circuitry in the display adapter is sending to the screen. Figures 8.1 and 8.2 illustrate the basic operation of page flipping. In Figure 8.1, the CRTC is programmed to fetch video data from the page of memory starting at offset 0 in display memory, and so page 0 is displayed. In Figure 8.2, the CRTC is programmed to fetch video data from the page of memory starting at offset 1000h, and so page 1 is displayed. The key point is that two text screens can be displayed in turn *without the contents of display memory being altered in any way.*

Two fundamental requirements must be met for a given graphics adapter to support page flipping. First, the adapter must have enough memory to store information for at least two screens at once. Second, the adapter must be programmable as regards the address at which it starts scanning display memory for video data.

The CGA, EGA, and VGA all meet the above requirements and support video paging, while the MDA, which has only 4K bytes of display memory (just slightly more than enough for one screen), does not. Since the Hercules Graphics Card has a programmable start address and has 64K bytes of display memory (and can, in fact, perform page flipping in a different way in graphics mode), it's theoretically capable of text paging, but my experiments indicate that the HGC does in fact provide only the single text page that the MDA supports. This makes some sense in that it provides maximum MDA compatibility.

The CGA has 16K bytes of display memory; since one text-mode screen requires 4K bytes of display memory, the CGA supports four 80-by-25 text pages. The CGA also supports eight 40-by-25 text pages, since a 40-by-25 text screen requires only 2K bytes. The EGA and VGA similarly support twice as many 40-by-25 as 80-by-25 text pages, but since 40-by-25 text is rarely used anymore, I'm going to ignore it for the remainder of this article.

CGA text paging is straightforward: The four pages are laid out one after the other in display memory, as shown in Figure 8.3, and you select a given text page for display simply by programming the Start Address High and Start Address Low registers of the 6845 CRTC (indexed registers 0Ch and 0Dh at I/O port 3D5h, respectively) to one-half the offset of the

---

Fig. 8.1 *Text paging with page 0, starting at offset 0 in display memory, selected.*

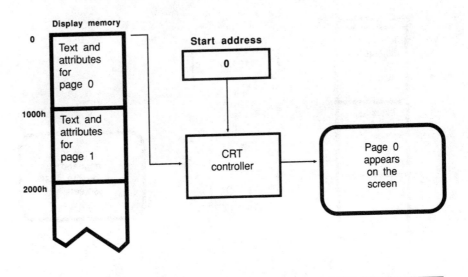

start of the desired text page in display memory. (The one-half is the result of the CRTC's characteristic of counting in units of character/attribute pairs in text mode rather than in units of bytes of display memory.) The code in Listing 8.1 [presented at the end of this chapter] flips through the four text pages of the CGA, advancing one page each time a key is pressed. (The EGA and VGA provide full compatibility with the CGA's four text pages; so, Listing 8.1 will run equally well on any of the three adapters.)

Each CGA text page is actually 4000 rather than 4K bytes long (80 columns times 25 lines times 2 bytes—character code and attribute—per character); 96 bytes are wasted at the end of each page. This means that you could, if you wished, pack the pages more tightly by starting them at addresses 0, 4000, 8000, and 12,000 instead of the addresses 0, 1000h, 2000h, and 3000h that we used above. It doesn't much matter which page organization is used; either way, there's room for only four text pages. Since IBM's BIOS uses 1000h for the text page length, that's what I'll use.

By the way, you may get the clever idea of using those extra bytes of display memory to store program data (or even code, if you're *really* clever); why let good memory go to waste? Don't do it! Display memory is *much* slower than normal system memory, because of the wait states inserted while the CRTC fetches video data. In fact, an AT can slow down to PC*jr* speeds when accessing display memory. So, don't use display

Fig. 8.2   *Text paging with page 1, starting at offset 1000h in display memory, selected.*

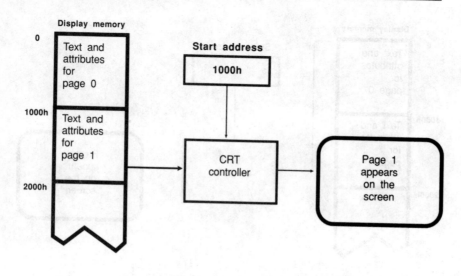

memory for anything other than video data unless you have absolutely no alternative.

That's really all there is to CGA text paging. One handy feature of CGA text paging is that the BIOS supports text paging to some extent, maintaining a separate cursor for each text page and allowing you to write text to and scroll whichever page you've selected to be active. Both the EGA BIOS and the VGA BIOS support the text-paging BIOS functions, as well. (In fact, the EGA and VGA BIOSes support all CGA BIOS functions.) Beware, though: I've heard that some versions of the IBM BIOS have bugs in their page-handling code; so, test your code on several machines before you rely on the BIOS for text paging. You might also want to take a close look at the video BIOS listings in IBM's PC, XT, and AT technical reference manuals if you're using BIOS text paging, to make sure the BIOS code really does what you expect it to. I'm not going to discuss the BIOS functions related to text paging here, since they're documented in several of IBM's manuals, included the aforementioned Technical Reference manuals and the BIOS Technical Reference manual.

Be aware that the cursor location is programmed with an address, not a screen position. That is, the cursor isn't positioned by setting an (X,Y) coordinate; instead the Cursor Location High and Cursor Location Low registers (CRTC registers 0Eh and 0Fh) are set to cause the cursor to appear when a specific memory address is read by the CRTC for video data. The cursor can be made to appear in any page by setting the cursor location to fall within that page. Cursor locations correspond directly to start addresses; for example, a cursor-location setting of 800h would position the cursor at the first character of page 1, just as a start-address setting of 800h would cause page 1 to be displayed. Likewise, a cursor-location setting of 1001h would position the cursor at the second character of page 2. (As with start addresses, a given cursor-location value is one-half the value of the CPU address of the corresponding page. Page 1 starts at offset 1000h, but the cursor location required to position the cursor at the start of page 1 is 800h.)

The EGA and VGA are by far the most interesting adapters in terms of text paging, since each is capable of supporting up to thirty-two 80-by-25 text pages. Now, given past experience, you might well guess that text paging is more complex on the EGA and VGA than on the CGA—and you'd be entirely correct. The first 4 pages are the same as the CGA's, and the next 4 pages lie just above the first 4 pages, but the remaining 24 pages are somewhat harder to find. It's just a matter of knowing where to look, though, and that's what this installment's about.

By the way, while the VGA does have text-paging capabilities that the EGA lacks, everything discussed in this installment will work on both the

EGA and VGA; from now on, any references to the VGA apply to the EGA as well, unless otherwise noted.

The Eight Basic Text Pages

In text mode, the VGA offers 32K bytes of display memory starting at B800:0000, rather than the 16K bytes of the CGA. Consequently, the VGA

Fig. 8.3   *The four text pages of the CGA.*

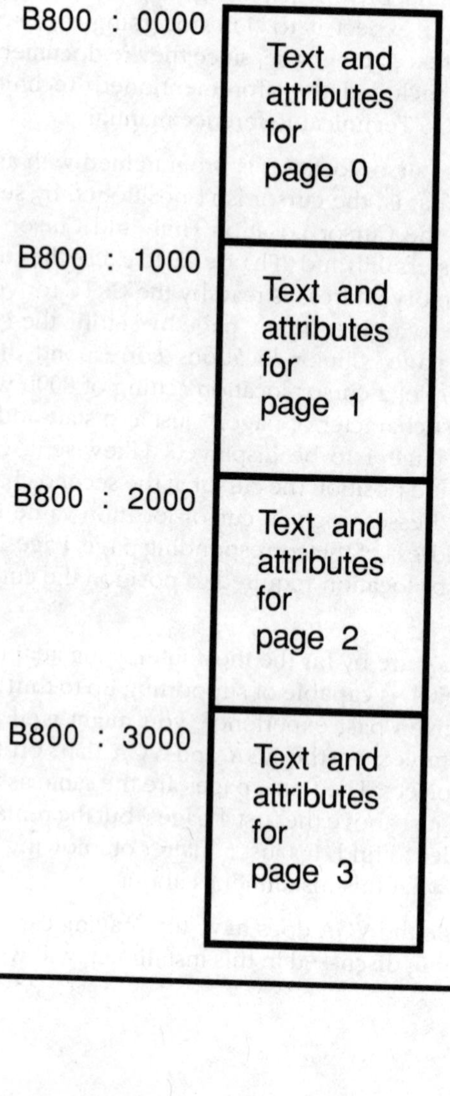

B800 : 0000

Text and attributes for page 0

B800 : 1000

Text and attributes for page 1

B800 : 2000

Text and attributes for page 2

B800 : 3000

Text and attributes for page 3

readily supports eight text pages in just the same way that the CGA supports four, as shown in Figure 8.4. Accessing one of the four pages the VGA adds (pages 4 through 7) is simply a matter of reading from or writing to the appropriate address in the range B800:4000 through B800:7FFF in display memory, and displaying one of the four pages merely requires the use of the appropriate start address for that page (2000h, 2800h, 3000h, or 3800h).

Fig. 8.4   *The eight standard text pages of the VGA.*

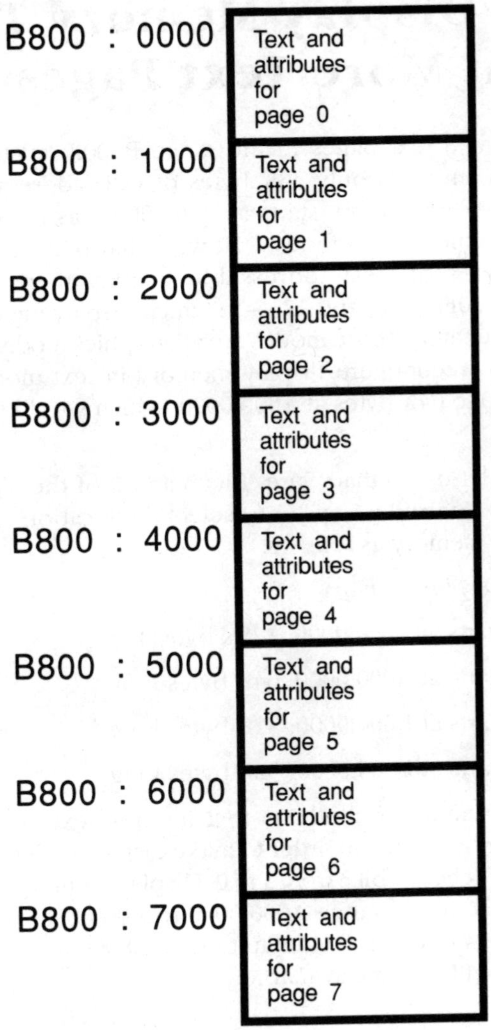

B800 : 0000	Text and attributes for page 0
B800 : 1000	Text and attributes for page 1
B800 : 2000	Text and attributes for page 2
B800 : 3000	Text and attributes for page 3
B800 : 4000	Text and attributes for page 4
B800 : 5000	Text and attributes for page 5
B800 : 6000	Text and attributes for page 6
B800 : 7000	Text and attributes for page 7

In order to see the eight basic text pages of the VGA in action, just change the value of NUMBER_OF_PAGES in Listing 8.1 from 4 to 8. Incidentally, Listing 8.1 illustrates an important concept in text paging: At any time, the page that your program is modifying does not have to be the page that is being displayed. In fact, the opposite situation is often desirable, since you generally won't want the user to see a given page while you're in the middle of updating it. The cleanest approach is to display one page, redraw a second page, and then switch to displaying the second page once it's fully updated.

Moving Display Memory Turns Up Eight More Text Pages

We're limited to 8 text pages in the range B800:0000 to B800:7FFF because the VGA supports only 32K bytes of CPU-addressable display memory when display memory starts at B800:0000 (as is the case in all BIOS-supported color text modes). Now, it happens that the VGA supports 64K bytes of CPU-addressable display memory in those modes—0Dh, 0Eh, 0Fh, 10h, and 12h—in which display memory starts at A000:0000; unfortunately, those modes are all graphics modes. What we'd really like to do is reconfigure display memory in text mode from 32K bytes at B800:0000 to 64K bytes at A000:0000, which would give us room for 16 text pages.

Does the VGA let us do that? Sure. Bits 3 and 2 of the Miscellaneous register (Graphics Controller register 6) select the location and length of the VGA's display memory as follows:

Bit 3	Bit 2	Display Memory
0	0	Starts at A000:0000; 128K bytes long
0	1	Starts at A000:0000; 64K bytes long
1	0	Starts at B000:0000; 32K bytes long
1	1	Starts at B800:0000; 32K bytes long

Normally, bits 3 and 2 are both set to 1 in color text modes. All you need to do in color text mode in order to make display memory 64K bytes long at A000:0000 is change bit 3 from 1 to 0. Display memory will instantly become addressable in the range A000:0000 to A000:FFFF, organized in just the same way as it was in the default range B800:0000 to B800:7FFF, and 16 text pages will become available.

The text pages are located just where you'd expect, as shown in Figure 8.5. Likewise, the start-address settings for displaying the text pages are a straightforward extension of the start addresses we've already encountered. Basically, text paging at A000:0000 is just like text paging at B800:0000, except that the segment address is different and display memory covers a greater memory range. In order to see the 16 text pages

Fig. 8.5   *The 16 VGA text pages that are available when display memory is moved to the segment at A000.*

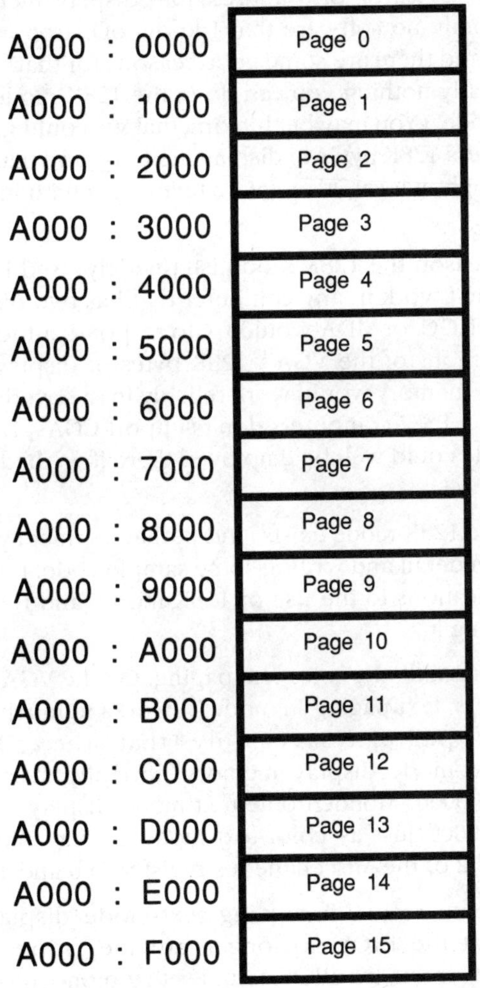

A000 : 0000	Page 0
A000 : 1000	Page 1
A000 : 2000	Page 2
A000 : 3000	Page 3
A000 : 4000	Page 4
A000 : 5000	Page 5
A000 : 6000	Page 6
A000 : 7000	Page 7
A000 : 8000	Page 8
A000 : 9000	Page 9
A000 : A000	Page 10
A000 : B000	Page 11
A000 : C000	Page 12
A000 : D000	Page 13
A000 : E000	Page 14
A000 : F000	Page 15

of the VGA in action, modify the value of NUMBER_OF_PAGES in Listing 8.1 from 8 to 16 and modify the value of RELOCATE_TO_A000 from 0 to 1.

Setting RELOCATE_TO_A000 to a nonzero value has two effects on the program in Listing 8.1. First, a nonzero setting for RELOCATE_TO_A000 causes MASM to assemble a section of the program that instructs the VGA to move display memory from the segment at B800 to the segment at A000 by way of the Miscellaneous register. Second, a nonzero setting causes the program to set ES to point to the relocated display memory at A000.

By the way, the 128K-byte display-memory configuration noted earlier is an interesting aspect of the VGA. While the VGA is indeed capable of supporting 128K bytes of CPU-addressable display memory, no BIOS mode (and virtually no software that I know of) supports this memory configuration—and there are some good reasons for that. The first reason is that there's really nothing you can do in the 128K mode that you can't do in the 64K mode. (You may be thinking that we could get 32 text pages if we could address 128K bytes of display memory, and that's true; as we'll see shortly, though, we can also get 32 text pages with just 64K bytes of display memory.)

The second reason the 128K mode isn't widely used is that the 128K mode flat-out can't work in any computer that has two display adapters, because a CGA, HGC, or MDA would try to respond at the same memory addresses as portions of the VGA's 128K bytes of display memory, and neither adapter's memory would work reliably in the overlapping address range. (Of course, PS/2 computers don't support CGAs, HGCs, or MDAs, so the 128K mode could well be employed there if we had a good reason to use it.)

At any rate, the 128K mode exists, and perhaps someday I'll get around to discussing it in detail and writing some sample code, but on the whole there are complications to the use of 128K mode, and relatively little to be gained by using it.

So far I've discussed only color text paging. On the VGA, monochrome text paging (that is, text paging in mode 7) works in much the same way as color text paging, save only that the 32K bytes of monochrome-text-mode display memory normally start at B000:0000 rather than B800:0000. Monochrome-text-mode display memory can be moved to A000:0000 just as color-text-mode display memory can: by setting bits 3 and 2 of the Miscellaneous register to 0 and 1, respectively.

One unfortunate result of moving text-mode display memory to A000:0000 is that the BIOS no longer provides support for placing characters on the screen; the BIOS assumes that monochrome-text-mode display memory starts at B000:0000 and that color-text-mode display memory starts at B800:0000, and it can't be convinced otherwise. The solution is to follow the approach I've used in Listing 8.1: Access display memory directly to place characters on the screen, rather than going through the BIOS **write_tty** or **write_character** functions. While this is a bit more work, you'd probably want to modify display memory directly in any case, since code that accesses display memory directly can update the screen much more rapidly than can code that uses the BIOS functions. After all, virtually all screen-oriented software that's worth anything, including text editors, word processors, and spreadsheets, goes directly to display memory rather than through the BIOS.

Finally, I'd like to point out that there's nothing to prevent you from moving display memory to A000:0000 to modify the upper 8 text pages and then moving display memory back to B800:0000 so that you can use the BIOS to access the lower 8 text pages. You can readily display the contents of the upper 8 pages while display memory is located at B800:0000; the CPU just can't read or write those pages until display memory is moved back to A000:0000. In order to see this admittedly unusual feature in action, set NUMBER_OF_PAGES to 16, RELOCATE_TO_A000 to 1, and RELOCATE_BACK_TO_B800 to 1 in Listing 8.1. This causes the program in Listing 8.1 to switch the display-memory segment back to B800 before displaying the 16 pages; the upper 8 pages are displayed even though the CPU can't read from or write to them, given the currently selected display-memory address range.

How is it that the code in Listing 8.1 can display eight text pages that the CPU can't get at? Basically, the VGA simply reads video data from display memory, beginning at the start address you've specified; the address at which the CPU can (or can't) address display memory is irrelevant as far as fetching video data is concerned, just as the start address is irrelevant as far as CPU addressing of display memory is concerned. Consequently, the same video data is displayed whether display memory resides in the segment at A000, B000, or B800. The only difference is that the CPU can't get at the upper eight pages when display memory lies in the segment at B000 or B800.

The Page Bit Reveals
16 More Text Pages

We've found 16 text pages thus far. Since 16 times 4K bytes equals 64K bytes, it would seem that's all the text pages we can have (given that we're not going to use 128K mode). There is, however, a very interesting bit that lets us get at 16 *more* text pages, for a grand total of 32 text pages. That bit is the Page bit, bit 5 of the Miscellaneous Output register at port 3C2h.

The Page bit is normally 1 in text mode; this causes CPU reads and writes to access the portion of display memory that's displayed with start addresses in the range 0 through 7000h. When the Page bit is set to 0, CPU reads and writes go to the portion of display memory that's displayed with start addresses in the range 8000h through 0F000h. This portion of display memory is normally untouched in text mode, since no BIOS mode supports access to it, but there's no reason not to use it. Figure 8.6 shows the locations of all 32 text pages and the start addresses for displaying those pages.

The 16 additional text pages that can be accessed when the Page bit is 0 are a mirror copy of the 16 pages we've already encountered. If display memory is located in the segment at 0B000h or 0B800h, then 8 text pages are accessible when the Page bit is 0 and 8 more text pages are accessible when the Page bit is 1, and the BIOS will draw text to whichever set of pages is currently selected by the Page bit. (However, the BIOS will always program the VGA to display the cursor in the normal set of pages—that is, the pages that the CPU accesses when the Page bit is 1.) If display memory is located at 0A000h, then the 16 text pages we've already seen are accessible when the Page bit is 1, and the 16 alternate text pages are accessible in exactly the same fashion when the Page bit is 0.

Listing 8.2 [presented at the end of this chapter] illustrates all 32 text pages of the VGA. One interesting aspect of Listing 8.2 is that the same text page, page 0, is displayed while all 32 pages are filled with text, and then the Page bit is left at the same value while each of the 32 pages is displayed in turn by a change of the start address. The key here is that the start address (which affects the portion of display memory shown on the screen) is independent of the Page bit (which affects the portion of display memory CPU reads and writes go to).

Setting the Page Bit

The process of setting the Page bit can be tricky, and it differs significantly on the EGA and VGA.

When assembled for the VGA (when the ADAPTER_IS_VGA equate is nonzero), the code in Listing 8.2 sets the Page bit to 0 by reading from port 3CCh and then ANDing off bit 5 and writing the new setting to port 3C2h. Note that on the VGA the Miscellaneous Output register is readable but must be read at 3CCh, because 3C2h reads back the Input Status 0 register. (Why this strange arrangement, rather than simply both reading and writing the Miscellaneous Output register at a single address? The Input Status 0 register is readable at 3C2h on the EGA; the VGA's designers had to leave it in the same place on the VGA for EGA compatibility. Similarly, the Miscellaneous Output register is writable at 3C2h on the EGA, and so there it had to stay on the VGA. Consequently, the only way to make the Miscellaneous Output register readable on the VGA was to make it readable at an address other than the one at which it is written to.)

On the EGA, the Miscellaneous Output register is not readable at all, and that poses a problem. The EGA requires you to know the value of the entire Miscellaneous Output register, since there's no way to read the current Miscellaneous Output setting and alter only the Page bit; the problem is that it's difficult to know what that value should be. A Miscellaneous Output register setting that works on the EGA won't necessarily work on the VGA, and vice-versa. Moreover, different Miscellaneous Output settings may be required on the EGA, depending on the type of monitor attached, and adapters that are compatible with only the VGA at the BIOS level may not work with either VGA or EGA settings.

What to do? Well, it's possible to look up the Miscellaneous Output register setting in the BIOS parameter table, but there is a problem even there, since the VGA's text modes are 400-scan-line modes and thus are located in a different area of the BIOS parameter table than are the EGA's 350-scan-line modes. While we could work around even that, it's not easy, and I've found BIOS parameter tables to be less than totally reliable in the past, especially on clone adapters. Yet another possible solution would be to set the Miscellaneous Output register according to the value of the BIOS points variable, which contains the height of the current font in pixels, but that's getting into very tricky territory. In short, manipulating the Page bit reliably on all VGAs and EGAs is no simple task.

Perhaps the simplest solution to the problem of how to program the Miscellaneous Output register is to use only the first 16 text pages. Another solution is to detect the installed adapter and handle the VGA with one set of instructions and the EGA with another set. There may well be a more elegant solution; if you know of one, please write and tell us.

By the way, Listing 8.2 doesn't detect adapter type but can be assembled specifically for either a VGA or an EGA; VGA code is assembled when ADAPTER_IS_VGA is nonzero, and EGA code is assembled when ADAPTER_IS_VGA is zero. The VGA code flat out won't work on an EGA. While the EGA code may work on some VGAs—it works, albeit with a bit of initial flicker, on a VGA attached to a MultiSync, for example—it won't work properly in all cases, since it changes the polarities of the sync pulses, and shouldn't be used on VGAs.

Where *Does* that Extra Memory Come From?

Finally, you may well wonder exactly where an additional 64K bytes of memory comes from when the Page bit is flipped. The answer is

Fig. 8.6 *The 32 VGA text pages that are available when the Page bit is used.*

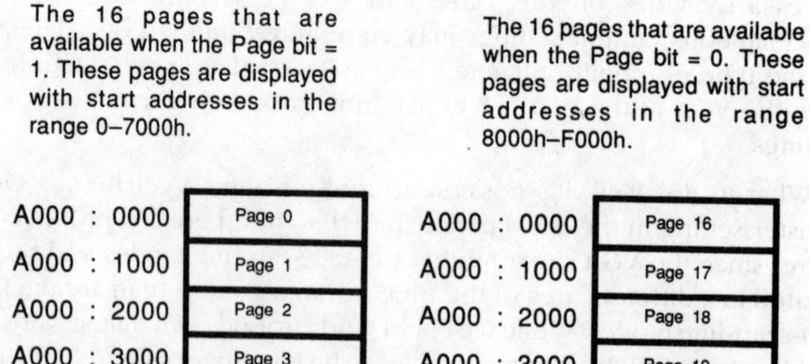

The 16 pages that are available when the Page bit = 1. These pages are displayed with start addresses in the range 0–7000h.

The 16 pages that are available when the Page bit = 0. These pages are displayed with start addresses in the range 8000h–F000h.

A000 : 0000	Page 0		A000 : 0000	Page 16
A000 : 1000	Page 1		A000 : 1000	Page 17
A000 : 2000	Page 2		A000 : 2000	Page 18
A000 : 3000	Page 3		A000 : 3000	Page 19
A000 : 4000	Page 4		A000 : 4000	Page 20
A000 : 5000	Page 5		A000 : 5000	Page 21
A000 : 6000	Page 6		A000 : 6000	Page 22
A000 : 7000	Page 7		A000 : 7000	Page 23
A000 : 8000	Page 8		A000 : 8000	Page 24
A000 : 9000	Page 9		A000 : 9000	Page 25
A000 : A000	Page 10		A000 : A000	Page 26
A000 : B000	Page 11		A000 : B000	Page 27
A000 : C000	Page 12		A000 : C000	Page 28
A000 : D000	Page 13		A000 : D000	Page 29
A000 : E000	Page 14		A000 : E000	Page 30
A000 : F000	Page 15		A000 : F000	Page 31

detailed in the VGA section of either the Model 50/60 or the Model 80 technical reference manual, as well as in the Display Adapter technical reference supplement—if you understand memory-addressing figures and tables. If you don't understand the explanations in those manuals, don't worry; there are few cases indeed in which you need to understand the byzantine ways in which the VGA organizes its memory, and the code in listings 8.1 and 8.2 will suffice for almost all text-paging needs. If you really need to know more—well, the information's all there in IBM's manuals!

In Conclusion

Once again, we've found that the VGA is much more complex and capable than one would expect, as the 4 simple text pages that were carried over from the CGA proved to be only the tip of the iceberg. The 32 text pages of the VGA are enough to support some animation, or to store many premade text screens without placing any demands on normal system memory.

Believe it or not, there's plenty more where that came from—the VGA is a seemingly inexhaustible source of new and useful tricks and techniques. Next time I'll probably look at saving and restoring VGA screens, but, as always, I'm open to suggestions.

See you then.

Listing 8.1

```
; Program to demonstrate the 4 text pages of the CGA.
;
; To demonstrate the 8 standard text pages of the VGA/EGA,
; change NUMBER_OF_PAGES from 4 to 8.
;
; To demonstrate the 16 text pages available on the VGA/EGA
; when display memory is relocated to A000, change NUMBER_OF_PAGES
; to 16 and change RELOCATE_TO_A000 from 0 to 1.
;
; To demonstrate that the upper 8 text pages can be displayed even
; when the CPU can't access them, change NUMBER_OF_PAGES to 16,
; RELOCATE_TO_A000 to 1, and RELOCATE_BACK_TO_B800 to 1.
;
; By Michael Abrash  5/22/88
;

NUMBER_OF_PAGES          equ     4
RELOCATE_TO_A000         equ     0
RELOCATE_BACK_TO_B800    equ     0
PAGE_LENGTH              equ     1000h    ;number of bytes per page
```

Listing 8.1 continues

Listing 8.1 *continued*

```
if RELOCATE_TO_A000
DISPLAY_MEMORY_SEGMENT     equ       0a000h
else
DISPLAY_MEMORY_SEGMENT     equ       0b800h
endif

GC_INDEX                   equ       3ceh
GC_MISCELLANEOUS           equ       6
CRTC_INDEX                 equ       3d4h
CRTC_START_ADDRESS_HIGH    equ       0ch
CRTC_START_ADDRESS_LOW     equ       0dh

stackseg         segment para stack 'STACK'
        db       512 dup (?)
stackseg         ends

code    segment para public 'CODE'
        assume   cs:code, ds:nothing
start   proc     near
;
; Set to text mode.
;
        mov      ax,3
        int      10h
;
; Relocate display memory to A000 if necessary, by reprogramming
; the Graphics Controller's Miscellaneous register.
;
if RELOCATE_TO_A000
        mov      dx,GC_INDEX
        mov      al,GC_MISCELLANEOUS
        out      dx,al
        inc      dx
        mov      al,06h
        out      dx,al
endif
;
; Point to the segment that display memory is currently
; addressed at.
;
        mov      ax,DISPLAY_MEMORY_SEGMENT
        mov      es,ax
;
; Fill each of the text screens in turn with an appropriate character.
; (Page 0 is filled with "A", page 1 with "B", and so on.)
;
        sub      ax,ax     ;start with page 0
        mov      bl,'A'    ;base letter
FillPageLoop:
        push     ax
        call     FillPage
        pop      ax
        inc      ax
        cmp      ax,NUMBER_OF_PAGES
        jb       FillPageLoop
;
; Relocate display memory back to B800 if necessary,
; by reprogramming the Graphics Controller's Miscellaneous
```

Listing 8.1 *continues*

Listing 8.1 *continued*

```
; register, to illustrate the principle that it's possible to
; display the upper 8 pages even when the CPU can't access them.
;
if RELOCATE_BACK_TO_B800
        mov     dx,GC_INDEX
        mov     al,GC_MISCELLANEOUS
        out     dx,al
        inc     dx
        mov     al,0Eh
        out     dx,al
endif
;
; Display each of the text pages in turn, waiting for a key
; before going to the next page.
;
        sub     ax,ax
ShowPageLoop:
        push    ax
        call    ShowPage
        call    WaitKey
        pop     ax
        inc     ax
        cmp     ax,NUMBER_OF_PAGES
        jb      ShowPageLoop
;
; Done-perform a mode set to reset all paging and clear
; the screen, then return to DOS.
;
        mov     ax,3
        int     10h
        mov     ah,4ch
        int     21h
start   endp
;
; Fills a text page with a corresponding character.
;
; Input:
;       AX = text page
;       BL = character for text page 0 (each text page
;               is filled with character BL + text page #)
;
FillPage        proc    near
        push    ax      ;save the page #
        mov     dx,PAGE_LENGTH
        mul     dx      ;calculate the start offset of the page
                        ; in the display memory segment
        mov     di,ax
        pop     ax      ;get back the page #
        add     al,bl   ;convert it to a unique letter
        mov     ah,7    ;attribute is white
        mov     cx,PAGE_LENGTH/2 ;page length as measured
                                 ; in character/attribute pairs
        cld
        rep     stosw   ;fill the page
        ret
FillPage        endp
;
; Programs the CRTC to display the desired text page.
```

Listing 8.1 *continues*

Listing 8.1 *continued*

```
;
; Input: AX = text page.
;
ShowPage        proc    near
        mov     dx,PAGE_LENGTH/2
        mul     dx                      ;start offset of the pages as
                                        ; measured in character/attribute
                                        ; pairs (which is how the CRTC
                                        ; counts in text mode)
        mov     dx,CRTC_INDEX           ;point to the CRTC Index register
        push    ax
        mov     al,CRTC_START_ADDRESS_HIGH
        out     dx,al
        inc     dx                      ;point to the CRTC Data register
        mov     al,ah
        out     dx,al                   ;set the high start address byte
        dec     dx                      ;point to the CRTC Index register
        mov     al,CRTC_START_ADDRESS_LOW
        out     dx,al
        inc     dx                      ;point to the CRTC Data register
        pop     ax
        out     dx,al                   ;set the low start address byte
        ret
ShowPage        endp
;
; Waits until a key is pressed.
;
WaitKey proc    near
        mov     ah,1
        int     16h
        jz      WaitKey
        sub     ah,ah
        int     16h     ;clear the key
        ret
WaitKey endp

code    ends
        end     start
```

Listing 8.2

```
; Program to demonstrate the 32 text pages of the VGA/EGA.
;
; To demonstrate the 32 text pages of the VGA, set
; ADAPTER_IS_VGA to 1.
;
; To demonstrate the 32 text pages of the EGA, set
; ADAPTER_IS_VGA to 0.
;
; By Michael Abrash  5/22/88
; Updated 6/29/89.
;

ADAPTER_IS_VGA          equ     0       ;set to 1 to assemble for VGA,
```

Listing 8.2 *continues*

Listing 8.2 continued

```
                                        ; 0 to assemble for EGA
PAGE_LENGTH              equ    1000h    ;number of bytes per page
MISCELLANEOUS_OUTPUT_W   equ    3c2h     ;Miscellaneous Output write port
MISCELLANEOUS_OUTPUT_R   equ    3cch     ;Miscellaneous Output read port
                                        ; (available only on VGA)

GC_INDEX                equ    3ceh
GC_MISCELLANEOUS        equ    6
CRTC_INDEX              equ    3d4h
CRTC_START_ADDRESS_HIGH equ    0ch
CRTC_START_ADDRESS_LOW  equ    0dh

stackseg        segment para stack 'STACK'
        db      512 dup (?)
stackseg        ends

code    segment para public 'CODE'
        assume  cs:code, ds:nothing
start   proc    near
;
; Set to text mode.
;
        mov     ax,3
        int     10h
;
; Relocate display memory to A000 by reprogramming
; the Graphics Controller's Miscellaneous register.
;
        mov     dx,GC_INDEX
        mov     al,GC_MISCELLANEOUS
        out     dx,al
        inc     dx
        mov     al,06h
        out     dx,al
;
; Point to display memory.
;
        mov     ax,0a000h
        mov     es,ax
;
; Fill text pages 0-15 (the pages that are accessible when
; the Page bit is 1, the setting after a mode set is performed).
; (Page 0 is filled with "A", page 1 with "B", and so on.)
;
        sub     ax,ax   ;start with page 0
        mov     bl,'A'  ;base letter for pages 0-15
FillPages0_15Loop:
        push    ax
        call    FillPage
        pop     ax
        inc     ax
        cmp     ax,16
        jb      FillPages0_15Loop
;
; Set the Page bit to 0.
;
if ADAPTER_IS_VGA
        mov     dx,MISCELLANEOUS_OUTPUT_R
        in      al,dx
```

Listing 8.2 continues

Listing 8.2 *continued*

```
        and     al,not 20h      ;Page bit (bit 5) -> 0
        mov     dx,MISCELLANEOUS_OUTPUT_W
        out     dx,al
else
        mov     dx,MISCELLANEOUS_OUTPUT_W
        mov     al,87h          ;Page bit (bit 5) -> 0
        out     dx,al
endif
;
; Now fill text pages 16-31 (the pages that are accessible when
; the Page bit is 0).
; (Page 16 is filled with "Q", page 17 with "R", and so on.)
;
        sub     ax,ax   ;start with page 0 in the second set of
                        ; 16 pages; pages in this set are accessed
                        ; exactly as pages 0-15 were
        mov     bl,'Q'  ;base letter for pages 16-31
FillPages16_31Loop:
        push    ax
        call    FillPage
        pop     ax
        inc     ax
        cmp     ax,16
        jb      FillPages16_31Loop
;
; Display each of the text pages in turn, waiting for a key
; before going to the next page. Note that all 32 pages can
; be displayed without changing the Page bit; the Page bit
; only affects CPU accesses, not video data fetching.
;
        sub     ax,ax
ShowPageLoop:
        push    ax
        call    ShowPage
        call    WaitKey
        pop     ax
        inc     ax
        cmp     ax,32
        jb      ShowPageLoop
;
; Done-perform a mode set to reset all paging and clear
; the screen, then return to DOS.
;
        mov     ax,3
        int     10h
        mov     ah,4ch
        int     21h
start   endp
;
; Fills a text page with a corresponding character.
;
; Input:
;       AX = text page
;       BL = character for text page 0 (each text page
;               is filled with character BL + text page #)
;
FillPage        proc    near
        push    ax      ;save the page #
```

Listing 8.2 *continues*

Listing 8.2 continued

```
        mov     dx,PAGE_LENGTH
        mul     dx          ;calculate the start offset of the page
                            ; in the display memory segment
        mov     di,ax
        pop     ax          ;get back the page #
        add     al,bl       ;convert it to a unique letter
        mov     ah,7        ;attribute is white
        mov     cx,PAGE_LENGTH/2 ;page length as measured
                                ; in character/attribute pairs
        cld
        rep     stosw       ;fill the page
        ret
FillPage        endp
;
; Programs the CRTC to display the desired text page.
;
; Input: AX = text page.
;
ShowPage        proc    near
        mov     dx,PAGE_LENGTH/2
        mul     dx                  ;start offset of the pages as
                                    ; measured in character/attribute
                                    ; pairs (which is how the CRTC
                                    ; counts in text mode)
        mov     dx,CRTC_INDEX       ;point to the CRTC Index register
        push    ax
        mov     al,CRTC_START_ADDRESS_HIGH
        out     dx,al
        inc     dx                  ;point to the CRTC Data register
        mov     al,ah
        out     dx,al       ;set the high start address byte
        dec     dx          ;point to the CRTC Index register
        mov     al,CRTC_START_ADDRESS_LOW
        out     dx,al
        inc     dx                  ;point to the CRTC Data register
        pop     ax
        out     dx,al       ;set the low start address byte
        ret
ShowPage        endp
;
; Waits until a key is pressed.
;
WaitKey proc    near
        mov     ah,1
        int     16h
        jz      WaitKey
        sub     ah,ah
        int     16h     ;clear the key
        ret
WaitKey endp

code    ends
        end     start
```

CHAPTER 9

Saving Screens, Color Selection, and More

Your typical magazine article is published, perhaps draws a few letters to the editor, and then vanishes forever. There's no way to know how many people it helped (or, indeed, if anyone even read it), and there's no real exchange of ideas, just a one-way lecture. That's okay, but it's not so rewarding as an ongoing two-way dialogue, where both sides develop and learn over time.

Of course, "On Graphics" has been just such an ongoing dialogue, and that's what makes the column so rewarding for me. For one thing, I get to build on ideas from column to column, allowing me to explore complex subjects—such as the EGA and VGA—that simply can't be handled properly in a single article. More important, though, is the feedback that I get from readers. That feedback lets me know that the column is useful to many people, and it also teaches me things that I could learn nowhere else. (See Listing 9.6 [presented at the end of this chapter] for one remarkable example.)

The ongoing dialogue with readers is also just plain *fun*. This chapter, which consists entirely of my answers to reader questions and reader answers to my questions, covers color control, saving and loading graphics screens, screen blanking, and MASM tricks. Imagine—all that in one short article . . . and with the knowledge that *someone* is eager to learn about each and every one of those topics.

To me, that's learning at its best—and at its most enjoyable.

171

Installment 9: In which we answer questions about screen saving and color selection and look at ingenious reader solutions to yet another MASM mystery.

A couple of interesting reader questions arrived recently, as well as solutions to my latest MASM puzzle, and together they'll make for a varied and interesting column. First, we'll look at saving and restoring hi-res EGA and VGA screens. Next, we'll unravel the 16-out-of-64-colors mess. We'll wind up by discussing MASM locals within REPT blocks.

That's a lot of ground to cover, so let's get started!

Saving and Restoring EGA and VGA Screens

Frank Baker, of the University of Wisconsin–Madison, wrote to ask how one goes about saving and restoring EGA hi-res (640-by-350) graphics screens to and from disk. Well, Frank, if you've understood everything we've discussed in the first eight installments of the "On Graphics" series, you *should* be able to solve this one on your own . . . but I agree that it's not obvious, and it certainly is useful.

The basic principle for saving EGA and VGA hi-res graphics screens is astonishingly simple: Write each plane to disk separately. All we need do is enable reads from plane 0 and write the 28,000 bytes of plane 0 that are displayed in mode 10h to disk, then enable reads from plane 1 and write the displayed portion of that plane to disk, and so on for planes 2 and 3. The result is a file that's 112,000 (28,000 × 4) bytes long, with the planes stored as four distinct 28,000-byte blocks, as shown in Figure 9.1.

The program shown in Listing 9.1 [presented at the end of this chapter] does just what I've described, putting the screen into mode 10h, putting up some bit-mapped text so there's something to save, and creating the 112K file SNAPSHOT.SCR, which contains the visible portion of the hi-res bit map.

The only part of Listing 9.1 that's even remotely tricky is the use of the Read Map register (Graphics Controller register 4) to make each of the four planes of display memory readable in turn. The same code is used to write 28,000 bytes of display memory to disk four times, and 28,000 bytes of memory starting at A000:0000 are written to disk each time; however, a different plane is read each time, thanks to the changing setting of the Read Map register. (If this is unclear, refer back to Figure 9.1; you may also want to reread Chapter 7 to brush up on the operation of the Read Map register in particular and reading EGA memory in general.)

Of course, we'll want the ability to restore what we've saved, and Listing 9.2 [presented at the end of this chapter] does this. Listing 9.2 reverses the action of Listing 9.1, selecting mode 10h and then loading 28,000 bytes from SNAPSHOT.SCR into each plane of display memory. The Map Mask register (Sequence Controller register 2) is used to select the plane to be written to. If your computer is slow enough, you can see the colors of the text change as each plane is loaded when Listing 9.2 runs. Note that Listing 9.2 does not itself draw any text but simply loads the bit map saved by Listing 9.1 back into the hi-res bit map.

If you compare listings 9.1 and 9.2, you will see that the Map Mask register setting used to load a given plane does not match the Read Map register setting used to read that plane. This is because while only one

Fig. 9.1 *EGA/VGA memory is saved by copying the 28,000 displayed bytes of each plane in turn to the file SNAPSHOT.SCR. The Read Map register is used to select which of the four planes is readable at A000:0000 at any given time.*

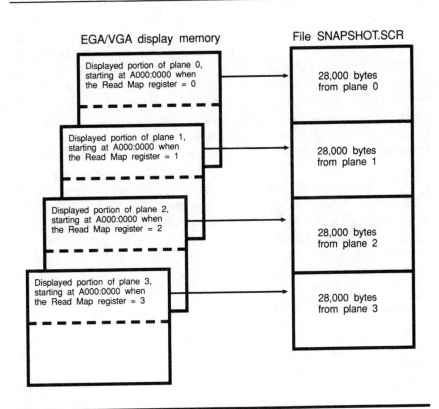

plane can ever be read at a time, anywhere from zero to four planes can be written to at once; consequently, Read Map register settings are plane selections from 0 to 3, while Map Mask register settings are plane *masks* from 0 to 15, where a bit 0 setting of 1 enables writes to plane 0, a bit 1 setting of 1 enables writes to plane 1, and so on. (Again, Chapter 7 provides a detailed explanation of the differences between the Read Map and Map Mask registers.)

Screen saving and restoring is pretty simple, eh? There are a few caveats, of course, but nothing serious. First, the EGA's registers must be programmed properly for screen saving and restoring to work. For screen saving, you must be in read mode 0; if you're in color compare mode, there's no telling what bit pattern you'll save, but it's not very likely to be the desired screen image. For screen restoring, you must be in write mode 0, with the Bit Mask register set to 0FFh and the Data Rotate register set to 0 (no data rotation and the logical function set to pass the data through unchanged).

While these requirements are no problem if you're simply calling a subroutine to save an image from your program, they pose a considerable problem if you're designing a hot-keyed TSR that can capture a screen image at any time. With the EGA, there's never any way to tell what state the registers are currently in, since the registers aren't readable. As a result, any TSR that sets the Bit Mask to 0FFh, the Data Rotate register to 0, and so on runs the risk of interfering with the drawing code of the program that was running when the TSR was activated.

What's the solution? Frankly, the solution is to get a VGA. A TSR designed for the VGA can simply read out and save the states of the registers of interest, program those registers as needed, save the screen image, and restore the original settings. From a programmer's perspective, readable registers are certainly near the top of the list of things to like about the VGA!

If you are going to write a hi-res VGA version of the screen capture program, be sure to account for the increased size of the VGA's mode 12h bit map. The mode 12h (640-by-480) screen uses 37.5K per plane of display memory; so, for mode 12h, the displayed-screen-size equate in listings 9.1 and 9.2 should be changed to

```
DISPLAYED_SCREEN_SIZE    equ        (640/8) × 480
```

Similarly, if you're capturing a graphics screen that starts at an offset other than 0 in the segment at A000, you must change the memory offset used by the disk functions to match. You can, if you so desire, read the start offset of the display memory providing the information shown on the screen from the Start Address registers (CRT Controller registers 0Ch and 0Dh).

Finally, be aware that the screen capture and restore programs in listings 9.1 and 9.2 are appropriate only for EGA/VGA modes 0Dh, 0Eh, 0Fh, 010h, and 012h, since they assume a four-plane configuration of EGA/VGA memory. In all text modes and in CGA graphics modes, and in VGA modes 11h and 13h as well, display memory can simply be written to disk and read back as a linear block of memory, just like a normal array.

While listings 9.1 and 9.2 are written in assembly language, the principles they illustrate apply equally well to high-level languages. In fact, there's no need for any assembly language at all when saving an EGA/VGA screen, so long as the high-level language you're using can perform direct port I/O to set up the adapter and can read and write display memory directly.

One tip if you're saving and restoring the screen from a high-level language on an EGA, though: After you've completed each save or restore operation, be sure to put any EGA registers that you've changed back to their default settings. Some high-level languages (and the BIOS as well) assume that some of the EGA's registers are in their default states; so, on the EGA, it's safest to leave the registers programmed to their defaults when you're done. On the VGA, of course, you can just read the registers out before you change them and then leave them as you found them when you're done.

16 Colors out of 64

Eric Klien, of Chelmsford, Massachusetts, wrote to ask how one produces the 64 colors from which the 16 colors displayed by the EGA can be chosen. The answer is simple enough: There's a BIOS function that lets you select the mappings of the 16 possible pixel values to the 64 possible colors. Let's establish a bit of background before proceeding, however.

The EGA sends pixel information to the monitor on six pins. This means that there are 2^6, or 64, colors that an EGA can generate. However, in 200-scan-line modes, Enhanced Color Display–compatible monitors ignore two of the signals, and so in CGA-compatible modes (modes 4, 5, 6, and the 200-scan-line versions of modes 0, 1, 2, and 3) you can select from only 16 colors (although the colors can still be remapped, as described below). If you're not hooked up to a monitor capable of displaying 350 scan lines (such as the old IBM Color Display), you can never select from more than 16 colors, since those monitors accept only four input signals. For now, we'll assume we're in one of the 350-scan-line color modes, a group that includes modes 0Dh, 0Eh, and 10h and the 350-scan-line versions of modes 0, 1, 2, and 3.

Each pixel comes out of memory (or, in text mode, out of the attribute-handling portion of the EGA) as a four-bit value, denoting 1 of 16 possible colors. In graphics modes, the four-bit pixel value is made up of one bit from each plane, with eight pixels' worth of data stored at any given byte address in display memory.

Normally, we think of the four-bit value of a pixel as being that pixel's color, with a pixel value of 0 being black, a pixel value of 1 being blue, and so on, as if that's a built-in feature of the EGA.

Fig. 9.2   *The 16 palette registers translate each four-bit pixel value from display memory or a text attribute into a six-bit pixel color to send to the display.*

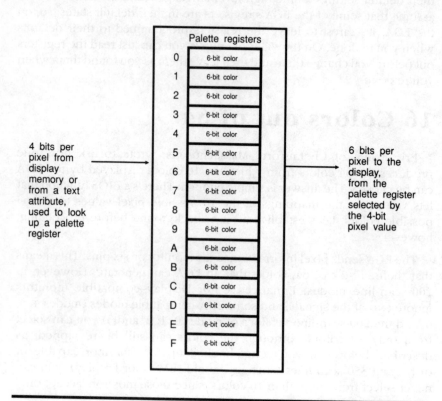

Hah! The correspondence of pixel values to color is absolutely arbitrary, depending solely on how the color-mapping portion of the EGA containing the palette registers is programmed. If you cared to have color 0 be bright red and color 1 be black, that could easily be arranged, as could a mapping in which all 16 colors were yellow. What's more, these mappings affect text-mode characters as readily as they do graphics-mode pixels, and so you could map text attribute 0 to white and text attribute 15 to black to produce a Mac-like black-on-white display, if you wished.

Each of the 16 palette registers stores the mapping of one of the 16 possible four-bit pixel values from memory to one of 64 possible six-bit pixel values to be sent to the monitor as video data, as shown in Figure 9.2. A four-bit pixel value of 0 causes the six-bit value stored in palette register 0 to be sent to the display as the color of that pixel; a pixel value of 1 causes the contents of palette register 1 to be sent to the display; and so on. Since there are only four input bits, it stands to reason that only 16 colors are available at any one time; since there are six output bits, however, those 16 colors can be mapped to any of 64 colors. The mapping for each of the 16 pixel values is controlled by the lower six bits of the corresponding palette register, as shown in Figure 9.3. Secondary red, green, and blue are less-intense versions of red, green, and blue, although their exact effects vary from monitor to monitor. The best way to figure out what the 64 colors look like on your monitor is to see them, and that's just what the program in Listing 9.3 [presented at the end of this chapter], which we'll discuss shortly, lets you do.

Fig. 9.3   *The organization of color bits within a palette register.*

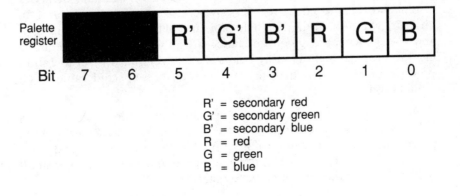

How are the palette registers set? Well, it's certainly possible to set the palette registers directly, addressed at registers 0 through 0Fh of the Attribute Controller. However, setting the palette registers is a bit tricky—bit 5 of the Attribute Controller Index register must be 0 while the palette registers are written to, and glitches can occur if the updating doesn't take place during the blanking interval—and besides, it turns out that there's no need at all to go straight to the hardware on this one. Conveniently, the EGA BIOS provides us with video function 10h, which supports setting either any one palette register or all 16 palette registers (and the overscan register as well) with a single video interrupt.

You invoke video function 10h by performing an INT 10h with AH set to 10h. If AL is 0 (subfunction 0), then BL contains the number of the palette register to set, and BH contains the value to set that register to. If AL is 1 (subfunction 1), then BH contains the value to set the overscan register to. Finally, if AL is 2 (subfunction 2), then ES:DX points to a 17-byte array containing the values to set palette registers 0–15 and the overscan register to. For completeness, although it's unrelated to the palette registers, there is one more subfunction of video function 10h: If AL = 3 (subfunction 3), BL is set to 1, to cause bit 7 of text attributes to select blinking, or is set to 0, to cause bit 7 of text attributes to select high-intensity reverse video.

Listing 9.3 uses video function 10h, subfunction 2, to step through all 64 possible colors. This is accomplished by putting up 16 color bars, one for each of the 16 possible four-bit pixel values, and then changing the mapping provided by the palette registers to select a different group of 16 colors from the set of 64 each time a key is pressed. Initially, colors 0–0Fh are displayed, then 1–10h, then 2–11h, and so on up to color 3Fh wrapping around to colors 0–0Eh and, finally, back to colors 0–0Fh.

By the way, at mode set, the 16 palette registers do not default to the colors 0–0Fh in any of the BIOS-supported modes. For example, in modes 3, 10h, and 12h, the palette registers are set to 0h, 1h, 2h, 3h, 4h, 5h, 14h, 7h, 38h, 39h, 3Ah, 3Bh, 3Ch, 3Dh, 3Eh, and 3Fh, respectively. Bits 6, 5, and 4—secondary red, green, and blue—are all set to 1 in palette registers 8–15 to produce high-intensity colors. Palette register 6 is set to 14h to produce brown, rather than the yellow that the expected value of 6h would produce.

When you run Listing 9.3, you'll see that the whole screen changes color as each new color set is selected. This occurs because most of the pixels on the screen have a value of 0 (selecting the background color stored in palette register 0), and we're reprogramming palette register 0 right along with the other 15 palette registers.

It's important to understand that in Listing 9.3, the bytes of display memory that make up the color bars are never changed after initialization. The only change is the mapping from the four-bit pixel data coming out of display memory to the six-bit data going to the monitor. For this reason, it's technically inaccurate to speak of bits in display memory as representing colors; more accurately, they represent attributes in the range 0–15, which are mapped to colors 0–3Fh by the palette registers.

While we're at it, I'm going to touch on overscan. Overscan is the color of the border of the display, the rectangular area around the edge of the monitor that's outside the region displaying active video data but inside the blanking area. The overscan (or border) color can be programmed to any of the 64 possible colors either by setting Attribute Controller register 11h directly or by calling video function 10h, subfunction 1. On ECD-compatible monitors, however, there's too little scan time to display a proper border when the EGA is in 350-scan-line mode, and so overscan should always be 0 (black), unless you're in 200-scan-line mode. Note, though, that a VGA can easily display a border on a VGA-compatible monitor, and VGAs are in fact programmed at mode set for an eight-pixel-wide border in all modes; all you need do is set the overscan color on any VGA to see the border.

An interesting point: The Attribute Controller provides a very convenient way to blank the screen, in the form of the aforementioned bit 5 of the Attribute Controller Index register (at address 3C0h after the Input Status register 1—3DAh in color, 3BAh in monochrome—has been read and on every other write to 3C0h thereafter). Whenever bit 5 of the AC Index register is 0, video data is cut off, effectively blanking the screen. Setting bit 5 of the AC Index back to 1 restores video data immediately. Listing 9.4 [presented at the end of this chapter] illustrates this simple but effective form of screen blanking.

Does that do it for color selection? Yes and no. For the EGA, we've covered the whole of color selection—but not so for the VGA. The VGA can emulate everything we've discussed, but it actually performs one 4-bit-to-8-bit translation, followed by yet another translation, this one 8-bit to 18-bit. What's more, the VGA has the ability to flip instantly through as many as sixteen 16-color sets. The VGA's color selection capabilities, which are supported by another set of BIOS functions, can be used to produce stunning color effects. Then, too, there are modes 11h and 13h of the VGA, which don't fit neatly into the 16-color scheme we've been discussing. However, I'm running out of room, and since everything we've discussed applies equally well to the EGA and VGA, we've covered the most broadly useful information about color selection; I'll try to get to VGA-specific color selection soon.

MASM Stuff:
Readers to the Rescue

A few chapters back, I pointed out that although the MASM manual indicated otherwise, the LOCAL directive didn't work properly inside a REPT block, and I asked if any *PJ* readers had workarounds. As usual, several readers did; all the solutions are good, and one is a wonderful illustration of the lengths to which people are willing to go to get MASM to cooperate.

First the simple solution. Both Michael Liebert, of Custom Real-Time Software in Caldwell, New Jersey, and Bradford Levy, of BKL Consulting in Lawrence, Kansas, sent in the solution shown in Listing 9.5 [presented at the end of this chapter]. (I've reproduced Brad's code, since it was in source form rather than assembly listing format, but the two solutions are essentially the same.) The solution is reasonably simple, although it seems like a lot of trouble to have to go through just to use local labels in REPT blocks. As Brad commented, "There are a number of things that you would think that MASM 5.0 should let you do more directly." Indeed there are.

The third solution, submitted by Adrian Crum, of La Habra, California, is shown in Listing 9.6. Adrian has come up with the ingenious solution of creating and maintaining *his own temporary label names!* This is exactly what MASM is supposed to do with local labels inside REPT blocks, of course; since MASM doesn't do it, Adrian simply did it himself. It's not so convenient as if LOCAL worked properly in REPT blocks—the local label counter ?CNT1 has to be explicitly initialized and incremented—but it's certainly a creative use of MASM's macro capabilities . . . and it does work. Listing 9.6 is an excellent tutorial on some advanced aspects of macro usage; if you're interested in making good use of macros, I suggest you study this listing until you understand every bit of it.

In Conclusion

Gosh. We certainly get into interesting areas when you folks come up with the questions and answers. I've cleared the queue of pending reader feedback, and so at the moment, I'm not sure what I'll look at next; as always, I welcome your suggestions. At any rate, rest assured that many unexplored mysteries yet lurk within the EGA and VGA, and we'll look into at least one of those next time.

See you then.

Listing 9.1

```
; Program to put up a mode 10h EGA graphics screen, then save it
; to the file SNAPSHOT.SCR.
;
; Updated 6/29/89.
;
VGA_SEGMENT        equ     0a000h
GC_INDEX           equ     3ceh     ;Graphics Controller Index register
READ_MAP           equ     4        ;Read Map register index in GC
DISPLAYED_SCREEN_SIZE equ (640/8)*350
                            ;# of displayed bytes per plane in a
                            ; hi-res graphics screen

;
stackseg           segment para stack 'STACK'
        db         512 dup (?)
stackseg           ends
;
Data    segment word 'DATA'
SampleText db      'This is bit-mapped text, drawn in hi-res '
        db         'EGA graphics mode 10h.', 0dh, 0ah, 0ah
        db         'Saving the screen (including this text)...'
        db         0dh, 0ah, '$'
Filename db        'SNAPSHOT.SCR',0        ;name of file we're saving to
ErrMsg1 db         '*** Couldn''t open SNAPSHOT.SCR ***',0dh,0ah,'$'
ErrMsg2 db         '*** Error writing to SNAPSHOT.SCR ***',0dh,0ah,'$'
WaitKeyMsg db      0dh, 0ah, 'Done. Press any key to end...',0dh,0ah,'$'
Handle  dw         ?        ;handle of file we're saving to
Plane   db         ?        ;plane being read
Data    ends
;
Code    segment
        assume     cs:Code, ds:Data
Start   proc       near
        mov        ax,Data
        mov        ds,ax
;
; Go to hi-res graphics mode.
;
        mov        ax,10h   ;AH = 0 means mode set, AL = 10h selects
                            ; hi-res graphics mode
        int        10h      ;BIOS video interrupt
;
; Put up some text, so the screen isn't empty.
;
        mov        ah,9     ;DOS print string function
        mov        dx,offset SampleText
        int        21h
;
; Delete SNAPSHOT.SCR if it exists.
;
        mov        ah,41h   ;DOS unlink file function
        mov        dx,offset Filename
        int        21h
;
; Create the file SNAPSHOT.SCR.
;
        mov        ah,3ch   ;DOS create file function
        mov        dx,offset Filename
        sub        cx,cx              ;make it a normal file
```

Listing 9.1 continues

Listing 9.1 *continued*

```
        int     21h
        mov     [Handle],ax     ;save the handle
        jnc     SaveTheScreen   ;we're ready to save if no error
        mov     ah,9            ;DOS print string function
        mov     dx,offset ErrMsg1
        int     21h             ;notify of the error
        jmp     short Done      ;and done
;
; Loop through the 4 planes, making each readable in turn and
; writing it to disk. Note that all 4 planes are readable at
; A000:0000; the Read Map register selects which plane is readable
; at any one time.
;
SaveTheScreen:
        mov     [Plane],0       ;start with plane 0
SaveLoop:
        mov     dx,GC_INDEX
        mov     al,READ_MAP     ;set GC Index to Read Map register
        out     dx,al
        inc     dx
        mov     al,[Plane]      ;get the # of the plane we want
                                ; to save
        out     dx,al   ;set to read from the desired plane
        mov     ah,40h  ;DOS write to file function
        mov     bx,[Handle]
        mov     cx,DISPLAYED_SCREEN_SIZE ;# of bytes to save
        sub     dx,dx   ;write all displayed bytes at A000:0000
        push    ds
        mov     si,VGA_SEGMENT
        mov     ds,si
        int     21h      ;write the displayed portion of this plane
        pop     ds
        jc      WriteError      ;handle write error, if any
        cmp     ax,DISPLAYED_SCREEN_SIZE ;did all bytes get written?
        jz      SaveLoopBottom  ;yes, no error
WriteError:
                                ;a error occurred while writing
        mov     ah,9            ;DOS print string function
        mov     dx,offset ErrMsg2
        int     21h             ;notify about the error
        jmp     short DoClose   ;and done
SaveLoopBottom:
        mov     al,[Plane]
        inc     ax              ;point to the next plane
        mov     [Plane],al
        cmp     al,3    ;have we done all planes?
        jbe     SaveLoop ;no, so do the next plane
;
; Close SNAPSHOT.SCR.
;
DoClose:
        mov     ah,3eh  ;DOS close file function
        mov     bx,[Handle]
        int     21h
;
; Wait for a keypress.
;
        mov     ah,9     ;DOS print string function
        mov     dx,offset WaitKeyMsg
```

Listing 9.1 *continues*

Listing 9.1 *continued*

```
        int     21h      ;prompt
        mov     ah,8     ;DOS input without echo function
        int     21h
;
; Restore text mode.
;
        mov     ax,3
        int     10h
;
; Done.
;
Done:
        mov     ah,4ch   ;DOS terminate function
        int     21h
Start   endp
Code    ends
        end     Start
```

Listing 9.2

```
; Program to restore a mode 10h EGA graphics screen from
; the file SNAPSHOT.SCR.
;
; Updated 6/29/89.
;
VGA_SEGMENT     equ     0a000h
SC_INDEX        equ     3c4h     ;Sequence Controller Index register
MAP_MASK        equ     2        ;Map Mask register index in SC
DISPLAYED_SCREEN_SIZE equ (640/8)*350
                                 ;# of displayed bytes per plane in a
                                 ; hi-res graphics screen
;
stackseg        segment para stack 'STACK'
        db      512 dup (?)
stackseg        ends
;
Data    segment word 'DATA'
Filename db     'SNAPSHOT.SCR',0 ;name of file we're restoring from
ErrMsg1 db      '*** Couldn''t open SNAPSHOT.SCR ***',0dh,0ah,'$'
ErrMsg2 db      '*** Error reading from SNAPSHOT.SCR ***',0dh,0ah,'$'
WaitKeyMsg db   0dh, 0ah, 'Done. Press any key to end...',0dh,0ah,'$'
Handle  dw      ?        ;handle of file we're restoring from
Plane   db      ?        ;plane being written
Data    ends
;
Code    segment
        assume  cs:Code, ds:Data
Start   proc    near
        mov     ax,Data
        mov     ds,ax
;
; Go to hi-res graphics mode.
;
        mov     ax,10h   ;AH = 0 means mode set, AL = 10h selects
```

Listing 9.2 *continues*

Listing 9.2 *continued*

```
                              ; hi-res graphics mode
            int       10h         ;BIOS video interrupt
;
; Open SNAPSHOT.SCR.
;
            mov       ah,3dh   ;DOS open file function
            mov       dx,offset Filename
            sub       al,al              ;open for reading
            int       21h
            mov       [Handle],ax     ;save the handle
            jnc       RestoreTheScreen ;we're ready to restore if no error
            mov       ah,9            ;DOS print string function
            mov       dx,offset ErrMsg1
            int       21h             ;notify of the error
            jmp       short Done      ;and done
;
; Loop through the 4 planes, making each writable in turn and
; reading it from disk. Note that all 4 planes are writable at
; A000:0000; the Map Mask register selects which planes are writable
; at any one time. We only make one plane writable at a time.
;
RestoreTheScreen:
            mov       [Plane],0       ;start with plane 0
RestoreLoop:
            mov       dx,SC_INDEX
            mov       al,MAP_MASK     ;set SC Index to Map Mask register
            out       dx,al
            inc       dx
            mov       cl,[Plane]      ;get the # of the plane we want
                                      ; to restore
            mov       al,1
            shl       al,cl    ;set the bit enabling writes to
                               ; only the one desired plane
            out       dx,al    ;set to write to the desired plane
            mov       ah,3fh   ;DOS read from file function
            mov       bx,[Handle]
            mov       cx,DISPLAYED_SCREEN_SIZE ;# of bytes to read
            sub       dx,dx    ;start loading bytes at A000:0000
            push      ds
            mov       si,VGA_SEGMENT
            mov       ds,si
            int       21h      ;read the displayed portion of this plane
            pop       ds
            jc        ReadError                  ;handle error, if any
            cmp       ax,DISPLAYED_SCREEN_SIZE ;did all bytes get read?
            jz        RestoreLoopBottom          ;yes, no error
ReadError:
                                      ;an error occurred
            mov       ah,9            ;DOS print string function
            mov       dx,offset ErrMsg2
            int       21h             ;notify about the error
            jmp       short DoClose   ;and done
RestoreLoopBottom:
            mov       al,[Plane]
            inc       ax       ;point to the next plane
            mov       [Plane],al
            cmp       al,3     ;have we done all planes?
            jbe       RestoreLoop ;no, so do the next plane
;
```

Listing 9.2 *continues*

Listing 9.2 continued

```
; Close SNAPSHOT.SCR.
;
DoClose:
        mov     ah,3eh   ;DOS close file function
        mov     bx,[Handle]
        int     21h
;
; Wait for a keypress.
;
        mov     ah,8     ;DOS input without echo function
        int     21h
;
; Restore text mode.
;
        mov     ax,3
        int     10h
;
; Done.
;
Done:
        mov     ah,4ch   ;DOS terminate function
        int     21h
Start   endp
Code    ends
        end     Start
```

Listing 9.3

```
; Program to illustrate the color mapping capabilities of the
; EGA's palette registers.
;
; Updated 6/29/89.
;
VGA_SEGMENT     equ     0a000h
SC_INDEX        equ     3c4h     ;Sequence Controller Index register
MAP_MASK        equ     2        ;Map Mask register index in SC
BAR_HEIGHT      equ     14       ;height of each bar
TOP_BAR         equ     BAR_HEIGHT*6   ;start the bars down a bit to
                                       ; leave room for text
;
stackseg        segment para stack 'STACK'
        db      512 dup (?)
stackseg        ends
;
Data    segment word 'DATA'
KeyMsg  db      'Press any key to see the next color set. '
        db      'There are 64 color sets in all.'
        db      0dh, 0ah, 0ah, 0ah, 0ah
        db      13 dup (' '), 'Attribute'
        db      38 dup (' '), 'Color$'
;
; Used to label the attributes of the color bars.
;
AttributeNumbers        label   byte
```

Listing 9.3 continues

Listing 9.3 continued

```
x=        0
          rept    16
if x lt 10
          db      '0', x+'0', 'h', 0ah, 8, 8, 8
else
          db      '0', x+'A'-10, 'h', 0ah, 8, 8, 8
endif
x=        x+1
          endm
          db      '$'
;
; Used to label the colors of the color bars. (Color values are
; filled in on the fly.)
;
ColorNumbers    label   byte
          rept    16
          db      '000h', 0ah, 8, 8, 8, 8
          endm
COLOR_ENTRY_LENGTH      equ     ($-ColorNumbers)/16
          db      '$'
;
CurrentColor    db      ?
;
; Space for the array of 16 colors we'll pass to the BIOS, plus
; an overscan setting of black.
;
ColorTable      db      16 dup (?), 0
Data      ends
;
Code      segment
          assume  cs:Code, ds:Data
Start     proc    near
          cld
          mov     ax,Data
          mov     ds,ax
;
; Go to hi-res graphics mode.
;
          mov     ax,10h  ;AH = 0 means mode set, AL = 10h selects
                          ; hi-res graphics mode
          int     10h     ;BIOS video interrupt
;
; Put up relevant text.
;
          mov     ah,9    ;DOS print string function
          mov     dx,offset KeyMsg
          int     21h
;
; Put up the color bars, one in each of the 16 possible pixel values
; (which we'll call attributes).
;
          mov     cx,16   ;we'll put up 16 color bars
          sub     al,al   ;start with attribute 0
BarLoop:
          push    ax
          push    cx
          call    BarUp
          pop     cx
```

Listing 9.3 continues

Listing 9.3 continued

```
        pop     ax
        inc     ax          ;select the next attribute
        loop    BarLoop
;
; Put up the attribute labels.
;
        mov     ah,2        ;video interrupt set cursor position function
        sub     bh,bh       ;page 0
        mov     dh,TOP_BAR/14    ;counting in character rows, match to
                                 ; top of first bar, counting in
                                 ; scan lines
        mov     dl,16       ;just to left of bars
        int     10h
        mov     ah,9        ;DOS print string function
        mov     dx,offset AttributeNumbers
        int     21h
;
; Loop through the color set, one new setting per keypress.
;
        mov     [CurrentColor],0        ;start with color zero
ColorLoop:
;
; Set the palette registers to the current color set, consisting
; of the current color mapped to attribute 0, current color + 1
; mapped to attribute 1, and so on.
;
        mov     al,[CurrentColor]
        mov     bx,offset ColorTable
        mov     cx,16       ;we have 16 colors to set
PaletteSetLoop:
        and     al,3fh              ;limit to 6-bit color values
        mov     [bx],al     ;built the 16-color table used for setting
        inc     bx          ; the palette registers
        inc     ax
        loop    PaletteSetLoop
        mov     ah,10h      ;video interrupt palette function
        mov     al,2        ;subfunction to set all 16 palette registers
                            ; and overscan at once
        mov     dx,offset ColorTable
        push    ds
        pop     es          ;ES:DX points to the color table
        int     10h         ;invoke the video interrupt to set the palette
;
; Put up the color numbers, so we can see how attributes map
; to color values, and so we can see how each color # looks
; (at least on this particular screen).
;
        call    ColorNumbersUp
;
; Wait for a keypress, so they can see this color set.
;
WaitKey:
        mov     ah,8        ;DOS input without echo function
        int     21h
;
; Advance to the next color set.
;
        mov     al,[CurrentColor]
```

Listing 9.3 continues

Listing 9.3 *continued*

```
            inc     ax
            mov     [CurrentColor],al
            cmp     al,64
            jbe     ColorLoop
;
; Do a mode set to restore text mode to its default state.
;
            mov     ax,3
            int     10h
;
; Done.
;
Done:
            mov     ah,4ch   ;DOS terminate function
            int     21h
;
; Puts up a bar consisting of the specified attribute (pixel value),
; at a vertical position corresponding to the attribute.
;
; Input: AL = attribute
;
BarUp       proc    near
            mov     dx,SC_INDEX
            mov     ah,al
            mov     al,MAP_MASK
            out     dx,al
            inc     dx
            mov     al,ah
            out     dx,al    ;set the Map Mask register to produce
                             ; the desired color
            mov     ah,BAR_HEIGHT
            mul     ah       ;row of top of bar
            add     ax,TOP_BAR ;start a few lines down to leave room for
                             ; text
            mov     dx,80    ;rows are 80 bytes long
            mul     dx       ;offset in bytes of start of scan line bar
                             ; starts on
            add     ax,20    ;offset in bytes of upper left corner of bar
            mov     di,ax
            mov     ax,VGA_SEGMENT
            mov     es,ax    ;ES:DI points to offset of upper left
                             ; corner of bar
            mov     dx,BAR_HEIGHT
            mov     al,0ffh
BarLineLoop:
            mov     cx,40    ;make the bars 40 wide
            rep     stosb    ;do one scan line of the bar
            add     di,40    ;point to the start of the next scan line
                             ; of the bar
            dec     dx
            jnz     BarLineLoop
            ret
BarUp       endp
;
; Converts AL to a hex digit in the range 0-F.
;
BinToHexDigit   proc    near
            cmp     al,9
```

Listing 9.3 *continues*

Listing 9.3 continued

```
          ja       IsHex
          add      al,'0'
          ret
IsHex:
          add      al,'A'-10
          ret
BinToHexDigit    endp
;
; Displays the color values generated by the color bars given the
; current palette register settings off to the right of the color
; bars.
;
ColorNumbersUp   proc     near
          mov      ah,2     ;video interrupt set cursor position function
          sub      bh,bh    ;page 0
          mov      dh,TOP_BAR/14    ;counting in character rows, match to
                            ; top of first bar, counting in
                            ; scan lines
          mov      dl,20+40+1       ;just to right of bars
          int      10h
          mov      al,[CurrentColor]        ;start with the current color
          mov      bx,offset ColorNumbers+1
                            ;build the color number text string on the fly
          mov      cx,16    ;we've got 16 colors to do
ColorNumberLoop:
          push     ax                ;save the color #
          and      al,3fh            ;limit to 6-bit color values
          shr      al,1
          shr      al,1
          shr      al,1
          shr      al,1              ;isolate the high nibble of the
                                     ; color #
          call     BinToHexDigit     ;convert the high color # nibble
          mov      [bx],al           ; and put it into the text
          pop      ax                ;get back the color #
          push     ax                ;save the color #
          and      al,0fh            ;isolate the low color # nibble
          call     BinToHexDigit     ;convert the low nibble of the
                                     ; color # to ASCII
          mov      [bx+1],al         ; and put it into the text
          add      bx,COLOR_ENTRY_LENGTH    ;point to the next entry
          pop      ax                ;get back the color #
          inc      ax                ;next color #
          loop     ColorNumberLoop
          mov      ah,9              ;DOS print string function
          mov      dx,offset ColorNumbers
          int      21h               ;put up the attribute numbers
          ret
ColorNumbersUp   endp
;
Start     endp
Code      ends
          end      Start
```

Listing 9.4 follows

Listing 9.4

```
; Program to demonstrate screen blanking via bit 5 of the
; Attribute Controller Index register.
;
; Updated 6/29/89.
;
AC_INDEX          equ     3c0h      ;Attribute Controller Index register
INPUT_STATUS_1    equ     3dah      ;color-mode address of the Input
                                    ; Status 1 register
;
; Macro to wait for and clear the next keypress.
;
WAIT_KEY          macro
        mov       ah,8      ;DOS input without echo function
        int       21h
        endm
;
stackseg          segment para stack 'STACK'
        db        512 dup (?)
stackseg          ends
;
Data      segment word 'DATA'
SampleText db     'This is bit-mapped text, drawn in hi-res '
        db        'EGA graphics mode 10h.', 0dh, 0ah, 0ah
        db        'Press any key to blank the screen, then '
        db        'any key to unblank it,', 0dh, 0ah
        db        'then any key to end.$'
Data      ends
;
Code      segment
        assume    cs:Code, ds:Data
Start     proc     near
        mov       ax,Data
        mov       ds,ax
;
; Go to hi-res graphics mode.
;
        mov       ax,10h    ;AH = 0 means mode set, AL = 10h selects
                            ; hi-res graphics mode
        int       10h       ;BIOS video interrupt
;
; Put up some text, so the screen isn't empty.
;
        mov       ah,9      ;DOS print string function
        mov       dx,offset SampleText
        int       21h
;
        WAIT_KEY
;
; Blank the screen.
;
        mov       dx,INPUT_STATUS_1
        in        al,dx     ;reset port 3c0h to index (rather than data)
                            ; mode
        mov       dx,AC_INDEX
        sub       al,al     ;make bit 5 zero...
        out       dx,al     ;...which blanks the screen
;
        WAIT_KEY
```

Listing 9.4 continues

Listing 9.4 continued

```
;
; Unblank the screen.
;
        mov     dx,INPUT_STATUS_1
        in      al,dx   ;reset port 3c0h to index (rather than data)
                        ; mode
        mov     dx,AC_INDEX
        mov     al,20h  ;make bit 5 one...
        out     dx,al   ;...which unblanks the screen
;
        WAIT_KEY
;
; Restore text mode.
;
        mov     ax,2
        int     10h
;
; Done.
;
Done:
        mov     ah,4ch  ;DOS terminate function
        int     21h
Start   endp
Code    ends
        end     Start
```

Listing 9.5

```
; Solution to MASM 5.0 problem with local labels in REPT blocks.
; Brad Levy's solution (also offered by Michael Liebert).
;
        dosseg
        .model  small
        .code
mac1    macro
        local   testlabel
        jmp     testlabel
testlabel:
        endm
mac2    macro
        rept    10
        mac1
        endm
        endm

        mac2

        end
```

Listing 9.6 follows

Listing 9.6

```
; Solution to MASM 5.0 problem with local labels in REPT blocks.
; Adrian Crum's solution.
;
; Note: this code is relatively simple, it should be easy to follow.
; Make sure that the counter, (?CNT1) is initialized only one in
; your program. Otherwise, you will receive multi-defined errors.
;
DOSSEG
.MODEL SMALL
.CODE
;
;
SYM_SUPP1       MACRO   X
        ;; support macro #1 for SYMBOLS macro
        ;;
        jmp       ?TMPLBL&X&
        ;;
        ;; Note: if you're sure that these will always be short jumps,
        ;; then JMP SHORT ?TMPLBL&X&
        ;;
ENDM
SYM_SUPP2       MACRO   X
        ;; Support macro #2 for SYMBOLS macro
        ;;
        ?TMPLBL&X&:
        ;;
ENDM
;
SYMBOLS MACRO
        ;; This is the main macro. No calling parameters. This macro
        ;; calls two other macros to generate 10 JMP instructions to
        ;; 10 temporary labels and the temporary labels themselves.
        ;;
        REPT    10
                SYM_SUPP1       %?CNT1  ;; Generate JMP instruction
                SYM_SUPP2       %?CNT1  ;; Generate label
                ?CNT1 = ?CNT1 + 1       ;; Increment counter
        ENDM
        ;;
        ;; Note: you could also define the number of repeats executed
        ;; by this macro by including a dummy parameter X at the
        ;; beginning of the macro and changing REPT 10 to REPT &X. The
        ;; correct call in that case would be SYMBOLS n, where n is
        ;; the number of repetitions.
        ;;
ENDM
;
START:
        ?CNT1 = 0                       ; INITIALIZE COUNTER
        SYMBOLS                         ; GENERATE 10 TEMP LABELS
        SYMBOLS                         ; GENERATE 10 MORE LABELS
        REPT 3                          ; GENERATE 3 MORE LABELS
                SYM_SUPP1       %?CNT1
                SYM_SUPP2       %?CNT1
                ?CNT1 = ?CNT1 + 1
        ENDM
;
END     START
```

CHAPTER

10

Higher 256-Color Resolution on the VGA

By God, people do like lots of colors in their graphics, and they like it even better when those colors are combined with high resolution. This chapter, which covers a 256-color mode with twice the resolution—320 by 400—of the 256-color mode supported by the BIOS, drew by far the largest response of any installment of "On Graphics." Most of the feedback was positive; the only complaint was that I mentioned but didn't provide working code for a 256-color mode that offers still-higher resolution! (I remedied that in short order; a discussion of 360-by-480 256-color mode rounds out this book.)

This chapter is a perfect example of what I meant when I said that the official modes and techniques of EGA and VGA programming are just a few special cases among millions of possibilities. Hidden in the VGA are several high-resolution 256-color modes, including a 320-by-400 256-color mode that is set up by combining some of the parameters from 320-by-200 256-color mode with some of the parameters from 640-by-480 16-color mode. Other 256-color modes involve different combinations, including some register settings that aren't used by *any* mode supported by the BIOS.

When it comes to pushing the VGA to the limit, it's sort of a "roll-your-own" adapter. Once you understand all the pieces of the VGA, you can put them together as needed to meet the needs of a particular application. The more you know about the VGA and the cleverer you are, the better your graphics code will be. I can't make you any cleverer (although I can show you a few interesting tricks), but I can make you more knowledgeable. With that in mind, let's get on to today's topic: the VGA's hidden 256-color modes.

Installment 10: In which we find the answer to the riddle, "When is 320 by 200 really 320 by 400?" and chance upon some intriguing 256-color resolutions.

One of the more appealing features of the VGA is the ability to display 256 simultaneous colors. Unfortunately, one of the *less* appealing features of the VGA is the limited resolution (320 by 200) of the one 256-color mode the BIOS supports. More colors can often compensate for fewer pixels, but the resolution difference between the 640-by-480 16-color mode and the 320-by-200 256-color mode is so great that many programmers must regretfully decide that they simply can't afford to use the 256-color mode.

If there's one thing we've learned about the VGA, however, it's that there's *never* just one way to do things. With the VGA, alternatives always exist for the clever programmer, and that's more true than you might imagine with 256-color mode. Not only is there a high 256-color resolution, but there are *lots* of higher 256-color resolutions, going all the way up to 360 by 480! (Here I'm talking about the vanilla IBM VGA—third-party VGAs go all the way up to 800-by-600 256-color resolutions, but that's a story for another time.)

While I'd love to cover all of the 256-color resolutions, high-resolution 256-color programming is a fairly complex topic, and I've only so much space and time. Consequently, I'm going to take a quick look at the available 256-color resolutions and then focus on my favorite 256-color mode, which provides 320-by-400 resolution and two graphics pages and can be set up with very little reprogramming of the VGA.

So. Let's get started.

Why 320 by 200?
Only IBM Knows for Sure

The first question, of course, is, "How can it be possible to get higher 256-color resolutions out of the VGA?" After all, there were no unused higher resolutions to be found in the CGA, Hercules card, or EGA.

The answer is another question. "Why did IBM *not* use the higher-resolution 256-color modes of the VGA?" The VGA is easily capable of twice the 200-scan-line vertical resolution of mode 13h, the 256-color mode, and IBM clearly made a decision not to support a higher-resolution 256-color mode. In fact, mode 13h *does* display 400 scan lines, but each row of pixels is displayed on two successive scan lines, resulting in an effective resolution of 320 by 200. This is the same scan-doubling approach used by the VGA to convert the CGA's 200-scan-line modes to 400 scan lines; however, because the resolution of the CGA has long been fixed at 200 scan lines, IBM had no choice with the CGA modes but to scan-double the lines. Mode 13h has no such historical limitation—it's the first 256-color mode ever offered by IBM, if you don't count the late and unlamented Professional Graphics Controller. Why, then, would IBM choose to limit the resolution of mode 13h?

There's no way to know, but one good guess is that IBM wanted a standard 256-color mode across all PS/2 computers, and mode 13h is the highest-resolution 256-color mode that could fill the bill. You see, each 256-color pixel requires one byte of display memory, and so a 320-by-200 256-color mode requires 64,000 bytes of display memory. A 320-by-400 256-color mode would require twice as much memory—128,000 bytes, to be exact. That's no problem for the VGA, which has 256K of display memory, but it's a stretch for the MCGA of the Model 30, since the MCGA comes with only 64K.

On the other hand, the smaller display-memory size of the MCGA also limits the number of colors supported in 640-by-480 mode to 2, rather than the 16 supported by the VGA. In this case, though, IBM simply created two modes and made both available on the VGA: mode 11h for 640-by-480 two-color graphics and mode 12h for 640-by-480 sixteen-color graphics. The same could have been done for 256-color graphics—but wasn't. Why? I don't know. Maybe IBM just didn't like the odd aspect ratio of a 320-by-400 graphics mode. Heck, maybe they made a mistake in designing the chip. Whatever the reason, mode 13h is really a 400-scan-line mode masquerading as a 200-scan-line mode, and we can readily end that masquerade.

Higher 256-Color Resolutions

The VGA can actually display even higher 256-color resolutions than 320 by 400—resolutions of 320 by 480, 360 by 400, and 360 by 480 are all possible. I'm going to take a quick look at each of the three higher resolutions and then return to 320 by 400, which I think is the best of the lot.

The number of scan lines on the screen is a function of the number of vertical frames displayed each second, which in turn is controlled by the vertical timing registers of the CRT Controller (CRTC). Most VGA modes, including mode 13h, display 70 frames per second, with each frame 400 scan lines high. However, modes 11h and 12h both display sixty 480-scan-line frames per second. Getting 480 scan lines out of mode 13h is a simple matter of selecting mode 13h and then reprogramming the vertical timing registers, the vertical height registers, and the vertical and horizontal sync polarities along the lines of mode 12h. (The sync polarities tell the VGA monitor how rapidly to scan vertically. Slower scanning is needed to allow 480 scan lines to fit on the screen.)

Three-hundred-sixty-by-four-hundred 256-color mode requires a change in the horizontal scanning rate of the VGA. You accomplish this by selecting the faster VGA clock in the Miscellaneous Output register. This clock is normally used for scanning 720 pixels across the screen in nine-dots-per-character 80-column text modes but will serve equally well to scan 720 pixels across the screen in graphics mode in the form of 90 eight-dot characters. Of course, changing the clock speed and the number of characters per line requires reprogramming of the horizontal timing and horizontal width registers in the CRTC to match, just as changing the frame rate and number of scan lines per frame required reprogramming of the vertical timing registers. These parameters aren't similar to any existing mode—since there is no 90-column, eight-dot-per-character mode—and must be calculated from scratch or by trial and error.

Three-hundred-sixty-by-four-hundred-eighty 256-color mode is simply a combination of the two modes we just discussed. With VGA monitors, horizontal timings and vertical timings operate independently; so, all you need to do to get 360-by-480 resolution is combine the 320-by-480 and 360-by-400 modes. All of the above modes also require reprogramming to let your programs get at display memory properly, as we'll see shortly in our discussion of 320-by-400 mode.

You've surely noticed that I haven't given any specifics about register values and such for selecting these higher resolution modes. There's a good reason for that: Each of these modes comes with certain risks for the developer. For one thing, the modes with 360 pixels per scan line run the VGA's memory faster than any other VGA mode, and I don't know if that access speed is within the specs of the VGA's memory. For another, there's always danger in reprogramming the timing registers. Sure, every VGA clone claims register compatibility, but it's on just such nonstandard modes as these that compatibility tends to break.

Given the risks of the above modes, given that I have limited space, *and* given that there's a mode I consider safe and superior, I'm not going to pursue the three higher-resolution 256-color modes I've mentioned any further—at least not in this installment. Those of you who really want to use these modes should be able to figure out what to do from the thumbnail sketches I've given. If enough readers request it, however, I would be happy to devote a future installment to these three modes.

By the way, I'm probably overstating the risks of the three higher-resolution 256-color modes. I read recently that Rix is coming out with a 360-by-480 256-color program for the VGA. Those guys know the VGA awfully well, and they have access to just about every VGA clone in existence. If they think 360-by-480 256-color mode is safe enough to use in a commercial product, it's a pretty safe bet that it is.

Still and all, I like 320-by-400 256-color mode best: It requires very little VGA reprogramming (and none at all to the timing registers) and gives us two pages—ideal for animation and flicker-free drawing. So, it's onward to 320 by 400 and working code!

320-by-400 256-Color Mode

Okay, what's so great about 320-by-400 256-color mode? Two things: easy, safe mode sets and paging.

As I said before, mode 13h is really a 320-by-400 mode, albeit with each line doubled to produce an effective resolution of 320 by 200. That means that we don't need to change any display timings, widths, or heights to tweak mode 13h into 320-by-400 mode—and that makes 320 by 400 a safe choice. Basically, 320-by-400 mode differs from mode 13h only in the settings of *mode* bits, which are sure to be consistent from one VGA clone to the next and which work equally well with all monitors. The other hi-resolution 256-color modes differ from mode 13h not only in the settings of the mode bits but also in the settings of timing and dimension registers, which may not be exactly the same on all VGA clones and particularly not on all multiscanning monitors. (Because multiscanning monitors can sometimes shrink or expand VGA displays, some VGAs may use alternate register settings for multiscanning monitors that are optimized for those monitors.)

The other good thing about 320-by-400 256-color mode is that two pages are supported. Since each 320-by 400 256-color mode requires 128,000 bytes of display memory, we can just barely manage two pages in 320-by-400 mode, one starting at offset 0 in display memory and the other starting at offset 8000h. Those two pages are the largest pair that can fit in the VGA's 256K bytes of memory, though, and the higher-resolution 256-color modes, which use still larger bit maps, can't support two pages at all. As we've seen in earlier chapters, paging is very useful for off-screen construction of images and fast, smooth animation.

That's why I like 320-by-400 256-color mode. The next step is to understand how the bit map is organized in 320-by-400 mode, and that's not so simple.

Display-Memory Organization in 320-by-400 Mode

First, let's look at why display memory must be organized differently in 320-by-400 256-color mode than in mode 13h. The designers of the VGA intentionally limited the maximum size of the bit map in mode 13h to 64K, thereby limiting resolution to 320 by 200. This was accomplished *in hardware*, and so there is no way to extend the bit-map organization of mode 13h to 320-by-400 mode.

That's a shame, because mode 13h has the simplest bit-map organization of any mode: one long, linear bit map, with each byte controlling one pixel. We can't have that organization, though; so we'll have to find an acceptable substitute if we want to use a higher 256-color resolution.

With the VGA, of course, there are actually *several* bit-map organizations that let us use higher 256-color resolutions than mode 13h. The one I like best is shown in Figure 10.1. Each byte controls one 256-color pixel. Pixel 0 is at address 0 in plane 0, pixel 1 is at address 0 in plane 1, pixel 2 is at address 0 in plane 2, pixel 3 is at address 0 in plane 3, pixel 4 is at address 1 in plane 0, and so on.

Let's look at this another way. Ideally, we'd like one long bit map, with each pixel at the address that's just after the address of the pixel to the left. Well, that's true in this case too, *if* you consider the number of the plane that the pixel is in to be part of the pixel's address. View the pixel numbers on the screen as increasing from left to right and from the end of one scan line to the start of the next. Then the pixel number, n, of the pixel at display-memory address *address* in plane *plane* is

$$n = (address \times 4) + plane$$

To turn that around, the display-memory address of pixel number n is given by

$$address = n \: / \: 4$$

and the plane of pixel n is given by

$$plane = n \text{ modulo } 4$$

Basically, the full address of the pixel, its pixel number, is broken into two components: the display-memory address and the plane.

By the way, because 320-by-400 mode has a significantly different memory organization than mode 13h, the BIOS text routines won't work in 320-by-400 mode. If you want to draw text in 320-by-400 mode, you'll have to look up a font in the BIOS ROM and draw the text yourself. Likewise, the BIOS read pixel and write pixel routines won't work in 320-by-400 mode, but that's no problem: I'll provide equivalent routines in the next section.

Our next task is to convert standard mode 13h into 320-by-400 mode. That's accomplished by undoing many of the mode bits that are set up especially for mode 13h so that from a programming perspective, the VGA reverts to a straightforward planar model of memory. That means taking the VGA out of chain-4 mode and doubleword mode, turning off the double display of each scan line, making sure chain mode, odd/even mode, and word mode are turned off, and selecting byte mode for video data display. All that's done in the **Set320By400Mode** subroutine in Listing 10.1 [presented at the end of this chapter], which we'll discuss next.

Reading and Writing Pixels

The basic graphics functions in any mode are functions to read and write single pixels. Any more complex function can be built on these primitives, although that's not always the speediest solution. What's more, once you understand the operation of the read pixel and write pixel functions, you've got all the knowledge you need to create functions that perform more-complex graphics functions. Consequently, we'll start our exploration of 320-by-400 mode with pixel-at-a-time line drawing.

Listing 10.1 draws eight multicolored octagons in turn, drawing a new one on top of the old one each time a key is pressed. The main-loop code of Listing 10.1 should be easy to understand: A series of diagonal, horizontal, and vertical lines is drawn one pixel at a time based on a list of line descriptors, with the draw colors incremented for each successive time through the line list.

Three aspects of Listing 10.1 are particularly interesting:

1. The **Set320By400Mode** subroutine selects 320-by-400 256-color mode by performing a mode 13h-mode set and then putting the VGA into standard planar byte mode. **Set320By400Mode** zeros display memory as well. It's necessary to clear display memory even after a

---

Fig. 10.1 *Dashed lines show the order in which bytes are scanned to generate pixels. Solid lines show the correspondence of bytes in display memory to pixels on the screen. Each byte controls one 256-color pixel.*

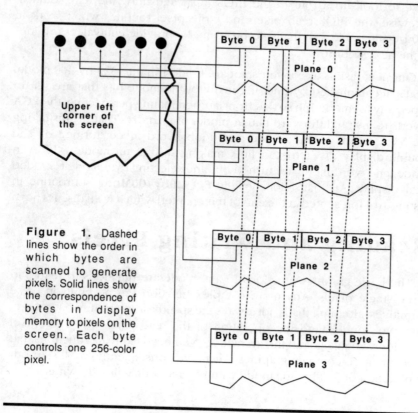

Figure 1. Dashed lines show the order in which bytes are scanned to generate pixels. Solid lines show the correspondence of bytes in display memory to pixels on the screen. Each byte controls one 256-color pixel.

mode-13h mode set, because the mode-13h mode set clears only the 64K of display memory that can be accessed in that mode, leaving 192K of display memory untouched.

2. The **WritePixel** subroutine draws a colored pixel at any x,y addressable location on the screen. Although it may not be obvious because I've optimized the code a little, the process of drawing a pixel is remarkably simple. First, the pixel's display-memory address is calculated as

$$address = [y \times (SCREEN\_WIDTH / 4)] + (x / 4)$$

which might be more recognizable as

$$address = [(y \times SCREEN\_WIDTH) + x] / 4$$

(There are 4 pixels at each display-memory address in 320-by-400 mode, hence the division by 4.) Then, the pixel's plane is calculated as

$$plane = x \text{ and } 3$$

which is equivalent to

$$plane = x \text{ modulo } 4$$

The pixel's color is then written to the addressed byte in the addressed plane. That's all there is to it!

3. The **ReadPixel** subroutine is virtually identical to **WritePixel** save that in **ReadPixel** the Read Map register is programmed with a plane number, while **WritePixel** uses a plane *mask* to set the Map Mask register. Of course, that merely reflects a fundamental difference in the operation of the two registers. **ReadPixel** isn't used in Listing 10.1, but I've included it because, as I said above, the read pixel and write pixel functions together can support a whole host of more-complex graphics functions.

How does 320-by-400 256-color mode stack up in terms of performance? As it turns out, the programming model of 320-by-400 mode is actually quite good for pixel drawing—very nearly on a par with the model of mode 13h. When you run Listing 10.1, you'll no doubt notice that the lines are drawn quite rapidly. (In fact, the drawing could be considerably faster still with a dedicated line-drawing subroutine, which would avoid the multiplication associated with each pixel in Listing 10.1.)

In 320-by-400 mode, the calculation of the memory address is not significantly slower than in mode 13h, and the calculation and selection of the target plane is quickly accomplished. As with mode 13h, 320-by-400 mode benefits tremendously from the byte-per-pixel organization of 256-color mode, which eliminates the need for the time-consuming pixel masking of the 16-color modes. Most important, byte-per-pixel modes never require read/modify/write operations (which can be extremely slow owing to display-memory wait states) to clip and draw pixels. To draw a pixel, you just store its color in display memory. What could be simpler?

More sophisticated operations than pixel drawing are less easy to accomplish in 320-by-400 mode, but with a little ingenuity it is possible to implement an efficient version of just about any useful graphics function. A fast line draw for 320-by-400 mode would be simple, and fast image copies could be implemented by copying one-quarter of the image to one plane, one-quarter to the next plane, and so on for all four planes. If you're really into performance, you could store your images with all the bytes for plane 0 grouped together, followed by all the bytes for plane 1, and so on. That would allow a single **rep movs** instruction to copy all the bytes for a given plane, with just four **rep movs** instructions copying the whole image.

It's all a bit complicated, but, as I say, you should be able to design for 320-by-400 mode a fast version of any graphics functions you may need. If you're not all that concerned about speed, **WritePixel** and **ReadPixel** should meet your needs.

Two 256-Color Pages

Listing 10.2 [presented at the end of this chapter] demonstrates the two pages of 320-by-400 256-color mode by drawing slanting color bars in page 0, drawing color bars slanting the other way in page 1, and flipping to page 1 on the next keypress. (Note that page 1 is accessed starting at offset 8000h in display memory and is—not surprisingly—displayed by setting the start address to 8000h.) Finally, Listing 10.2 draws vertical color bars in page 0 and flips back to page 0 when another key is pressed.

The color-bar routines don't use the **WritePixel** subroutine from Listing 10.1; they go straight to display memory instead for improved speed. As I mentioned above, yet-better speed could be achieved by a color-bar algorithm that draws all the pixels in plane 0, then all the pixels in plane 1, and so on, thereby avoiding the overhead of constantly reprogramming the Map Mask register.

When you run Listing 10.2, note the extremely smooth edges and fine gradations of color, especially in the screens with slanting color bars. The displays produced by Listing 10.2 make it clear that 320-by-400 256-color mode can produce effects that are simply not possible in the 16-color modes.

Also note that the initial screen takes some time to appear in its entirety when Listing 10.2 runs. The problem here is that you're seeing the drawing of the screen as it happens, and the screen isn't drawn all that rapidly. However, both the second and third screens appear in a flash. It takes just as long to draw these screens as it did the first screen; they *seem* to be drawn faster because they're drawn to off-screen memory and then made visible by a flip of the displayed page, thereby making the drawing process invisible to the user. These two features—seemingly instantaneous screen updating and hiding of drawing from the user—are the two great virtues of page flipping.

Something to Think About

You can, if you wish, use the display-memory organization of 320-by-400 mode in 320-by-200 mode by modifying **Set320By400Mode** to leave the maximum scan line setting at 1 in the mode set. (The version of **Set320x400Mode** in listings 10.1 and 10.2 forces the maximum scan line to 0, doubling the effective resolution of the screen.) Why would you want to do that? Simply because you could then choose from, not two, but *four* 320-by-200 256-color display pages, starting at offsets 0, 4000h, 8000h, and 0C000h in display memory.

In Conclusion

Who knows what resolutions lurk in the hearts of VGAs? Now you do. What an adapter, eh?

As always, I'm not sure what's next on the list for "On Graphics." Also as always, I'm open to your suggestions; drop me a line via MCI Mail or the U.S. mail.

See you next time.

Listing 10.1

```
; Program to demonstrate pixel drawing in 320x400 256-color
; mode on the VGA. Draws 8 lines to form an octagon, a pixel
; at a time. Draws 8 octagons in all, one on top of the other,
; each in a different color set. Although it's not used, a
; pixel read function is also provided.
;
; Updated 6/29/89.
;
VGA_SEGMENT          equ     0a000h
SC_INDEX             equ     3c4h        ;Sequence Controller Index register
GC_INDEX             equ     3ceh        ;Graphics Controller Index register
CRTC_INDEX           equ     3d4h        ;CRT Controller Index register
MAP_MASK             equ     2           ;Map Mask register index in SC
MEMORY_MODE          equ     4           ;Memory Mode register index in SC
MAX_SCAN_LINE        equ     9           ;Maximum Scan Line reg index in CRTC
START_ADDRESS_HIGH   equ     0ch         ;Start Address High reg index in CRTC
UNDERLINE            equ     14h         ;Underline Location reg index in CRTC
MODE_CONTROL         equ     17h         ;Mode Control register index in CRTC
READ_MAP             equ     4           ;Read Map register index in GC
GRAPHICS_MODE        equ     5           ;Graphics Mode register index in GC
MISCELLANEOUS        equ     6           ;Miscellaneous register index in GC
SCREEN_WIDTH         equ     320         ;# of pixels across screen
SCREEN_HEIGHT        equ     400         ;# of scan lines on screen
WORD_OUTS_OK         equ     1           ;set to 0 to assemble for
                                         ; computers that can't handle
                                         ; word outs to indexed VGA registers
;
stackseg        segment para stack 'STACK'
        db      512 dup (?)
stackseg        ends
;
Data    segment word 'DATA'
;
BaseColor       db      0
;
; Structure used to control drawing of a line.
;
LineControl     struc
StartX          dw      ?
StartY          dw      ?
LineXInc        dw      ?
LineYInc        dw      ?
BaseLength      dw      ?
LineColor       db      ?
LineControl     ends
;
; List of descriptors for lines to draw.
;
LineList        label   LineControl
        LineControl     <130,110,1,0,60,0>
        LineControl     <190,110,1,1,60,1>
        LineControl     <250,170,0,1,60,2>
        LineControl     <250,230,-1,1,60,3>
        LineControl     <190,290,-1,0,60,4>
        LineControl     <130,290,-1,-1,60,5>
        LineControl     <70,230,0,-1,60,6>
        LineControl     <70,170,1,-1,60,7>
        LineControl     <-1,0,0,0,0,0>
```

Listing 10.1 continues

Listing 10.1 *continued*

```
Data    ends
;
; Macro to output a word value to a port.
;
OUT_WORD        macro
if WORD_OUTS_OK
        out     dx,ax
else
        out     dx,al
        inc     dx
        xchg    ah,al
        out     dx,al
        dec     dx
        xchg    ah,al
endif
        endm
;
; Macro to output a constant value to an indexed VGA register.
;
CONSTANT_TO_INDEXED_REGISTER    macro   ADDRESS, INDEX, VALUE
        mov     dx,ADDRESS
        mov     ax,(VALUE shl 8) + INDEX
        OUT_WORD
        endm
;
Code    segment
        assume  cs:Code, ds:Data
Start   proc    near
        mov     ax,Data
        mov     ds,ax
;
; Set 320x400 256-color mode.
;
        call    Set320By400Mode
;
; We're in 320x400 256-color mode. Draw each line in turn.
;
ColorLoop:
        mov     si,offset LineList ;point to the start of the
                                   ; line descriptor list
LineLoop:
        mov     cx,[si+StartX]  ;set the initial X coordinate
        cmp     cx,-1
        jz      LinesDone       ;a descriptor with a -1 X
                                ; coordinate marks the end
                                ; of the list
        mov     dx,[si+StartY]     ;set the initial Y coordinate,
        mov     bl,[si+LineColor]  ; line color,
        mov     bp,[si+BaseLength] ; and pixel count
        add     bl,[BaseColor]  ;adjust the line color according
                                ; to BaseColor
PixelLoop:
        push    cx              ;save the coordinates
        push    dx
        call    WritePixel      ;draw this pixel
        pop     dx              ;retrieve the coordinates
        pop     cx
        add     cx,[si+LineXInc] ;set the coordinates of the
```

Listing 10.1 *continues*

Listing 10.1 *continued*

```
        add     dx,[si+LineYInc] ; next point of the line
        dec     bp              ;any more points?
        jnz     PixelLoop       ;yes, draw the next
        add     si,size LineControl ;point to the next line descriptor
        jmp     LineLoop        ; and draw the next line
LinesDone:
        call    GetNextKey      ;wait for a key, then
        inc     [BaseColor]     ; bump the color selection and
        cmp     [BaseColor],8   ; see if we're done
        jb      ColorLoop       ;not done yet
;
; Return to text mode.
;
        mov     ax,0003h
        int     10h     ;text mode
        mov     ah,4ch
        int     21h     ;done
;
Start   endp
;
; Sets up 320x400 256-color modes.
;
; Input: none
;
; Output: none
;
Set320By400Mode proc    near
;
; First, go to normal 320x200 256-color mode, which is really a
; 320x400 256-color mode with each line scanned twice.
;
        mov     ax,0013h  ;AH = 0 means mode set, AL = 13h selects
                          ; 256-color graphics mode
        int     10h       ;BIOS video interrupt
;
; Change CPU addressing of video memory to linear (not odd/even,
; chain, or chain 4), to allow us to access all 256K of display
; memory. When this is done, VGA memory will look just like memory
; in modes 10h and 12h, except that each byte of display memory will
; control one 256-color pixel, with 4 adjacent pixels at any given
; address, one pixel per plane.
;
        mov     dx,SC_INDEX
        mov     al,MEMORY_MODE
        out     dx,al
        inc     dx
        in      al,dx
        and     al,not 08h      ;turn off chain 4
        or      al,04h          ;turn off odd/even
        out     dx,al
        mov     dx,GC_INDEX
        mov     al,GRAPHICS_MODE
        out     dx,al
        inc     dx
        in      al,dx
        and     al,not 10h      ;turn off odd/even
        out     dx,al
        dec     dx
```

Listing 10.1 *continues*

Listing 10.1 *continued*

```
        mov     al,MISCELLANEOUS
        out     dx,al
        inc     dx
        in      al,dx
        and     al,not 02h      ;turn off chain
        out     dx,al
;
; Now clear the whole screen, since the mode 13h mode set only
; cleared 64K out of the 256K of display memory. Do this before
; we switch the CRTC out of mode 13h, so we don't see garbage
; on the screen when we make the switch.
;
        CONSTANT_TO_INDEXED_REGISTER SC_INDEX,MAP_MASK,0fh
                                ;enable writes to all planes, so
                                ; we can clear 4 pixels at a time
        mov     ax,VGA_SEGMENT
        mov     es,ax
        sub     di,di
        mov     ax,di
        mov     cx,8000h        ;# of words in 64K
        cld
        rep     stosw           ;clear all of display memory
;
; Tweak the mode to 320x400 256-color mode by not scanning each
; line twice.
;
        mov     dx,CRTC_INDEX
        mov     al,MAX_SCAN_LINE
        out     dx,al
        inc     dx
        in      al,dx
        and     al,not 1fh      ;set maximum scan line = 0
        out     dx,al
        dec     dx
;
; Change CRTC scanning from doubleword mode to byte mode, allowing
; the CRTC to scan more than 64K of video data.
;
        mov     al,UNDERLINE
        out     dx,al
        inc     dx
        in      al,dx
        and     al,not 40h      ;turn off doubleword
        out     dx,al
        dec     dx
        mov     al,MODE_CONTROL
        out     dx,al
        inc     dx
        in      al,dx
        or      al,40h  ;turn on the byte mode bit, so memory is
                        ; scanned for video data in a purely
                        ; linear way, just as in modes 10h and 12h
        out     dx,al
        ret
Set320By400Mode endp
;
; Draws a pixel in the specified color at the specified
; location in 320x400 256-color mode.
```

Listing 10.1 *continues*

Listing 10.1 *continued*

```
;
; Input:
;       CX = X coordinate of pixel
;       DX = Y coordinate of pixel
;       BL = pixel color
;
; Output: none
;
; Registers altered: AX, CL, DX, DI, ES
;
WritePixel      proc    near
        mov     ax,VGA_SEGMENT
        mov     es,ax   ;point to display memory
        mov     ax,SCREEN_WIDTH/4
                        ;there are 4 pixels at each address, so
                        ; each 320-pixel row is 80 bytes wide
                        ; in each plane
        mul     dx      ;point to start of desired row
        push    cx      ;set aside the X coordinate
        shr     cx,1    ;there are 4 pixels at each address
        shr     cx,1    ; so divide the X coordinate by 4
        add     ax,cx   ;point to the pixel's address
        mov     di,ax
        pop     cx      ;get back the X coordinate
        and     cl,3    ;get the plane # of the pixel
        mov     ah,1
        shl     ah,cl   ;set the bit corresponding to the plane
                        ; the pixel is in
        mov     al,MAP_MASK
        mov     dx,SC_INDEX
        OUT_WORD        ;set to write to the proper plane for
                        ; the pixel
        mov     es:[di],bl      ;draw the pixel
        ret
WritePixel      endp
;
; Reads the color of the pixel at the specified location in 320x400
; 256-color mode.
;
; Input:
;       CX = X coordinate of pixel to read
;       DX = Y coordinate of pixel to read
;
; Output:
;       AL = pixel color
;
; Registers altered: AX, CX, DX, SI, ES
;
ReadPixel       proc    near
        mov     ax,VGA_SEGMENT
        mov     es,ax   ;point to display memory
        mov     ax,SCREEN_WIDTH/4
                        ;there are 4 pixels at each address, so
                        ; each 320-pixel row is 80 bytes wide
                        ; in each plane
        mul     dx      ;point to start of desired row
        push    cx      ;set aside the X coordinate
        shr     cx,1    ;there are 4 pixels at each address
```

Listing 10.1 *continues*

Listing 10.1 *continued*

```
        shr     cx,1     ; so divide the X coordinate by 4
        add     ax,cx    ;point to the pixel's address
        mov     si,ax
        pop     ax       ;get back the X coordinate
        and     al,3     ;get the plane # of the pixel
        mov     ah,al
        mov     al,READ_MAP
        mov     dx,GC_INDEX
        OUT_WORD         ;set to read from the proper plane for
                         ; the pixel
        lods    byte ptr es:[si] ;read the pixel
        ret
ReadPixel       endp
;
; Waits for the next key and returns it in AX.
;
; Input: none
;
; Output:
;       AX = full 16-bit code for key pressed
;
GetNextKey      proc    near
WaitKey:
        mov     ah,1
        int     16h
        jz      WaitKey ;wait for a key to become available
        sub     ah,ah
        int     16h      ;read the key
        ret
GetNextKey      endp
;
Code    ends
;
        end     Start
```

Listing 10.2

```
; Program to demonstrate the two pages available in 320x400
; 256-color modes on a VGA.  Draws diagonal color bars in all
; 256 colors in page 0, then does the same in page 1 (but with
; the bars tilted the other way), and finally draws vertical
; color bars in page 0.
;
; Updated 6/29/89.
;
VGA_SEGMENT         equ     0a000h
SC_INDEX            equ     3c4h    ;Sequence Controller Index register
GC_INDEX            equ     3ceh    ;Graphics Controller Index register
CRTC_INDEX          equ     3d4h    ;CRT Controller Index register
MAP_MASK            equ     2       ;Map Mask register index in SC
MEMORY_MODE         equ     4       ;Memory Mode register index in SC
MAX_SCAN_LINE       equ     9       ;Maximum Scan Line reg index in CRTC
START_ADDRESS_HIGH  equ     0ch     ;Start Address High reg index in CRTC
UNDERLINE           equ     14h     ;Underline Location reg index in CRTC
```

Listing 10.2 continues

Listing 10.2 *continued*

```
MODE_CONTROL      equ     17h      ;Mode Control register index in CRTC
GRAPHICS_MODE     equ     5        ;Graphics Mode register index in GC
MISCELLANEOUS     equ     6        ;Miscellaneous register index in GC
SCREEN_WIDTH      equ     320      ;# of pixels across screen
SCREEN_HEIGHT     equ     400      ;# of scan lines on screen
WORD_OUTS_OK      equ     1        ;set to 0 to assemble for
                                   ; computers that can't handle
                                   ; word outs to indexed VGA registers
;
stackseg          segment para stack 'STACK'
        db        512 dup (?)
stackseg          ends
;
; Macro to output a word value to a port.
;
OUT_WORD          macro
if WORD_OUTS_OK
        out       dx,ax
else
        out       dx,al
        inc       dx
        xchg      ah,al
        out       dx,al
        dec       dx
        xchg      ah,al
endif
        endm
;
; Macro to output a constant value to an indexed VGA register.
;
CONSTANT_TO_INDEXED_REGISTER    macro   ADDRESS, INDEX, VALUE
        mov       dx,ADDRESS
        mov       ax,(VALUE shl 8) + INDEX
        OUT_WORD
        endm
;
Code    segment
        assume  cs:Code
Start   proc    near
;
; Set 320x400 256-color mode.
;
        call    Set320By400Mode
;
; We're in 320x400 256-color mode, with page 0 displayed.
; Let's fill page 0 with color bars slanting down and to the left.
;
        sub     di,di           ;page 0 starts at address 0
        mov     bl,1            ;make color bars slant down and
                                ; to the left
        call    ColorBarsUp     ;draw the color bars
;
; Now do the same for page 1, but with the color bars
; tilting the other way.
;
        mov     di,8000h        ;page 1 starts at address 8000h
        mov     bl,-1           ;make color bars slant down and
                                ; to the right
```

Listing 10.2 *continues*

Listing 10.2 *continued*

```
        call    ColorBarsUp     ;draw the color bars
;
; Wait for a key and flip to page 1 when one is pressed.
;
        call    GetNextKey
        CONSTANT_TO_INDEXED_REGISTER CRTC_INDEX,START_ADDRESS_HIGH,80h
                                ;set the Start Address High register
                                ; to 80h, for a start address of 8000h
;
; Draw vertical bars in page 0 while page 1 is displayed.
;
        sub     di,di           ;page 0 starts at address 0
        sub     bl,bl           ;make color bars vertical
        call    ColorBarsUp     ;draw the color bars
;
; Wait for another key and flip back to page 0 when one is pressed.
;
        call    GetNextKey
        CONSTANT_TO_INDEXED_REGISTER CRTC_INDEX,START_ADDRESS_HIGH,00h
                                ;set the Start Address High register
                                ; to 00h, for a start address of 0000h
;
; Wait for yet another key and return to text mode and end when
; one is pressed.
;
        call    GetNextKey
        mov     ax,0003h
        int     10h             ;text mode
        mov     ah,4ch
        int     21h             ;done
;
Start   endp
;
; Sets up 320x400 256-color modes.
;
; Input: none
;
; Output: none
;
Set320By400Mode proc    near
;
; First, go to normal 320x200 256-color mode, which is really a
; 320x400 256-color mode with each line scanned twice.
;
        mov     ax,0013h  ;AH = 0 means mode set, AL = 13h selects
                          ; 256-color graphics mode
        int     10h          ;BIOS video interrupt
;
; Change CPU addressing of video memory to linear (not odd/even,
; chain, or chain 4), to allow us to access all 256K of display
; memory. When this is done, VGA memory will look just like memory
; in modes 10h and 12h, except that each byte of display memory will
; control one 256-color pixel, with 4 adjacent pixels at any given
; address, one pixel per plane.
;
        mov     dx,SC_INDEX
        mov     al,MEMORY_MODE
        out     dx,al
```

Listing 10.2 *continues*

Listing 10.2 continued

```
        inc     dx
        in      al,dx
        and     al,not 08h      ;turn off chain 4
        or      al,04h          ;turn off odd/even
        out     dx,al
        mov     dx,GC_INDEX
        mov     al,GRAPHICS_MODE
        out     dx,al
        inc     dx
        in      al,dx
        and     al,not 10h      ;turn off odd/even
        out     dx,al
        dec     dx
        mov     al,MISCELLANEOUS
        out     dx,al
        inc     dx
        in      al,dx
        and     al,not 02h      ;turn off chain
        out     dx,al
;
; Now clear the whole screen, since the mode 13h mode set only
; cleared 64K out of the 256K of display memory. Do this before
; we switch the CRTC out of mode 13h, so we don't see garbage
; on the screen when we make the switch.
;
        CONSTANT_TO_INDEXED_REGISTER SC_INDEX,MAP_MASK,0fh
                                ;enable writes to all planes, so
                                ; we can clear 4 pixels at a time
        mov     ax,VGA_SEGMENT
        mov     es,ax
        sub     di,di
        mov     ax,di
        mov     cx,8000h        ;# of words in 64K
        cld
        rep     stosw           ;clear all of display memory
;
; Tweak the mode to 320x400 256-color mode by not scanning each
; line twice.
;
        mov     dx,CRTC_INDEX
        mov     al,MAX_SCAN_LINE
        out     dx,al
        inc     dx
        in      al,dx
        and     al,not 1fh      ;set maximum scan line = 0
        out     dx,al
        dec     dx
;
; Change CRTC scanning from doubleword mode to byte mode, allowing
; the CRTC to scan more than 64K of video data.
;
        mov     al,UNDERLINE
        out     dx,al
        inc     dx
        in      al,dx
        and     al,not 40h      ;turn off doubleword
        out     dx,al
        dec     dx
```

Listing 10.2 continues

Listing 10.2 continued

```
        mov     al,MODE_CONTROL
        out     dx,al
        inc     dx
        in      al,dx
        or      al,40h  ;turn on the byte mode bit, so memory is
                        ; scanned for video data in a purely
                        ; linear way, just as in modes 10h and 12h
        out     dx,al
        ret
Set320By400Mode endp
;
; Draws a full screen of slanting color bars in the specified page.
;
; Input:
;       DI = page start address
;       BL = 1 to make the bars slant down and to the left, -1 to
;            make them slant down and to the right, 0 to make
;            them vertical.
;
ColorBarsUp     proc    near
        mov     ax,VGA_SEGMENT
        mov     es,ax   ;point to display memory
        sub     bh,bh   ;start with color 0
        mov     si,SCREEN_HEIGHT ;# of rows to do
        mov     dx,SC_INDEX
        mov     al,MAP_MASK
        out     dx,al   ;point the SC Index reg to the Map Mask reg
        inc     dx      ;point DX to the SC Data register
RowLoop:
        mov     cx,SCREEN_WIDTH/4
                        ;there are 4 pixels at each address, so
                        ; each 320-pixel row is 80 bytes wide
                        ; in each plane
        push    bx      ;save the row-start color and the slant
                        ; direction
ColumnLoop:
MAP_SELECT = 1
        rept    4       ;do all 4 pixels at this address with
                        ; in-line code
        mov     al,MAP_SELECT
        out     dx,al   ;select planes 0, 1, 2, and 3 in turn
        mov     es:[di],bh ;write this plane's pixel
        inc     bh      ;set the color for the next pixel
MAP_SELECT = MAP_SELECT shl 1
        endm
        inc     di      ;point to the address containing the next
                        ; 4 pixels
        loop    ColumnLoop ;do any remaining pixels on this line
        pop     bx      ;get back the row-start color
        add     bh,bl   ;select next row-start color (controls
                        ; slanting of color bars)
        dec     si      ;count down lines on the screen
        jnz     RowLoop
        ret
ColorBarsUp     endp
;
; Waits for the next key and returns it in AX.
;
```

Listing 10.2 continues

Listing 10.2 continued

```
GetNextKey      proc    near
WaitKey:
        mov     ah,1
        int     16h
        jz      WaitKey ;wait for a key to become available
        sub     ah,ah
        int     16h     ;read the key
        ret
GetNextKey      endp
;
Code    ends
;
        end     Start
```

Bit-Plane Animation
on the EGA and VGA

For my money, animation is the most fun you can have on a microcomputer. It requires knowledge, creativity, and excellent code to implement—and it's a heck of a lot of fun to watch once it's up and running!

This chapter of *Power Graphics Programming*, which is about a particularly slick form of animation known as bit-plane animation, is one of my favorites. There's not much more to say about this chapter—the text and code speak for themselves. Actually, I *will* add one comment: Run the code yourself, just to see it in action. Unless I miss my guess, it will make you want to sit down and write some animation code of your own.

Installment 11: In which have some fun with animation, in the process refuting the claim that the PC is a lousy animation engine.

When it comes to computers, my first love is animation. There's nothing quite like the satisfaction of fooling the eye and creating a miniature reality simply by rearranging a few bytes of display memory. What makes animation particularly interesting is that it has to be performed fast (as measured in human time) and without blinking and flickering, which can destroy the illusion of motion and solidity. Those constraints make animation the toughest graphics challenge—and the most rewarding.

It pains me to hear industry pundits downgrade the PC—especially the EGA and VGA—when it comes to animation. Okay, I'll grant you that the PC isn't an Amiga and never will be, but then neither is anything else on the market. The EGA and VGA offer good resolution and color, and while their hardware wasn't *designed* for animation, that doesn't mean we can't put it to work in that capacity. One lesson that any good PC graphics or assembler programmer learns quickly is that it's what the PC's hardware *can* do—not what it was intended to do—that's important.

(By the way, if I were to pick one aspect of the PC to dump on, it would be sound, not animation. The PC's sound circuity really is lousy, and it's hard to understand why that should be, given that a cheap sound chip—which even the PC*jr* had—would have changed everything. I guess IBM figured "serious" computer users would be put off by a computer that could make fun noises.)

Anyway, my point is that the PC's animation capabilities are pretty good. There's a trick, though: You can push the EGA and VGA (henceforth referred to as the *EVGA*) to their animation limits only by stretching your mind a bit and using some unorthodox approaches to animation. In fact, stretching your mind is the key to producing good code for *any* task on the PC—that's the topic of my book *The Zen of Assembler* (Scott, Foresman & Co., 1989). For most software, however, it's not fatal if your code isn't excellent: There's slow but functional software all over the place. When it comes to EVGA animation, though, you won't get to first base without a clever approach.

So, what clever approaches do I have in mind? All sorts. The resources of the EVGA are many and varied, and they can be applied and combined in hundreds of ways to produce effective animation. For example, refer back to the first chapter of this book for a discussion of page flipping. Or look at the July 1986 issue of *PC Tech Journal*, which describes the basic block-move animation technique, or the August 1986 issue of *PC Tech Journal*, which shows a software-sprite scheme built around the EGA's vertical interrupt and the AND-OR image drawing technique. Or look back over the other nine chapters of this book—they contain literally dozens of graphics tips and tricks that can be applied to animation.

This month we're going to add another entry to the list. We're going to take advantage of the bit-plane architecture and color palette of the EVGA to develop an animation architecture that can handle several overlapping images with terrific speed and with virtually perfect visual quality. This technique produces no overlap effects or flicker and allows us to use the fastest possible method to draw images: the **rep movs** instruction.

As with any technique on the PC, there are tradeoffs involved with bit-plane animation. While bit-plane animation is extremely attractive as far as performance and visual quality are concerned, it is somewhat limited: It supports only four colors plus the background color at any one time, each image must consist of only one of the four colors, and images of the same color preferably should not intersect.

It doesn't much matter if bit-plane animation isn't perfect for all applications, though. The real point of showing you bit-plane animation is to bring home the reality that the EVGA is a complex adapter with many resources and that you can do remarkable things if you understand those resources and come up with creative ways to put them to work at specific tasks.

Bit Planes: The Basics

The underlying principle of bit-plane animation is extremely simple. The EVGA has four separate bit planes in mode 10h. Plane 0 normally contains data for the blue component of pixel color, plane 1 normally contains green pixel data, plane 2 contains red pixel data, and plane 3 contains intensity pixel data. I'm going to mix that up in a moment, and so I'll refer to them simply as planes 0, 1, 2, and 3 from now on.

Each bit plane can be written to independently. The contents of the four bit planes are used to generate pixels, with the four bits that control the color of each pixel coming from the four planes. However, the bits from the planes go through one stage on the way to becoming pixels: They're used to look up a six-bit color from one of the 16 palette registers. Figure 11.1 shows how the bits from the four planes feed into the palette registers to select the color of each pixel.

The preceding paragraph is nothing more than a restatement of basic EVGA operation. I don't have space to recap that information in detail—refer back to the first ten chapters if you're getting lost. If you're still with me, take a good look at Figure 11.1. Any light bulbs going on over your head yet? Pity. Well, let's continue.

The general problem with EVGA animation is that it's complex and time-consuming to manipulate images that span the four planes (as most do), and it's hard to avoid interference problems when images intersect, since those images share the same bits in display memory. Since the four bit planes can be written to and read independently, it should be apparent that if we could come up with a way to display images from any given plane independently of whatever images are stored in the other planes, we would have four sets of images that we could manipulate very easily.

There would be no interference effects between images in different planes, since images in one plane wouldn't share bits with images in another plane. What's more, since all the bits for a given image would reside in a single plane, we could do away with the cumbersome programming of the EVGA's complex hardware that is needed to manipulate images that span multiple planes.

All in all, it would be a good deal if we could store each image in a single plane, as shown in Figure 11.2. However, a problem arises when images in different planes overlap, as shown in Figure 11.3: Because the combined bits from overlapping images generate new colors, the overlapping parts of the images look like they don't belong to either of the two images. What we really want, of course, is for one of the images to appear to be in front of the other. It would be better yet if the rear image showed through transparent (background-colored) parts of the forward image. Can we do that? You bet.

Stacking the Palette Registers

Suppose that instead of viewing the four bits per pixel coming out of display memory as selecting one of sixteen colors, we view those bits as selecting one of *four* colors. If the bit from plane 0 is 1, that would select color 0 (say, red). The bit from plane 1 would select color 1 (say, green), the bit from plane 2 would select color 2 (say, blue), and the bit from plane 3 would select color 3 (say, white). Whenever more than 1 bit is 1, the 1 bit from the lowest-numbered plane would determine the color, and 1 bits from all other planes would be ignored. Finally, the absence of any 1 bits at all would select the background color (say, black).

That would give us four colors and the background color. It would also give us nifty image precedence, with images in plane 0 appearing to be in front of images from the other planes, images in plane 1 appearing to be in front of images from planes 2 and 3, and so on. It would even give us transparency, which allows rearward images to show through holes within and around the edges of images in forward planes. Finally, and most importantly, it would meet all the criteria needed to allow us to store each image in a single plane, letting us manipulate the images very quickly and with no reprogramming of the EVGA's hardware other than the few OUT instructions required to select the plane we want to write to.

Which leaves only one question: How do we get this magical pixel-precedence scheme to work? As it turns out, it's a simple matter of reprogramming the palette registers. All we need to do is reprogram the palette registers so that the 1 bit from the plane with the highest precedence determines the color. Table 11.1 lists the palette RAM settings for the colors described above.

Remember that the four-bit values coming from display memory select which palette register provides the actual pixel color. Given that, it's easy to see that the rightmost 1 bit of the four bits coming from display memory in the above table selects the pixel color. If the bit from plane 0 is 1, then the color is red, no matter what the other bits are, as shown in Figure 11.4. When the bit from plane 0 is 0 and the bit from plane 1 is 1, the color is green, and so on for planes 2 and 3. In other words, with the palette register settings given in Table 11.1, we instantly have exactly what we want, which is an approach that keeps images in one plane from interfering with images in other planes while providing precedence and transparency.

Fig. 11.1 *A summary of the path by which four bits of video data (one bit from each of the four planes) become a six-bit pixel color.*

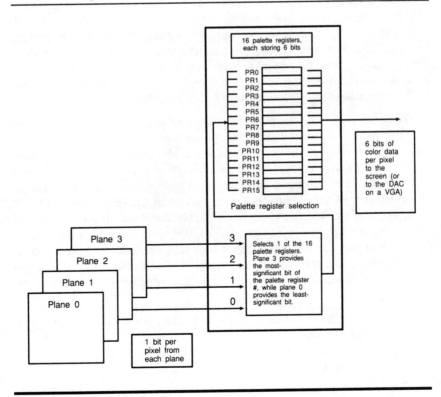

Seems almost too easy, doesn't it? It works beautifully, however, as we'll see very shortly. First, though, I'd like to point out that there's nothing sacred about plane 0 having precedence. We could rearrange the palette register settings so that any plane had the highest precedence, followed by the other planes in any order. I've chosen to give plane 0 the highest precedence only because it seems simplest to think of plane 0 as appearing in front of plane 1, which is in front of plane 2, which is in front of plane 3.

Bit-Plane Animation in Action

Without further ado, Listing 11.1 [presented at the end of this chapter] shows bit-plane animation in action. This program animates 13 rather large images (each 32 pixels on a side) over a complex background at a good clip—*even on a PC*. Five of the images move very quickly, while the other eight bounce back and forth at a steady pace.

I'm not going to discuss the listing in detail. For one thing, that would take too much space. For another, the code is very thoroughly commented and should speak for itself. In any case, most of the individual components of the listing—the Map Mask register, mode sets, word versus byte OUT instructions to the EVGA—have come up in earlier chapters. Do notice, however, that Listing 11.1 sets the palette exactly as I described earlier. This is accomplished by passing a pointer to a 17-byte array (1 byte for each of the 16 palette registers, and 1 byte for the border color) to the BIOS video interrupt (INT 10h), function 10h, subfunction 1.

There's a whole lot of animation going on in Listing 11.1. What's more, the animation is virtually flicker free, partly thanks to bit-plane animation and partly because images are never really erased but are simply overwritten. (The principle behind the animation is that of redrawing each image with a blank fringe around it when it moves so that the blank fringe erases the part of the old image that the new image doesn't overwrite. For details on this sort of animation, see Chapter 1 and the above-mentioned *PC Tech Journal* July 1986 article.) Better yet, the red images take precedence over the green images, which take precedence over the blue images, which take precedence over the white backdrop, and all obscured images show through holes in and around the edges of images in front of them.

In short, Listing 11.1 accomplishes everything we wished for earlier in an animation technique.

If you can, run the listing. The animation may be a revelation to those of you who are used to weak, slow animation on PCs and or EVGAs. Bit-plane animation makes the PC look an awful lot like—dare I say it?—a game machine. If you're running Listing 11.1 on an AT or a faster computer (and, considering the sophistication of *PJ*'s readership, I'd say that's a pretty safe bet), you'll have to crank up the SLOWDOWN equate at the start of the listing to slow things down. Even on a stock AT, the listing runs much too fast without a substantial delay (although it does look rather interesting at warp speed). We should all have such problems, eh? In fact, we could easily increase the number of animated images past 20 on an AT.

Fig. 11.2 *It would be useful if we could store each image in a single plane. The images would appear together on the screen but could be manipulated without the cumbersome programming of the EVGA's complex hardware that is required for images that span multiple planes.*

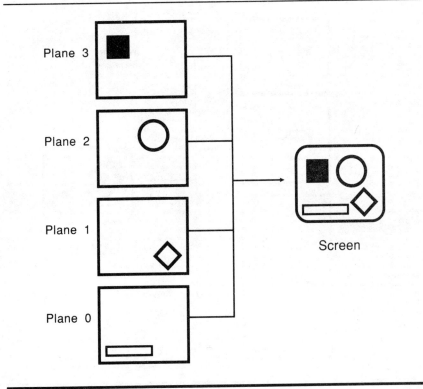

Bit-plane animation does have serious limitations, which we'll get to in a second. One limitation that is *not* inherent to bit-plane animation but simply a shortcoming of Listing 11.1 is somewhat choppy horizontal motion. In the interests of both clarity and keeping the listing to a reasonable length, I decided to byte-align all images horizontally. This saved the many tables needed to define the seven non–byte-aligned rotations of the images as well as the code needed to support rotation. Unfortunately, it also meant that the smallest possible horizontal movement was eight pixels (one byte of display memory), which is enough to be noticeable at certain speeds. The situation is, however, easily corrected with the additional rotations and code. Vertically, where there is no byte-alignment issue, the images move four or six pixels at a time, resulting in considerably smoother animation.

Fig. 11.3 *If we store each image in a single plane, undesirable color effects result when the images overlap.*

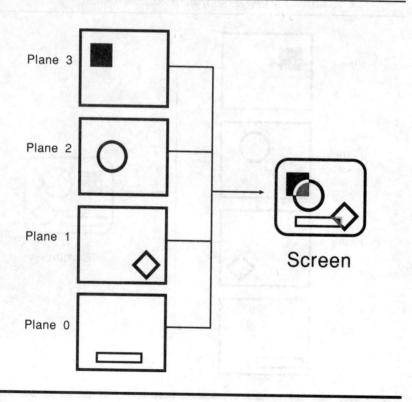

The addition of code to support rotated images also opens the door to support for internal animation, where the appearance of a given image changes over time to suggest that the image is an active entity. For example, propellers could whirl, jaws could snap, and jets could flare. Bit-plane animation with byte-aligned images and internal animation can look truly spectacular. Perhaps someday I can wangle space for an extra-long "On Graphics" and put all the animation pieces together in a single listing. It's a sight worth seeing, particularly for those who doubt the PC's worth when it comes to animation.

Limitations of Bit-Plane Animation

As I've said, bit-plane animation is not perfect. For starters, bit-plane animation can be used only in the EVGA's planar modes: modes 0Dh, 0Eh,

Table 11.1

Bit Value For Plane 3 2 1 0	Palette Register	Register Setting
0 0 0 0	0	00h (black)
0 0 0 1	1	3Ch (red)
0 0 1 0	2	3Ah (green)
0 0 1 1	3	3Ch (red)
0 1 0 0	4	9h (blue)
0 1 0 1	5	3Ch (red)
0 1 1 0	6	Ah (green)
0 1 1 1	7	3Ch (red)
1 0 0 0	8	3Fh (white)
1 0 0 1	9	3Ch (red)
1 0 1 0	10	3Ah (green)
1 0 1 1	11	Ch (red)
1 1 0 0	12	9h (blue)
1 1 0 1	13	Ch (red)
1 1 1 0	14	Ah (green)
1 1 1 1	15	3Ch (red)

0Fh, 10h, and 12h. Also, the reprogramming of the palette registers that provides image precedence also reduces the available color set from the normal 16 colors to just 5 (one color per plane plus the background color). Worse still, each image can be drawn in only one of the four colors. Mixing colors within an image is not allowed, since the bits for each image are limited to a single plane and therefore can select only one color. Finally, all images of the same precedence must be the same color.

It is possible to work around the color limitations to some extent by using only one or two planes for bit-plane animation while reserving the other planes for multicolor drawing. For example, you could use plane 3 for bit-plane animation while using planes 0, 1, and 2 for normal eight-color drawing. The images in plane 3 would then appear to be in front of the eight-color images. If we wanted the plane-3 images to be yellow, we could set up the palette registers as shown in Table 11.2.

As you can see, yellow is displayed whenever a pixel's bit from plane 3 is 1. This gives the images from plane 3 precedence while leaving us with the eight normal low-intensity colors for images drawn across the other three planes, as shown in Figure 11.5. Of course, this approach provides only one, rather than three, high-precedence planes, but that might be a good tradeoff for being able to draw multicolored images as a backdrop to the high-precedence images. For the right application, high-speed, flicker-free, plane-3 images moving in front of an eight-color backdrop could be a potent combination indeed.

Another limitation of bit-plane animation is that it's best if images stored in the same plane never cross each other. When images do cross, the blank fringe around each image can temporarily erase the overlapped parts of the other image or images, resulting in momentary flicker. While that's not fatal, it certainly detracts from the rock-solid animation effect of bit-plane animation.

Not allowing images in the same plane to overlap is actually less of a limitation than it seems. Run Listing 11.1 again. Unless you were looking for it, you'd never notice that images of the same color almost never overlap—there's plenty of action to distract the eye, and the trajectories of images of the same color are arranged so that they have a full range of motion without running into each other. The only exception is the chain of green images, which occasionally doubles back on itself when it bounces directly into a corner and reverses direction. Here, however, the images are moving so quickly that the brief moment during which one image's fringe blanks a portion of another image is noticeable only upon close inspection—and it's not particularly unaesthetic even then.

When a technique has such tremendous visual and performance advantages as bit-plane animation does, it behooves you to design your animation software so that the limitations of the animation technique don't get in the way. For example, you might design a shooting-gallery game with all the images in a given plane marching along in step in a continuous band. Since the images would never overlap, you could use bit-plane animation.

Shearing and Page Flipping

As Listing 11.1 runs, you may occasionally see an image shear, with the top and bottom parts of the image briefly offset. This is a consequence of drawing an image directly into memory as that memory is being scanned for video data. Occasionally, the CRT controller scans a given area of display memory for pixel data just as the program is changing that same memory. If the CRT controller scans memory faster than the CPU can modify that memory, then the CRT controller can scan out the bytes of display memory that have been already been changed, pass the point in the image that the CPU is currently drawing, and start scanning out bytes

Fig. 11.4 *When the palette registers are set up for bit-plane animation, with plane 0 given the highest precedence and mapped to red, then whenever a pixel's plane-0 bit is 1, red is displayed, no matter what the values of the bits from the other planes.*

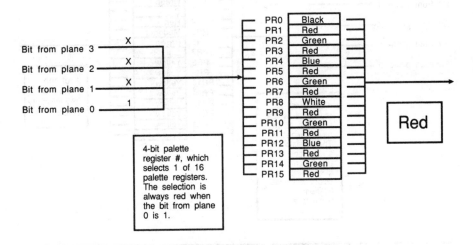

that haven't yet been changed. The result is mismatched upper and lower portions of the image.

If the CRT controller scans more slowly than the CPU can modify memory (likely with a 386, a fast VGA, and narrow images), then the CPU can pass the CRT controller, with the same net result of mismatched top and bottom parts of the image as the CRT controller scans out first unchanged bytes and then changed bytes. Basically, shear will occasionally occur unless the CPU and CRT proceed at exactly the same rate, which is most unlikely. Shear is more noticeable when there are fewer but larger images, since it's more apparent when a larger screen area is sheared and because it's easier to spot one out of three large images momentarily shearing than one out of twenty small images.

Image shear isn't terrible—I've written and sold several games in which images occasionally shear, and I've never heard anyone complain—but neither is it ideal. One solution is page flipping, in which drawing is done to a nondisplayed page of display memory while another page of display memory is shown on the screen. When the drawing is finished, the newly

Fig. 11.5 *When the palette registers are set up as shown for bit-plane animation, with one bit plane (plane 3) appearing in front of an eight-color backdrop, then whenever a pixel's plane-3 bit is 0, one of the eight normal, low-intensity colors is selected by the three bits from the other planes.*

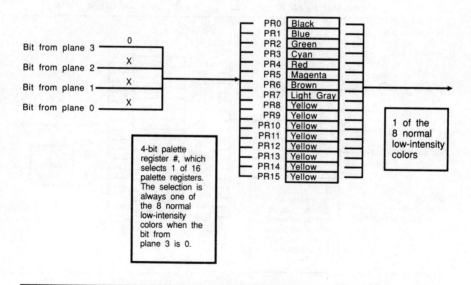

drawn part of display memory is made the displayed page so that the new screen is made visible all at once, with no shearing or flicker. The other page is then drawn to, and when the drawing is complete, the display is switched back to that page.

Page flipping can be used in conjunction with bit-plane animation, although page flipping does somewhat diminish the unique performance advantages of bit-plane animation. Page flipping also makes it possible to implement image precedence in other, slower ways. Whether or not it's used in conjunction with bit-plane animation, page flipping produces animation of the highest visual quality. There are a few drawbacks to page flipping, however:

❑ Page flipping requires two display memory buffers—one to draw in and one to display at any given time. Unfortunately, in mode 12h there just isn't enough memory for two buffers, and so page flipping is not an option in that mode.

❑ Page flipping requires that you keep the contents of both buffers up to date, which can necessitate a good deal of extra drawing.

Table 11.2

Palette Register	Register Setting
0	00h (black)
1	01h (blue)
2	02h (green)
3	03h (cyan)
4	4h (red)
5	05h (magenta)
6	14h (brown)
7	07h (light gray)
8	3Eh (yellow)
9	3Eh (yellow)
10	3Eh (yellow)
11	3Eh (yellow)
12	3Eh (yellow)
13	3Eh (yellow)
14	3Eh (yellow)
15	Eh (yellow)

❏ Page flipping requires that you wait until you're sure the page has flipped before you start drawing to the other page. Otherwise, you could end up modifying a page while it's still being displayed, defeating the whole purpose of page flipping. Waiting for pages to flip takes time and can slow overall performance significantly. What's more, it's sometimes difficult to be sure when the page has flipped, since not all EVGA clones implement the EVGA status bits and page-flip timing identically.

To sum up, bit-plane animation by itself is very fast and looks good. In conjunction with page flipping, bit-plane animation looks a little better but is slower, and the overall animation scheme is more difficult to implement and perhaps a bit less reliable on some computers.

In Conclusion

Bit-plane animation is neat stuff. Heck, good animation of *any* sort is fun, and the PC is as good a place as any (well, almost any) to make people's jaws drop. Don't let anyone tell you that you can't have good animation on the PC. You can—*if* you stretch your mind to find ways to bring the full power of the EGA and VGA to bear on your applications. Bit-plane animation isn't for every task; neither are page flipping, exclusive ORing, pixel panning, or any of the host of other techniques we've discussed. One or more tricks from that grab bag should give you what you need for any given task, though, and the bigger your grab bag, the better your programs. What we're doing in "On Graphics" is making the biggest grab bag of graphics tricks we can. Let me know if you've got some nifty tricks to add or if there's anything you'd like to see covered.

See you next time.

Listing 11.1

```
;
; Program to demonstrate bit-plane animation. Performs
; flicker-free animation with image transparency and
; image precedence across four distinct planes, with
; 13 32x32 images kept in motion at once.
;
; Updated 6/29/89.
;
; Set to higher values to slow down on faster computers.
; 0 is fine for a PC. 500 is a reasonable setting for an AT.
; Slowing animation further allows a good look at
; transparency and the lack of flicker and color effects
; when images cross.
;
SLOWDOWN          equ     0
;
; Plane selects for the four colors we're using.
;
RED       equ     01h
GREEN     equ     02h
BLUE      equ     04h
WHITE     equ     08h
;
VGA_SEGMENT       equ     0a000h  ;mode 10h display memory
                                  ; segment
SC_INDEX          equ     3c4h    ;Sequence Controller Index
                                  ; register
MAP_MASK          equ     2       ;Map Mask register index in
                                  ; Sequence Controller
SCREEN_WIDTH      equ     80      ;# of bytes across screen
SCREEN_HEIGHT     equ     350     ;# of scan lines on screen
WORD_OUTS_OK      equ     1       ;set to 0 to assemble for
                                  ; computers that can't
                                  ; handle word outs to
                                  ; indexed VGA regs
;
stackseg          segment para stack 'STACK'
        db        512 dup (?)
stackseg          ends
;
; Complete info about one object that we're animating.
;
ObjectStructure struc
Delay             dw      ?       ;used to delay for n passes
                                  ; through the loop to
                                  ; control animation speed
BaseDelay         dw      ?       ;reset value for Delay
Image             dw      ?       ;pointer to drawing info
                                  ; for object
XCoord            dw      ?       ;object X location in pixels
XInc              dw      ?       ;# of pixels to increment
                                  ; location by in the X
                                  ; direction on each move
XLeftLimit        dw      ?       ;left limit of X motion
XRightLimit       dw      ?       ;right limit of X motion
YCoord            dw      ?       ;object Y location in pixels
YInc              dw      ?       ;# of pixels to increment
                                  ; location by in the Y
```

Listing 11.1 continues

Listing 11.1 continued

```
                                    ; direction on each move
YTopLimit       dw      ?           ;top limit of Y motion
YBottomLimit    dw      ?           ;bottom limit of Y motion
PlaneSelect     db      ?           ;mask to select plane to
                                    ; which object is drawn
                db      ?           ;to make an even # of words
                                    ; long, for better 286
                                    ; performance (keeps the
                                    ; following structure
                                    ; word-aligned)
ObjectStructure ends
;
Data    segment word 'DATA'
;
; Palette settings to give plane 0 precedence, followed by
; planes 1, 2, and 3. Plane 3 has the lowest precedence (is
; obscured by any other plane), while plane 0 has the
; highest precedence (displays in front of any other plane).
;
Colors  db      000h ;background color=black
        db      03ch ;plane 0 only=red
        db      03ah ;plane 1 only=green
        db      03ch ;planes 0&1=red (plane 0 priority)
        db      039h ;plane 2 only=blue
        db      03ch ;planes 0&2=red (plane 0 priority)
        db      03ah ;planes 1&2=green (plane 1 priority)
        db      03ch ;planes 0&1&2=red (plane 0 priority)
        db      03fh ;plane 3 only=white
        db      03ch ;planes 0&3=red (plane 0 priority)
        db      03ah ;planes 1&3=green (plane 1 priority)
        db      03ch ;planes 0&1&3=red (plane 0 priority)
        db      039h ;planes 2&3=blue (plane 2 priority)
        db      03ch ;planes 0&2&3=red (plane 0 priority)
        db      03ah ;planes 1&2&3=green (plane 1 priority)
        db      03ch ;planes 0&1&2&3=red (plane 0 priority)
        db      000h ;border color=black
;
; Image of a hollow square.
; There's an 8-pixel-wide blank border around all edges
; so that the image erases the old version of itself as
; it's moved and redrawn.
;
Square  label   byte
        dw      48,6    ;height in pixels, width in bytes
        rept    8
        db      0,0,0,0,0,0     ;top blank border
        endm
        .radix  2
```

Listing 11.1 continues

Listing 11.1 *continued*

```
        db      0,11111111,11111111,11111111,11111111,0
        db      0,11111111,11111111,11111111,11111111,0
        db      0,11111111,11111111,11111111,11111111,0
        db      0,11111111,11111111,11111111,11111111,0
        db      0,11111111,11111111,11111111,11111111,0
        db      0,11111111,11111111,11111111,11111111,0 ·
        db      0,11111111,11111111,11111111,11111111,0
        db      0,11111111,11111111,11111111,11111111,0
        db      0,11111111,00000000,00000000,11111111,0
        db      0,11111111,00000000,00000000,11111111,0
        db      0,11111111,00000000,00000000,11111111,0
        db      0,11111111,00000000,00000000,11111111,0
        db      0,11111111,00000000,00000000,11111111,0
        db      0,11111111,00000000,00000000,11111111,0
        db      0,11111111,00000000,00000000,11111111,0
        db      0,11111111,00000000,00000000,11111111,0
        db      0,11111111,00000000,00000000,11111111,0
        db      0,11111111,00000000,00000000,11111111,0
        db      0,11111111,00000000,00000000,11111111,0
        db      0,11111111,00000000,00000000,11111111,0
        db      0,11111111,00000000,00000000,11111111,0
        db      0,11111111,00000000,00000000,11111111,0
        db      0,11111111,00000000,00000000,11111111,0
        db      0,11111111,00000000,00000000,11111111,0
        db      0,11111111,11111111,11111111,11111111,0
        db      0,11111111,11111111,11111111,11111111,0
        db      0,11111111,11111111,11111111,11111111,0
        db      0,11111111,11111111,11111111,11111111,0
        db      0,11111111,11111111,11111111,11111111,0
        db      0,11111111,11111111,11111111,11111111,0
        db      0,11111111,11111111,11111111,11111111,0
        db      0,11111111,11111111,11111111,11111111,0
        .radix  10
        rept    8
        db      0,0,0,0,0,0          ;bottom blank border
        endm
;
; Image of a hollow diamond with a smaller diamond in the
; middle.
; There's an 8-pixel-wide blank border around all edges
; so that the image erases the old version of itself as
; it's moved and redrawn.
;
Diamond label   byte
        dw      48,6        ;height in pixels, width in bytes
        rept    8
        db      0,0,0,0,0,0          ;top blank border
        endm
        .radix  2
```

Listing 11.1 *continues*

Listing 11.1 continued

```
        db      0,00000000,00000001,10000000,00000000,0
        db      0,00000000,00000011,11000000,00000000,0
        db      0,00000000,00000111,11100000,00000000,0
        db      0,00000000,00001111,11110000,00000000,0
        db      0,00000000,00011111,11111000,00000000,0
        db      0,00000000,00111110,01111100,00000000,0
        db      0,00000000,01111100,00111110,00000000,0
        db      0,00000000,11111000,00011111,00000000,0
        db      0,00000001,11110000,00001111,10000000,0
        db      0,00000011,11100000,00000111,11000000,0
        db      0,00000111,11000000,00000011,11100000,0
        db      0,00001111,10000001,10000001,11110000,0
        db      0,00011111,00000011,11000000,11111000,0
        db      0,00111110,00000111,11100000,01111100,0
        db      0,01111100,00001111,11110000,00111110,0
        db      0,11111000,00011111,11111000,00011111,0
        db      0,11111000,00011111,11111000,00011111,0
        db      0,01111100,00001111,11110000,00111110,0
        db      0,00111110,00000111,11100000,01111100,0
        db      0,00011111,00000011,11000000,11111000,0
        db      0,00001111,10000001,10000001,11110000,0
        db      0,00000111,11000000,00000011,11100000,0
        db      0,00000011,11100000,00000111,11000000,0
        db      0,00000001,11110000,00001111,10000000,0
        db      0,00000000,11111000,00011111,00000000,0
        db      0,00000000,01111100,00111110,00000000,0
        db      0,00000000,00111110,01111100,00000000,0
        db      0,00000000,00011111,11111000,00000000,0
        db      0,00000000,00001111,11110000,00000000,0
        db      0,00000000,00000111,11100000,00000000,0
        db      0,00000000,00000011,11000000,00000000,0
        db      0,00000000,00000001,10000000,00000000,0
        .radix  10
        rept    8
        db      0,0,0,0,0,0      ;bottom blank border
        endm
;
; List of objects to animate.
;
        even    ;word-align for better 286 performance
;
ObjectList      label   ObjectStructure
 ObjectStructure <1,21,Diamond,88,8,80,512,16,0,0,350,RED>
 ObjectStructure <1,15,Square,296,8,112,480,144,0,0,350,RED>
 ObjectStructure <1,23,Diamond,88,8,80,512,256,0,0,350,RED>
 ObjectStructure <1,13,Square,120,0,0,640,144,4,0,280,BLUE>
 ObjectStructure <1,11,Diamond,208,0,0,640,144,4,0,280,BLUE>
 ObjectStructure <1,8,Square,296,0,0,640,144,4,0,288,BLUE>
 ObjectStructure <1,9,Diamond,384,0,0,640,144,4,0,288,BLUE>
 ObjectStructure <1,14,Square,472,0,0,640,144,4,0,280,BLUE>
 ObjectStructure <1,8,Diamond,200,8,0,576,48,6,0,280,GREEN>
 ObjectStructure <1,8,Square,248,8,0,576,96,6,0,280,GREEN>
 ObjectStructure <1,8,Diamond,296,8,0,576,144,6,0,280,GREEN>
 ObjectStructure <1,8,Square,344,8,0,576,192,6,0,280,GREEN>
 ObjectStructure <1,8,Diamond,392,8,0,576,240,6,0,280,GREEN>
ObjectListEnd   label   ObjectStructure
;
Data    ends
```

Listing 11.1 continues

Listing 11.1 continued

```
;
; Macro to output a word value to a port.
;
OUT_WORD        macro
if WORD_OUTS_OK
        out     dx,ax
else
        out     dx,al
        inc     dx
        xchg    ah,al
        out     dx,al
        dec     dx
        xchg    ah,al
endif
        endm
;
; Macro to output a constant value to an indexed VGA
; register.
;
CONSTANT_TO_INDEXED_REGISTER    macro ADDRESS, INDEX, VALUE
        mov     dx,ADDRESS
        mov     ax,(VALUE shl 8) + INDEX
        OUT_WORD
        endm
;
Code    segment
        assume  cs:Code, ds:Data
Start   proc    near
        cld
        mov     ax,Data
        mov     ds,ax
;
; Set 640x350 16-color mode.
;
        mov     ax,0010h        ;AH=0 means select mode
                                ;AL=10h means select
                                ; mode 10h
        int     10h             ;BIOS video interrupt
;
; Set the palette up to provide bit-plane precedence. If
; planes 0 & 1 overlap, the plane 0 color will be shown;
; if planes 1 & 2 overlap, the plane 1 color will be
; shown; and so on.
;
        mov     ax,(10h shl 8) + 2      ;AH = 10h means
                                        ; set palette
                                        ; registers fn
                                        ;AL = 2 means set
                                        ; all palette
                                        ; registers
        push    ds                      ;ES:DX points to
        pop     es                      ; the palette
        mov     dx,offset Colors        ; settings
        int     10h                     ;call the BIOS to
                                        ; set the palette
;
; Draw the static backdrop in plane 3. All the moving images
; will appear to be in front of this backdrop, since plane 3
```

Listing 11.1 continues

Listing 11.1 *continued*

```
; has the lowest precedence the way the palette is set up.
;
        CONSTANT_TO_INDEXED_REGISTER SC_INDEX, MAP_MASK, 08h
                                ;allow data to go to
                                ; plane 3 only
;
; Point ES to display memory for the rest of the program.
;
        mov     ax,VGA_SEGMENT
        mov     es,ax
;
        sub     di,di
        mov     bp,SCREEN_HEIGHT/16     ;fill in the screen
                                        ; 16 lines at a time
BackdropBlockLoop:
        call    DrawGridCross           ;draw a cross piece
        call    DrawGridVert            ;draw the rest of a
                                        ; 15-high block
        dec     bp
        jnz     BackdropBlockLoop
        call    DrawGridCross           ;bottom line of grid
;
; Start animating!
;
AnimationLoop:
        mov     bx,offset ObjectList    ;point to the first
                                        ; object in the list
;
; For each object, see if it's time to move and draw that
; object.
;
ObjectLoop:
;
; See if it's time to move this object.
;
        dec     [bx+Delay]      ;count down delay
        jnz     DoNextObject    ;still delaying--don't move
        mov     ax,[bx+BaseDelay]
        mov     [bx+Delay],ax   ;reset delay for next time
;
; Select the plane that this object will be drawn in.
;
        mov     dx,SC_INDEX
        mov     ah,[bx+PlaneSelect]
        mov     al,MAP_MASK
        OUT_WORD
;
; Advance the X coordinate, reversing direction if either
; of the X margins has been reached.
;
        mov     cx,[bx+XCoord]          ;current X location
        cmp     cx,[bx+XLeftLimit]      ;at left limit?
        ja      CheckXRightLimit        ;no
        neg     [bx+XInc]               ;yes-reverse
CheckXRightLimit:
        cmp     cx,[bx+XRightLimit]     ;at right limit?
        jb      SetNewX                 ;no
        neg     [bx+XInc]               ;yes-reverse
```

Listing 11.1 *continues*

Listing 11.1 continued

```
SetNewX:
        add     cx,[bx+XInc]            ;move the X coord
        mov     [bx+XCoord],cx          ; & save it
;
; Advance the Y coordinate, reversing direction if either
; of the Y margins has been reached.
;
        mov     dx,[bx+YCoord]          ;current Y location
        cmp     dx,[bx+YTopLimit]       ;at top limit?
        ja      CheckYBottomLimit       ;no
        neg     [bx+YInc]               ;yes-reverse
CheckYBottomLimit:
        cmp     dx,[bx+YBottomLimit]    ;at bottom limit?
        jb      SetNewY                 ;no
        neg     [bx+YInc]               ;yes-reverse
SetNewY:
        add     dx,[bx+YInc]            ;move the Y coord
        mov     [bx+YCoord],dx          ; & save it
;
; Draw at the new location. Because of the plane select
; above, only one plane will be affected.
;
        mov     si,[bx+Image]           ;point to the
                                        ; object's image
                                        ; info

        call    DrawObject
;
; Point to the next object in the list until we run out of
; objects.
;
DoNextObject:
        add     bx,size ObjectStructure
        cmp     bx,offset ObjectListEnd
        jb      ObjectLoop
;
; Delay as specified to slow things down.
;
if SLOWDOWN
        mov     cx,SLOWDOWN
DelayLoop:
        loop    DelayLoop
endif
;
; If a key's been pressed, we're done, otherwise animate
; again.
;
CheckKey:
        mov     ah,1
        int     16h                     ;is a key waiting?
        jz      AnimationLoop           ;no
        sub     ah,ah
        int     16h                     ;yes-clear the key & done
;
; Back to text mode.
;
        mov     ax,0003h                ;AH=0 means select mode
                                        ;AL=03h means select
                                        ; mode 03h
```

Listing 11.1 continues

Listing 11.1 *continued*

```
        int     10h
;
; Back to DOS.
;
        mov     ah,4ch          ;DOS terminate function
        int     21h             ;done
;
Start   endp
;
; Draws a single grid cross-element at the display memory
; location pointed to by ES:DI. 1 horizontal line is drawn
; across the screen.
;
; Input: ES:DI points to the address at which to draw
;
; Output: ES:DI points to the address following the
;               line drawn
;
; Registers altered: AX, CX, DI
;
DrawGridCross   proc    near
        mov     ax,0ffffh       ;draw a solid line
        mov     cx,SCREEN_WIDTH/2-1
        rep     stosw           ;draw all but the rightmost
                                ; edge
        mov     ax,0080h
        stosw                   ;draw the right edge of the
                                ; grid
        ret
DrawGridCross   endp
;
; Draws the noncross part of the grid at the display-memory
; location pointed to by ES:DI. 15 scan lines are filled.
;
; Input: ES:DI points to the address at which to draw
;
; Output: ES:DI points to the address following the
;               part of the grid drawn
;
; Registers altered: AX, CX, DX, DI
;
DrawGridVert    proc    near
        mov     ax,0080h        ;pattern for a vertical line
        mov     dx,15           ;draw 15 scan lines (all of
                                ; a grid block except the
                                ; solid cross line)
BackdropRowLoop:
        mov     cx,SCREEN_WIDTH/2
        rep     stosw           ;draw this scan line's bit
                                ; of all the vertical lines
                                ; on the screen
        dec     dx
        jnz     BackdropRowLoop
        ret
DrawGridVert    endp
;
; Draws the specified image at the specified location.
; Images are drawn on byte boundaries horizontally, pixel
```

Listing 11.1 *continues*

Listing 11.1 *continued*

```
; boundaries vertically.
; The Map Mask register must already have been set to enable
; access to the desired plane.
;
; Input:
;       CX - X coordinate of upper left corner
;       DX - Y coordinate of upper left corner
;       DS:SI - pointer to draw info for image
;       ES - display memory segment
;
; Output: none
;
; Registers altered: AX, CX, DX, SI, DI, BP
;
DrawObject      proc    near
        mov     ax,SCREEN_WIDTH
        mul     dx          ;calculate the start offset in
                            ; display memory of the row the
                            ; image will be drawn at
        shr     cx,1
        shr     cx,1
        shr     cx,1        ;divide the X coordinate in pixels
                            ; by 8 to get the X coordinate in
                            ; bytes
        add     ax,cx       ;destination offset in display
                            ; memory for the image
        mov     di,ax       ;point ES:DI to the address to
                            ; which the image will be copied
                            ; in display memory
        lodsw
        mov     dx,ax       ;# of lines in the image
        lodsw               ;# of bytes across the image
        mov     bp,SCREEN_WIDTH
        sub     bp,ax       ;# of bytes to add to the display
                            ; memory offset after copying a line
                            ; of the image to display memory in
                            ; order to point to the address
                            ; where the next line of the image
                            ; will go in display memory
DrawLoop:
        mov     cx,ax       ;width of the image
        rep     movsb       ;copy the next line of the image
                            ; into display memory
        add     di,bp       ;point to the address at which the
                            ; next line will go in display
                            ; memory
        dec     dx          ;count down the lines of the image
        jnz     DrawLoop
        ret
DrawObject      endp
;
Code    ends
        end     Start
```

CHAPTER 12

Fast Line Drawing for the EGA and VGA

This chapter is about two aspects of drawing lines: understanding how lines are drawn, and drawing lines *fast*. The design and implementation of fast line-drawing code pulls together much of what we've learned so far: set/reset, the bit mask, the organization of EGA/VGA memory, and crafting good assembler code. Line drawing is particularly interesting because it's complex, but not *too* complex; it's a big-enough problem to pose a challenge, but it's small enough to be amenable to serious optimization. In other words, it's the sort of task that's hard enough to make you sweat, but it's manageable enough so that, with a bit of thought, it can be implemented well without undue frustration or wasted time.

As a bonus, we get to see lines drawn in a *big* hurry when we're done with the line-drawing code. That's one of the best things about graphics: After putting your best efforts into graphics code, you immediately get to *see* just how good that code is. Talk about positive (or negative) feedback!

Installment 12: In which we draw lines like a bat out of hell. (This article was originally written for Turbo Technix *magazine. However, it first appeared in print in* Programmer's Journal.*)*

This installment of "On Graphics" is going to be a little bit different from the norm. You see, some time ago I wrote an article about fast line drawing for the late, lamented *Turbo Technix*, the Borland magazine. The article explained Bresenham's line-drawing algorithm in some detail and presented a clear and reasonably fast EGA/VGA implementation of the algorithm in C so that anyone with a mind to could understand how the process of drawing a line worked. Then, with the theoretical and educational aspects taken care of, the article presented a *very* fast assembly language implementation of the algorithm. (If something is worth doing, it's worth doing right, and lines should be drawn with assembly code!)

Pleased with the result, I shipped the article off to *Turbo Technix,* where it was queued up for publication in the seventh issue. Alas, issue six was the last of its line, and there I was, with an article I was sure a good many people would be interested in reading . . . and no way to get it into print.

Well, thanks to cooperation from the people at Borland and *PJ*, I'm able to run the article here. It's not in the usual "On Graphics" style, since it was written for a different audience. It spends more time explaining details, such as the organization of display memory, that most of you know like the back of your hand by now. Still, a little extra detail never hurts, and even if all you look at is the assembly code in Listing 12.3 [presented at the end of this chapter], it *is* good code. But if you want to know whether it's the fastest Bresenham's implementation possible, I must tell you that it isn't.

First, the code could be sped up a bit by a shuffling and combining of the various error-term manipulations, but that would result in *truly* cryptic code. Since I want you to be able to relate the original algorithm to the final code, I skipped those optimizations. Also, write mode 3, which is unique to the VGA, could be used for faster drawing.

Second, horizontal, vertical, and diagonal lines could be made special cases, since those particular lines require little calculation and so can be drawn very rapidly. This is especially true of horizontal lines, which can be drawn eight pixels at a time.

Third, in-line code or duplicated code (or both) could be used to eliminate most of the branches in Listing 12.3. Because the 8088 is notoriously slow at branching, that would make quite a difference in overall performance. If you're interested in in-line code and similar assembly techniques, I refer you to my book on high-performance assembly programming, *The Zen of Assembler* (Scott, Foresman & Co., 1989).

That brings us neatly to my final point: Even if I didn't know that there were further optimizations to be made to my line-drawing implementation, I'd *assume* that there were. As I'm sure the experienced assembly programmers among you know, there are dozens of ways to tackle any problem in assembly, and someone else always seems to have come up with a trick that never occurred to you. I've incorporated a suggestion made by Jim Mackraz in the code in this article, and I'd be most interested in hearing of any other tricks or tips you readers may have.

The line-drawing implementation in Listing 12.3 is fast enough for most purposes, though. Let's get to it.

Line Drawing

For all the complexity of graphics design and programming, surprisingly few primitive functions lie at the heart of most graphics software. Heavily used primitives include routines that draw dots, circles, area fills, bit block logical transfers, and, of course, lines. For many years, computer graphics were created primarily with specialized line-drawing hardware, and so lines are in a way the lingua franca of computer graphics. Lines are used in a wide variety of microcomputer graphics applications today, notably CAD/CAM and computer-aided engineering.

There are two important characteristics of any line-drawing function. First, it must draw a reasonable approximation of a line. Since a computer screen has limited resolution, a line-drawing function must actually approximate a straight line by drawing a series of dots in what amounts to a jagged pattern that generally proceeds in the desired direction. That pattern of dots must reliably suggest to the human eye the true line it represents.

Second, to be usable a line-drawing function must be *fast*. As mentioned above, minicomputers and mainframes generally have hardware that performs line drawing, but most microcomputers offer no such assistance. When drawing lines on the CGA, the EGA, or the VGA, the PC's CPU must draw lines on its own, and, as many users of graphics-oriented software know, that can be a slow process indeed.

Line-drawing quality and speed derive from two factors: the algorithm used to draw the line and the implementation of that algorithm. In this chapter, I will present two implementations for the EGA and VGA (henceforth referred to collectively as the *EVGA*) of Bresenham's line-drawing algorithm, an algorithm that provides adequate line quality and excellent drawing speed. (Bresenham also has circle-drawing and ellipse-drawing algorithms.) The first implementation, written in Turbo C, illustrates the workings of the algorithm and draws lines at a good rate. The second implementation, written in assembly language and callable directly from Turbo C, draws lines at an extremely high speed, four to six times faster than the C version. Between them, the two implementations illuminate Bresenham's line-drawing algorithm and provide high-performance line-drawing capability.

What's So Tough About Drawing a Line?

The difficulty in drawing a line lies in generating a set of dots that, taken together, are a reasonable facsimile of a true line. Only horizontal, vertical,

---

Fig. 12.1 *Approximation of a true line on a finite-resolution graphics display. Black circles are screen dots turned on to approximate the true line; white dots are screen dots that are not turned on.*

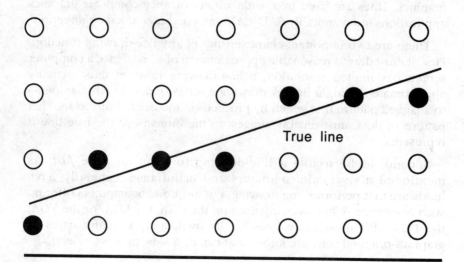

and diagonal lines can be drawn precisely along the true line being represented; all other lines must be approximated from the array of dots that a given video mode supports, as shown in Figure 12.1.

Considerable thought has gone into the design of line-drawing algorithms, and a number of techniques for drawing high-quality lines have been developed. (See the references listed at the end of this chapter for discussions of several line-drawing approaches.) Unfortunately, most of these techniques were developed for powerful, expensive graphics workstations and require very high resolution, a large color palette, or floating-point hardware. These techniques tend to perform poorly and produce less visually impressive results on PCs.

Bresenham's line-drawing algorithm, on the other hand, is uniquely suited to microcomputer implementation in that it requires no floating-point operations, no divides, and no multiplies inside the line-drawing loop. Moreover, it can be implemented with surprisingly little code.

Bresenham's Line-Drawing Algorithm

The key to grasping Bresenham's algorithm is to understand that when you draw an approximation of a line on a finite-resolution display, each dot drawn will lie either exactly on the true line or to one side or the other of the true line. The amount by which the dot deviates from the true line is the error of the line drawing at that point. As the drawing of the line progresses from one dot to the next, the cumulative error can be used to tell when, given the resolution of the display, a more accurate approximation of the line could be drawn by placing a given dot one unit of screen resolution away from its predecessor in the horizontal direction, the vertical direction, or both.

Let's examine the case of drawing a line where the horizontal, or x, length of the line is greater than the vertical, or y, length and both lengths are greater than 0. For example, suppose we are drawing a line from (0,0) to (5,2), as shown in Figure 12.2. Note that the figure shows the upper left corner of the screen as (0,0), rather than having (0,0) at its more traditional lower-left-corner location. Because of the way the PC's graphics are mapped to memory, it is simpler to work within this framework, although a translation of y from increasing downward to increasing upward could be effected easily enough simply by subtracting the x coordinate from the screen height minus one. (If you are more comfortable with the traditional coordinate system, feel free to modify the code in listings 12.1 and 12.3 [presented at the end of this chapter].)

In Figure 12.2, the endpoints of the line fall exactly on displayed dots. However, no other part of the line squarely intersects the center of a dot, meaning that all other dots will have to be plotted as approximations of the line. The approach to approximation that Bresenham's algorithm takes is to move exactly one dot along the major dimension of the line each time a new dot is drawn while moving one dot along the minor dimension each time the line moves more than halfway between dots along the minor dimension.

In Figure 12.2, the *x* dimension is the major dimension. This means that six dots—one at each *x* coordinate (0, 1, 2, 3, 4, and 5)—will be drawn. The trick, then, is to decide on the correct *y* coordinates to accompany those *x* coordinates.

It's easy enough to select the *y* coordinates by eye in Figure 12.2 on the basis of the *y* coordinate closest to the line for each *x* coordinate: The appropriate *y* coordinates are 0, 0, 1, 1, 2, and 2. Bresenham's algorithm makes the same selections, based on the same criterion, by keeping a running record of the error of the line—that is, how far from the true line the current *y* coordinate is—at each *x* coordinate, as shown in Figure 12.3.

Fig. 12.2 *Drawing a line from (0,0) to (5,2). Only the endpoints fall squarely on a dot on the screen. All other points must be approximated by the drawing of nearby dots.*

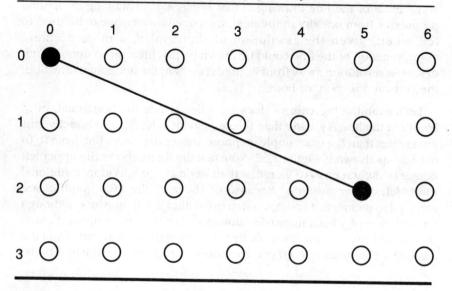

When the running error of the line indicates that the current y coordinate deviates from the true line to the extent that the adjacent y coordinate would be closer to the line, then the current y coordinate is changed to that adjacent y coordinate.

Let's take a moment to follow the steps Bresenham's algorithm would take in drawing the line in Figure 12.3. The initial dot is drawn at (0,0), the start point of the line. At this point, the error of the line is 0.

Since x is the major dimension, the next dot has an x coordinate of 1. The y coordinate of this dot will be either 0 (the last y coordinate) or 1 (the adjacent y coordinate in the direction of the end point of the line), depending on which is closer to the true line at this x coordinate. The running error at this point is B minus A. Since this amount is less than one-half (that is, less than halfway to the next y coordinate), the y coordinate does not change at $x = 1$; consequently, the second dot is drawn at (1,0).

The third dot has an x coordinate of 2. The running error at this point is C minus A, which is greater than one-half and therefore closer to the next y coordinate than to the current one. The third dot is drawn at (2,1), and 1 is subtracted from the running error to compensate for the

Fig. 12.3 *When drawing a line from (0,0) to (5,2), Bresenham's algorithm uses the error term to decide at which y coordinate the closest approximation to the line for each x coordinate lies.*

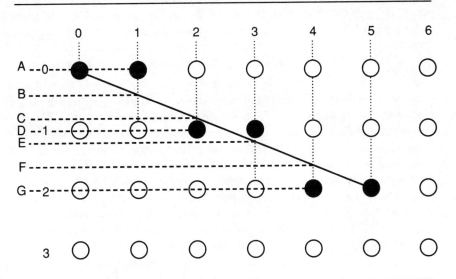

adjustment of one dot in the current y coordinate. The running error of the dot actually drawn at this point is C minus D.

The fourth dot has an x coordinate of 3. The running error at this point is E minus D; since this is less than one-half, the current y coordinate doesn't change, and the fourth dot is drawn at (3,1).

The fifth dot has an x coordinate of 4. The running error at this point is F minus D; since this is greater than one-half, the current y coordinate advances. The third dot is drawn at (4,2), and 1 is subtracted from the running error. The error of the dot drawn at this point is F minus G.

Finally, the sixth dot is the end point of the line. This dot has an x coordinate of 5. The running error at this point is G minus G, or 0, indicating that this point is squarely on the true line—as of course it should be, given that it's the end point—so the current y coordinate remains the same. The end point of the line is drawn at (5,2), and the line is complete.

Conceptually, that's really all there is to Bresenham's algorithm. The algorithm is a process of drawing a dot at each possible coordinate along the major dimension of the line, in each case at the closest possible coordinate along the minor dimension. The running error is used to keep track of when the coordinate along the minor dimension must change to remain as close as possible to the true line. Bresenham's algorithm is particularly fast because it allows the running error to be maintained without any divides, multiplies, or floating-point arithmetic, as you'll see in Listing 12.1.

While we've discussed line-drawing in only one of the octants (an octant is one-eighth of a circle or one-half of a quadrant), the above description of the case where x is the major dimension, y is the minor dimension, and both dimensions are greater than 0 can readily be generalized to all eight octants in which lines could be drawn—and we'll do just that in Listing 12.1.

Now, I realize full well that the above is nothing more than a seat-of-the-pants overview of Bresenham's line-drawing algorithm. Given the "working-code" orientation of *PJ* readers, I'm going the leave the explanation at that, especially since a full explanation would require many pages and a cryptic mathematical derivation. If you want or need a full mathematical treatment, refer to pages 433–436 of Foley and Van Dam's *Fundamentals of Interactive Computer Graphics* (see the references listed at the end of this chapter). This source provides the derivation of the integer-only, divide-free version of the algorithm as well as Pascal code for drawing lines in one of the eight possible octants.

Strengths and Weaknesses

The overwhelming strength of Bresenham's line-drawing algorithm is speed. With no divides, no floating-point operations, and no need for variables that won't fit in 16 bits, it is perfectly suited for IBM PCs and compatibles.

The weakness of Bresenham's algorithm is that it produces relatively low quality lines by comparison with most other line-drawing algorithms. In particular, lines generated with Bresenham's algorithm can tend to look somewhat jagged. On the PC, however, jagged lines are an inevitable consequence of relatively low resolution and a small color set; so, lines drawn with Bresenham's algorithm don't look all that much different from lines drawn in other ways. Besides, in most applications users are far more interested in the overall picture than in the primitive elements the picture is built from. As a general rule, any collection of dots that trend from point A to point B in a straight fashion is accepted by the eye as a line.

Bresenham's algorithm is successfully used by many current PC programs, and by the standard of this wide acceptance, the algorithm is certainly good enough. Then, too, users hate waiting for their computers to finish drawing. By any standard of drawing performance, Bresenham's algorithm excels.

A Turbo C Implementation of Bresenham's Algorithm

Listing 12.1 is a Turbo C implementation of Bresenham's line-drawing algorithm for modes 0Eh, 0Fh, 10h, and 12h of the EVGA, called as function **EVGALine**. Listing 12.2 [presented at the end of this chapter] is a sample program that demonstrates the use of **EVGALine**.

The **EVGALine** function itself performs four operations. **EVGALine** first sets up the EVGA's hardware so that all dots drawn will be in the desired colors. This is accomplished by setting two of the EVGA's registers: the Enable Set/Reset register and the Set/Reset register. Setting the Enable Set/Reset to the value 0Fh, as is done in **EVGALine**, causes all drawing to produce dots in the color contained in the Set/Reset register. Setting the Set/Reset register to the passed color, in conjunction with the Enable Set/Reset setting of 0Fh, causes all drawing done by **EVGALine** and the functions it calls to generate the passed color. In summary, setting up the Enable Set/Reset and Set/Reset registers in this way causes the remainder of **EVGALine** to draw a line in the specified color.

EVGALine next performs a simple check to cut in half the number of line orientations that must be handled separately. Figure 12.4 shows the eight possible line orientations among which a Bresenham's algorithm implementation must distinguish. (In interpreting Figure 12.4, assume that lines radiate outward from the center of the figure, falling into one of eight octants delineated by the horizontal and vertical axes and the two diagonals.) The need to identify these line orientations falls out of the nature of the algorithm; the orientations are distinguished by which coordinate forms the major axis and by whether x and y each increases or decreases from the line start to the line end.

A moment of thought will show, however, that four of the line orientations are redundant. Each of the four orientations for which *DeltaY*, the y component of the line, is less than 0 (that is, for which the line-start y coordinate is greater than the line-end y coordinate) can be transformed

Fig. 12.4 *The eight line orientations among which the implementation of Bresenham's algorithm must distinguish. Lines in the four upper octants are converted to equivalent lines in the four lower octants by a switching of the start and end coordinates. Lines start at the center of the figure and radiate outward.*

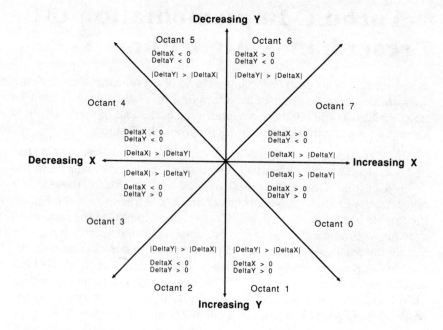

into one of the four orientations for which the line-start y coordinate is less than the line-end y coordinate simply by a reversal of the line-start and line-end coordinates, which causes the line to be drawn in the other direction. **EVGALine** does this by swapping $(x0, y0)$ (the line-start coordinates) with $(x1, y1)$ (the line-end coordinates) whenever $y0$ is greater than $y1$.

With this accomplished, **EVGALine** must still distinguish among the four remaining line orientations. Those four orientations form two major categories: orientations for which the x dimension is the major axis of the line and orientations for which the y dimension is the major axis. As shown in Figure 12.4, octant 1 (where x increases from start to finish) and octant 2 (where x decreases from start to finish) fall into the latter category and differ in only one respect: the direction in which the x coordinate moves when it changes. Handling of the running error of the line is exactly the same value for both cases—as one would expect, given the symmetry of lines differing only in the sign of *DeltaX*, the x coordinate of the line. Consequently, for those cases where *DeltaX* is less than zero, the direction of x movement is made negative, and the absolute value of *DeltaX* is used for error-term calculations.

Similarly, octants 0 (where x increases from start to finish) and 3 (where x decreases from start to finish) differ only in the direction in which the x coordinate moves when it changes. The difference between line drawing in octants 0 and 3 and line drawing in octants 1 and 2 is that in octants 0 and 3, since x is the major axis, the x coordinate changes on every dot of the line and the y coordinate changes only when the running error of the line dictates. In octants 1 and 2, the y coordinate changes on every dot and the x coordinate changes only when the running error dictates, since y is the major axis.

There is one line-drawing function for octants 0 and 3—**Octant0**—and one line-drawing function for octants 1 and 2—**Octant1**. A single function with **if** statements could certainly be used to handle all four octants, but at a significant performance cost. There is, on the other hand, very little performance cost to grouping octants 0 and 3 together and octants 1 and 2 together, since the two octants in each pair differ only in the direction of change of the x coordinate.

EVGALine determines which line-drawing function to call and with what value for the direction of change of the x coordinate on the basis of two criteria: whether *DeltaX* is negative or not and whether the absolute value of *DeltaX* ($|DeltaX|$) is less than *DeltaY* or not, as shown in Figure 12.5. Recall that the value of *DeltaY*, and hence the direction of change of the y coordinate, is guaranteed to be nonnegative as a result of the earlier elimination of four of the line orientations.

After calling the appropriate function to draw the line (more on those functions shortly), **EVGALine** restores the state of the Enable Set/Reset register to its default of 0. In this state, the Set/Reset register has no effect, and so it is not necessary to restore the state of the Set/Reset register as well. **EVGALine** also restores the state of the Bit Mask register (which, as we will see, is modified by **EVGADot**, the dot-drawing routine actually used to draw each dot of the lines produced by **EVGALine**) to its default of 0FFh. While it would be more modular to have **EVGADot** restore the state of the Bit Mask register after drawing each dot, it would also be considerably slower to do so. The same could be said of having **EVGADot** set the Enable Set/Reset and Set/Reset registers for each dot: While modularity would improve, speed would suffer markedly.

Drawing Each Line

The **Octant0** and **Octant1** functions draw lines for which | *DeltaX*| is greater than *DeltaY* and lines for which | *DeltaX*| is less than or equal to *DeltaY*, respectively. The parameters to **Octant0** and **Octant1** are the starting point of the line, the length of the line in each dimension, and *XDirection*, the amount by which the *x* coordinate should be changed when it moves. *XDirection* must be either 1 (to draw toward the right edge of the screen) or -1 (to draw toward the left edge of the screen). No value is required for the amount by which the *y* coordinate should be changed: Since *DeltaY* is guaranteed to be positive, the *y* coordinate always changes by 1 dot.

Octant0 draws lines for which | *DeltaX*| is greater than *DeltaY*. For such lines, the *x* coordinate of each dot drawn differs from the previous dot by either 1 or -1, depending on the value of *XDirection*. (This makes it possible for **Octant0** to draw lines in both octant 0 and octant 3.) Whenever *ErrorTerm* becomes nonnegative, indicating that the next *y* coordinate is a better approximation of the line being drawn, the *y* coordinate is increased by one.

Octant1 draws lines for which | *DeltaX*| is less than or equal to *DeltaY*. For these lines, the *y* coordinate of each dot drawn is one greater than the *y* coordinate of the previous dot. Whenever *ErrorTerm* becomes nonnegative, indicating that the next *x* coordinate is a better approximation of the line being drawn, the *x* coordinate is advanced by either 1 or -1, depending on the value of *XDirection*. (This makes it possible for **Octant1** to draw lines in both octant 1 and octant 2.)

Drawing Each Dot

At the core of **Octant0** and **Octant1** is a dot-drawing function, **EVGADot**. This function draws a dot at the specified coordinates in whatever color the hardware of the EVGA happens to be set up for. As described earlier, since the entire line drawn by **EVGALine** is of the same color, line-drawing performance is improved by setting the EVGA's hardware up once in **EVGALine** before the line is drawn and then drawing all the dots in the line in the same color via **EVGADot**.

EVGADot makes certain assumptions about the screen. First, it assumes that the address of the byte controlling the dots at the start of a given row on the screen is 80 bytes after the start of the row immediately above it; in other words, this implementation of **EVGADot** works only for screens configured to be 80 bytes wide. Since this is the standard configuration of all the modes **EVGALine** is designed to work in, the assumption of 80 bytes per row should be no problem. If it is a problem, however, **EVGADot** could easily be modified to retrieve the BIOS integer variable at address 0040:004A, which contains the number of bytes per row for the current video mode.

Second, **EVGADot** assumes that screen memory is organized as a linear bit map starting at address A000:0000, with the dot at the upper left of the screen controlled by bit 7 of the byte at offset 0, the next dot to the right controlled by bit 6, the ninth dot controlled by bit 7 of the byte at offset 1, and so on. Further, it assumes that the graphics adapter's hardware is configured so that setting the Bit Mask register to allow modification of only the bit controlling the dot of interest and then ORing a value of 0FFh with display memory will draw that dot correctly without affecting any other dots. Again, this is the normal way in which modes 0Eh, 0Fh, 10h, and 12h operate. **EVGADot** also assumes that the EVGA is set up so that each dot will be drawn in the correct color, as described earlier.

Given those assumptions, **EVGADot** becomes a surprisingly simple function. First, **EVGADot** builds a far pointer that points to the byte of display memory controlling the dot to be drawn. Second, a mask is generated consisting of 0s for all bits except the bit controlling the dot to be drawn. Third, the Bit Mask register is set to that mask so that when display memory is read and then written, all bits except the one that controls the dot to be drawn will be left unmodified.

Finally, 0FFh is ORed with the display-memory byte controlling the dot to be drawn. ORing with 0FFh first reads display memory, thereby loading the EVGA's internal latches with the contents of the display-memory byte controlling the dot to be drawn, and then writes display memory with the value 0FFh. Because of the unusual way in which the EVGA's data paths work and the way in which **EVGALine** sets up the EVGA's Enable Set/Reset and Set/Reset registers, the value of 0FFh that is written by the program is ignored. Instead, the value that actually gets placed in display memory is the color that was passed to **EVGALine** and placed in the Set/Reset register. The Bit Mask register (set as described above) allows only the single bit controlling the dot to be drawn to be set to this color value.

The result of all this is simply a single dot drawn in the color set up in **EVGALine**. **EVGADot** may seems excessively complex for a function that does nothing more that draw one dot, but programming the EVGA isn't trivial (as we've seen over the course of many installments of "On Graphics"). Besides, while the explanation of **EVGADot** is lengthy, the code itself is only five lines long.

Line drawing would be somewhat faster if the code of **EVGADot** were made an in-line part of **Octant0** and **Octant1**, thereby saving the overhead of preparing parameters and calling the function. Feel free to

Fig. 12.5 *How **EVGALine** determines which line-drawing function to call and with what direction of change for the x coordinate. Lines start at the center of the figure and radiate outward.*

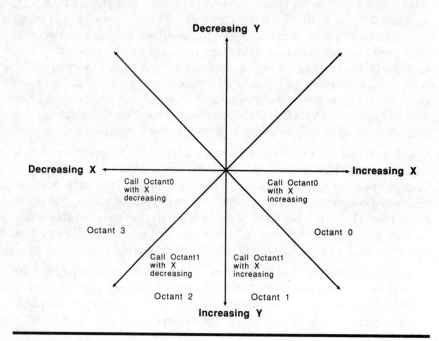

do this if you wish. I maintained **EVGADot** as a separate function for clarity and for ease of inserting a dot-drawing function for a different graphics adapter, should that be desired. If you do install a dot-drawing function for a different adapter, remember to remove the EVGA-specific **outportb** lines in **EVGALine** itself.

Comments on the Turbo C Implementation

EVGALine does no error checking whatsoever. My assumption in writing **EVGALine** was that it would ultimately be used as the lowest-level primitive of a graphics software package, with operations such as error checking and clipping performed at a higher level. Similarly, **EVGALine** is tied to the EVGA's screen-coordinate system of (0,0) to (639,199) (in mode 0Eh), (0,0) to (639,349) (in modes 0Fh and 10h), or (0,0) to (639,479) (in mode 12h), with the upper left corner considered to be (0,0). Again, transformation from any coordinate system to the coordinate system used by **EVGALine** can be performed at a higher level. **EVGALine** is specifically designed to do one thing: draw lines into the display memory of the EVGA. Additional operations can be supplied by the code that calls **EVGALine**.

The version of **EVGALine** shown in Listing 12.1 is reasonably fast, but not so fast as it might be. Inclusion of **EVGADot** directly in **Octant0** and **Octant1** and, indeed, inclusion of **Octant0** and **Octant1** directly in **EVGALine** would speed execution by saving the overhead of calling and parameter passing. Handpicked register variables might speed performance as well, as would the use of word OUTs (**outport**) rather than byte OUTs (**outportb**). A more significant performance increase would come from eliminating separate calculation of the address and mask for each dot. Since the location of each dot relative to the previous dot is known, the address and mask could be adjusted from one dot to the next rather than recalculated from scratch.

These enhancements are not incorporated into the code in Listing 12.1, for a couple of reasons. One reason is that it's important that the workings of the algorithm be clearly visible in the code for learning purposes; once the implementation is understood, rewriting it for improved performance would certainly be a worthwhile exercise. Another reason is that when flat-out speed is needed, assembly language is the best way to go; why produce hard-to-understand C code to boost speed a bit when assembly language code can perform the same task at two or more times the speed?

A high-speed assembly language version of **EVGALine** would seem to be a logical next step.

An Assembly Language Implementation of Bresenham's Algorithm

Listing 12.3 is a high-performance implementation of Bresenham's algorithm, written entirely in assembly language. The code is callable from Turbo C just like Listing 12.1—with the same name (**EVGALine**) and with the same parameters. Either of the two can be linked to any program that calls **EVGALine**, since they appear to be identical to the calling program. The only difference between the two versions is that the sample program in Listing 12.2 runs over six times as fast on a PC when calling the assembly language version of **EVGALine** as when calling the Turbo C version and over four times as fast on an AT. Link each version with Listing 12.2 and compare performance—the difference is startling.

An explanation of the workings of the code in Listing 12.3 would be a lengthy one and would be redundant: The basic operation of the code is no different from that of the code in Listing 12.1, although the implementation is much changed, owing to the nature of assembly language and to its being designed for speed rather than clarity. Given that you thoroughly understand the C implementation in Listing 12.1, the assembler implementation in Listing 12.3, being well commented, should speak for itself.

Listing 12.3 incorporates a clever notion for which credit is due to Jim Mackraz, who described the notion in a letter written in response to an article I wrote in *PJ*. Jim's suggestion was that when drawing lines for which | *DeltaX* | is greater than | *DeltaY* |, bits set to 1 for each of the dots controlled by a given byte can be accumulated in a register. Rather than each dot being drawn individually, all the dots controlled by that byte can be drawn at once, with a single access to display memory, when all dot processing associated with that byte has been completed. This approach can save many display-memory reads and writes when drawing nearly horizontal lines, and that's important, since EGAs and VGAs hold the CPU up for a considerable time on each display-memory access.

Conclusion

All too many PC programmers fall into the high-level-language trap of thinking that a good algorithm guarantees good performance. Not so. As our two implementations of Bresenham's algorithm graphically illustrate (pun not originally intended but allowed to stand once recognized), truly good PC code requires both a good algorithm *and* a good assembly language implementation. In Listing 12.3, we've got both—and my, oh my, isn't it fun?

There are several other matters I'd like to attend to, but I've long since overrun my allotted space. In particular, much as I want to get to John Bridges' mode-set code for the 360-by-480 256-color mode of the VGA, it'll just have to wait. Let me know if there's anything else you'd like to see covered, and I'll try to get to it.

See you next time.

References

Foley, J. D., and Van Dam, A. *Fundamentals of Interactive Computer Graphics.* Reading, Massachusetts: Addison-Wesley, 1982.

Newman, W. M., and Sproull, R. F. *Principles of Interactive Computer Graphics.* New York: McGraw-Hill, 1979.

Listing 12.1

```
/* Turbo C implementation of Bresenham's line-drawing algorithm
 * for the EGA and VGA. Works in modes 0xE, 0xF, 0x10, and 0x12.
 *
 * Compiled with Turbo C 2.0.
 *
 * By Michael Abrash.   2/4/89.
 */
#include <dos.h>        /* contains MK_FP macro */

#define EVGA_SCREEN_WIDTH_IN_BYTES      80
                                        /* memory offset from start of
                                           one row to start of next */
#define EVGA_SCREEN_SEGMENT             0xA000
                                        /* display-memory segment */
#define GC_INDEX                        0x3CE
                                        /* Graphics Controller
                                           Index register port */
#define GC_DATA                         0x3CF
```

Listing 12.1 continues

Listing 12.1 continued

```
                                   /* Graphics Controller
                                      Data register port */
#define SET_RESET_INDEX          0  /* indexes of needed */
#define ENABLE_SET_RESET_INDEX   1  /* Graphics Controller */
#define BIT_MASK_INDEX           8  /* registers */

/*
 * Draws a dot at (X0,Y0) in whatever color the EGA/VGA hardware is
 * set up for. Leaves the bit mask set to whatever value the
 * dot required.
 */
void EVGADot(X0, Y0)
unsigned int X0;      /* coordinates at which to draw dot, with */
unsigned int Y0;      /* (0,0) at the upper left of the screen */
{
    unsigned char far *PixelBytePtr;
    unsigned char PixelMask;

    /* Calculate the offset in the screen segment of the byte in
       which the pixel lies */
    PixelBytePtr = MK_FP(EVGA_SCREEN_SEGMENT,
        ( Y0 * EVGA_SCREEN_WIDTH_IN_BYTES ) + ( X0 / 8 ));

    /* Generate a mask with a 1 bit in the pixel's position within the
       screen byte */
    PixelMask = 0x80 >> ( X0 & 0x07 );

    /* Set up the Graphics Controller's Bit Mask register to allow
       only the bit corresponding to the pixel being drawn to
       be modified */
    outportb(GC_INDEX, BIT_MASK_INDEX);
    outportb(GC_DATA, PixelMask);

    /* Draw the pixel. Because of the operation of the set/reset
       feature of the EGA/VGA, the value written doesn't matter.
       The screen byte is ORed in order to perform a read to latch the
       display memory, then perform a write in order to modify it. */
    *PixelBytePtr |= 0xFF;
}


/*
 * Draws a line in octant 0 or 3 ( |DeltaX| >= DeltaY ).
 * |DeltaX|+1 points are drawn.
 */
void Octant0(X0, Y0, DeltaX, DeltaY, XDirection)
unsigned int X0, Y0;            /* coordinates of start of the line */
unsigned int DeltaX, DeltaY;    /* length of the line */
int XDirection;                 /* 1 if line is drawn left to right,
                                     -1 if drawn right to left */
{
    int DeltaYx2;
    int DeltaYx2MinusDeltaXx2;
    int ErrorTerm;

    /* Set up initial error term and values used inside drawing loop */
    DeltaYx2 = DeltaY * 2;
    DeltaYx2MinusDeltaXx2 = DeltaYx2 - (int) ( DeltaX * 2 );
    ErrorTerm = DeltaYx2 - (int) DeltaX;
```

Listing 12.1 continues

Listing 12.1 *continued*

```
    /* Draw the line */
    EVGADot(X0, Y0);                    /* draw the first pixel */
    while ( DeltaX-- ) {
        /* See if it's time to advance the Y coordinate */
        if ( ErrorTerm >= 0 ) {
            /* Advance the Y coordinate & adjust the error term
               back down */
            Y0++;
            ErrorTerm += DeltaYx2MinusDeltaXx2;
        } else {
            /* Add to the error term */
            ErrorTerm += DeltaYx2;
        }
        X0 += XDirection;               /* advance the X coordinate */
        EVGADot(X0, Y0);                /* draw a pixel */
    }
}

/*
 * Draws a line in octant 1 or 2 ( |DeltaX| < DeltaY ).
 * |DeltaY|+1 points are drawn.
 */
void Octant1(X0, Y0, DeltaX, DeltaY, XDirection)
unsigned int X0, Y0;            /* coordinates of start of the line */
unsigned int DeltaX, DeltaY;    /* length of the line */
int XDirection;                 /* 1 if line is drawn left to right,
                                   -1 if drawn right to left */

{
    int DeltaXx2;
    int DeltaXx2MinusDeltaYx2;
    int ErrorTerm;

    /* Set up initial error term and values used inside drawing loop */
    DeltaXx2 = DeltaX * 2;
    DeltaXx2MinusDeltaYx2 = DeltaXx2 - (int) ( DeltaY * 2 );
    ErrorTerm = DeltaXx2 - (int) DeltaY;

    EVGADot(X0, Y0);                    /* draw the first pixel */
    while ( DeltaY-- ) {
        /* See if it's time to advance the X coordinate */
        if ( ErrorTerm >= 0 ) {
            /* Advance the X coordinate & adjust the error term
               back down */
            X0 += XDirection;
            ErrorTerm += DeltaXx2MinusDeltaYx2;
        } else {
            /* Add to the error term */
            ErrorTerm += DeltaXx2;
        }
        Y0++;                           /* advance the Y coordinate */
        EVGADot(X0, Y0);                /* draw a pixel */
    }
}

/*
 * Draws a line on the EGA or VGA.
 */
```

Listing 12.1 *continues*

Listing 12.1 continued

```
void EVGALine(X0, Y0, X1, Y1, Color)
int X0, Y0;     /* coordinates of one end of the line */
int X1, Y1;     /* coordinates of the other end of the line */
char Color;     /* color to draw line in */
{
    int DeltaX, DeltaY;
    int Temp;

    /* Set the drawing color */

    /* Put the drawing color in the Set/Reset register */
    outportb(GC_INDEX, SET_RESET_INDEX);
    outportb(GC_DATA, Color);
    /* Cause all planes to be forced to the Set/Reset color */
    outportb(GC_INDEX, ENABLE_SET_RESET_INDEX);
    outportb(GC_DATA, 0xF);

    /* Save half the line-drawing cases by swapping Y0 with Y1
       and X0 with X1 if Y0 is greater than Y1. As a result, DeltaY
       is always > 0, and only the octant 0-3 cases need to be
       handled. */
    if ( Y0 > Y1 ) {
        Temp = Y0;
        Y0 = Y1;
        Y1 = Temp;
        Temp = X0;
        X0 = X1;
        X1 = Temp;
    }

    /* Handle as four separate cases, for the four octants in which
       Y1 is greater than Y0 */
    DeltaX = X1 - X0;     /* calculate the length of the line
                             in each coordinate */
    DeltaY = Y1 - Y0;
    if ( DeltaX > 0 ) {
        if ( DeltaX > DeltaY ) {
            Octant0(X0, Y0, DeltaX, DeltaY, 1);
        } else {
            Octant1(X0, Y0, DeltaX, DeltaY, 1);
        }
    } else {
        DeltaX = -DeltaX;                /* absolute value of DeltaX */
        if ( DeltaX > DeltaY ) {
            Octant0(X0, Y0, DeltaX, DeltaY, -1);
        } else {
            Octant1(X0, Y0, DeltaX, DeltaY, -1);
        }
    }

    /* Return the state of the EGA/VGA to normal */
    outportb(GC_INDEX, ENABLE_SET_RESET_INDEX);
    outportb(GC_DATA, 0);
    outportb(GC_INDEX, BIT_MASK_INDEX);
    outportb(GC_DATA, 0xFF);
}
```

Listing 12.2

```
/* Sample program to illustrate EGA/VGA line-drawing routines.
 *
 * Must be linked with Listing 12.1 with a command line like:
 *
 *     tcc lst12-2 lst12-1.asm
 *
 * Compiled with Turbo C 2.0.
 *
 * By Michael Abrash.   2/4/89.
 * Updated 6/30/89.
 */
#include <dos.h>       /* contains geninterrupt */

#define GRAPHICS_MODE   0x10
#define TEXT_MODE       0x03
#define BIOS_VIDEO_INT  0x10
#define X_MAX           640     /* working screen width */
#define Y_MAX           348     /* working screen height */

extern void EVGALine();

/*
 * Subroutine to draw a rectangle full of vectors, of the specified
 * length and color, around the specified rectangle center.
 */
void VectorsUp(XCenter, YCenter, XLength, YLength, Color)
int XCenter, YCenter;     /* center of rectangle to fill */
int XLength, YLength;     /* distance from center to edge
                             of rectangle */
int Color;                /* color to draw lines in */
{
    int WorkingX, WorkingY;

    /* Lines from center to top of rectangle */
    WorkingX = XCenter - XLength;
    WorkingY = YCenter - YLength;
    for ( ; WorkingX < ( XCenter + XLength ); WorkingX++ )
       EVGALine(XCenter, YCenter, WorkingX, WorkingY, Color);

    /* Lines from center to right of rectangle */
    WorkingX = XCenter + XLength - 1;
    WorkingY = YCenter - YLength;
    for ( ; WorkingY < ( YCenter + YLength ); WorkingY++ )
       EVGALine(XCenter, YCenter, WorkingX, WorkingY, Color);

    /* Lines from center to bottom of rectangle */
    WorkingX = XCenter + XLength - 1;
    WorkingY = YCenter + YLength - 1;
    for ( ; WorkingX >= ( XCenter - XLength ); WorkingX-- )
       EVGALine(XCenter, YCenter, WorkingX, WorkingY, Color);

    /* Lines from center to left of rectangle */
    WorkingX = XCenter - XLength;
    WorkingY = YCenter + YLength - 1;
    for ( ; WorkingY >= ( YCenter - YLength ); WorkingY-- )
       EVGALine(XCenter, YCenter, WorkingX, WorkingY, Color );
}
```

Listing 12.2 continues

Listing 12.2 *continued*

```c
/*
 * Sample program to draw four rectangles full of lines.
 */
int main()
{
   char temp;

   /* Set graphics mode */
   _AX = GRAPHICS_MODE;
   geninterrupt(BIOS_VIDEO_INT);

   /* Draw each of four rectangles full of vectors */
   VectorsUp(X_MAX / 4, Y_MAX / 4, X_MAX / 4,
      Y_MAX / 4, 1);
   VectorsUp(X_MAX * 3 / 4, Y_MAX / 4, X_MAX / 4,
      Y_MAX / 4, 2);
   VectorsUp(X_MAX / 4, Y_MAX * 3 / 4, X_MAX / 4,
      Y_MAX / 4, 3);
   VectorsUp(X_MAX * 3 / 4, Y_MAX * 3 / 4, X_MAX / 4,
      Y_MAX / 4, 4);

   /* Wait for the enter key to be pressed */
   scanf("%c", &temp);

   /* Back to text mode */
   _AX = TEXT_MODE;
   geninterrupt(BIOS_VIDEO_INT);
}
```

Listing 12.3

```asm
; Fast assembler implementation of Bresenham's line-drawing algorithm
; for the EGA and VGA. Works in modes 0Dh, 0Eh, 0Fh, 10h, and 12h.
; Turbo C version 2.0 near-callable.
; Bit mask accumulation technique when |DeltaX| >= |DeltaY|
;  suggested by Jim Mackraz.
;
; Assemble and link with the program of Listing 12.2 with a command
; line like:
;
;        tcc lst12-2 lst12-3.asm
;
; (requires Turbo C and either TASM or MASM).
;
; Assembled with TASM 1.0.
;
; By Michael Abrash.  2/4/89.
; Updated 6/29/89.
;
;******************************************************************
; C-compatible line-drawing entry point at _EVGALine.             *
; Called from Turbo C with:                                       *
;        EVGALine(X0, Y0, X1, Y1, Color);                         *
;******************************************************************
```

Listing 12.3 *continues*

Listing 12.3 *continued*

```
;

_TEXT    segment byte public 'CODE'
         assume cs: _TEXT


;
; Equates.
;
EVGA_SCREEN_WIDTH_IN_BYTES equ  80        ;memory offset from start of
                                          ; one row to start of next
                                          ; in display memory
EVGA_SCREEN_SEGMENT        equ  0a000h    ;display-memory segment
GC_INDEX                   equ  3ceh      ;Graphics Controller
                                          ; Index register port

SET_RESET_INDEX            equ  0         ;indexes of needed
ENABLE_SET_RESET_INDEX     equ  1         ; Graphics Controller
BIT_MASK_INDEX             equ  8         ; registers


;
; Stack frame.
;
EVGALineParms    struc
         dw      ?                        ;pushed BP
         dw      ?                        ;pushed return address (make double
                                          ; word for far call)
X0       dw      ?                        ;starting X coordinate of line
Y0       dw      ?                        ;starting Y coordinate of line
X1       dw      ?                        ;ending X coordinate of line
Y1       dw      ?                        ;ending Y coordinate of line
Color    db      ?                        ;color of line
         db      ?                        ;dummy to pad to word size
EVGALineParms    ends

;****************************************************************
; Line-drawing macros.                                         *
;****************************************************************


;
; Macro to loop through length of line, drawing each pixel in turn.
; Used for case of |DeltaX| >= |DeltaY|.
; |DeltaX|+1 points are drawn.
;
; Input:
;        MOVE_LEFT: 1 if DeltaX < 0, 0 else
;        AL: pixel mask for initial pixel
;        BX: |DeltaX| (X distance between start and end points)
;        DX: address of GC data register, with index register set to
;                  index of Bit Mask register
;        SI: DeltaY (Y distance between start and end points)
;        ES:DI: display-memory address of byte containing initial
;                  pixel
;
; Output: none
;
LINE1    macro   MOVE_LEFT
         local   LineLoop, MoveXCoord, NextPixel, Line1End
         local   MoveToNextByte, ResetBitMaskAccumulator
         mov     cx,bx   ;# of pixels in line
```

Listing 12.3 *continues*

Listing 12.3 *continued*

```
        jcxz    Line1End ;done if there are no more pixels
                         ; (there's always at least the one pixel
                         ; at the start location)
        shl     si,1     ;DeltaY * 2
        mov     bp,si    ;error term
        sub     bp,bx    ;error term starts at DeltaY * 2 - DeltaX
        shl     bx,1     ;DeltaX * 2
        sub     si,bx    ;DeltaY * 2 - DeltaX * 2 (used in loop)
        add     bx,si    ;DeltaY * 2 (used in loop)
        mov     ah,al    ;set aside pixel mask for initial pixel
                         ; with AL (the pixel mask accumulator) set
                         ; for the initial pixel
LineLoop:
;
; See if it's time to advance the Y coordinate yet.
;
        and     bp,bp           ;see if error term is negative
        js      MoveXCoord      ;yes, stay at the same Y coordinate
;
; Advance the Y coordinate, first writing all pixels in the current
; byte, then move the pixel mask either left or right, depending
; on MOVE_LEFT.
;
        out     dx,al    ;set up bit mask for pixels in this byte
        xchg    byte ptr [di],al
                         ;load latches and write pixels, with bit mask
                         ; preserving other latched bits. Because
                         ; set/reset is enabled for all planes, the
                         ; value written actually doesn't matter
        add     di,EVGA_SCREEN_WIDTH_IN_BYTES   ;increment Y coordinate
        add     bp,si    ;adjust error term back down
;
; Move pixel mask one pixel (either right or left, depending
; on MOVE_LEFT), adjusting display-memory address when pixel mask wraps.
;
if MOVE_LEFT
        rol     ah,1     ;move pixel mask 1 pixel to the left
else
        ror     ah,1     ;move pixel mask 1 pixel to the right
endif
        jnc     ResetBitMaskAccumulator ;didn't wrap to next byte
        jmp     short MoveToNextByte     ;did wrap to next byte
;
; Move pixel mask one pixel (either right or left, depending
; on MOVE_LEFT), adjusting display-memory address and writing pixels
; in this byte when pixel mask wraps.
;
MoveXCoord:
        add     bp,bx    ;increment error term & keep same Y coordinate
if MOVE_LEFT
        rol     ah,1     ;move pixel mask 1 pixel to the left
else
        ror     ah,1     ;move pixel mask 1 pixel to the right
endif
        jnc     NextPixel ;if still in same byte, no need to
                          ; modify display memory yet
        out     dx,al    ;set up bit mask for pixels in this byte.
        xchg    byte ptr [di],al
```

Listing 12.3 continues

Listing 12.3 continued

```
                      ;load latches and write pixels, with bit mask
                      ; preserving other latched bits. Because
                      ; set/reset is enabled for all planes, the
                      ; value written actually doesn't matter
MoveToNextByte:
if MOVE_LEFT
        dec     di      ;next pixel is in byte to left
else
        inc     di      ;next pixel is in byte to right
endif
ResetBitMaskAccumulator:
        sub     al,al   ;reset pixel mask accumulator
NextPixel:
        or      al,ah   ;add the next pixel to the pixel mask
                      ; accumulator
        loop    LineLoop
;
; Write the pixels in the final byte.
;
Line1End:
        out     dx,al   ;set up bit mask for pixels in this byte.
        xchg    byte ptr [di],al
                      ;load latches and write pixels, with bit mask
                      ; preserving other latched bits. Because
                      ; set/reset is enabled for all planes, the
                      ; value written actually doesn't matter

        endm


;
; Macro to loop through length of line, drawing each pixel in turn.
; Used for case of DeltaX < DeltaY.
; |DeltaY|+1 points are drawn.
;
; Input:
;       MOVE_LEFT: 1 if DeltaX < 0, 0 else
;       AL: pixel mask for initial pixel
;       BX: |DeltaX| (X distance between start and end points)
;       DX: address of GC data register, with index register set to
;               index of Bit Mask register
;       SI: DeltaY (Y distance between start and end points)
;       ES:DI: display-memory address of byte containing initial
;               pixel
;
; Output: none
;
LINE2   macro   MOVE_LEFT
        local   LineLoop, MoveYCoord, ETermAction, Line2End
        mov     cx,si   ;# of pixels in line
        shl     bx,1    ;DeltaX * 2
        mov     bp,bx   ;error term
        sub     bp,si   ;error term starts at DeltaX * 2 - DeltaY
        shl     si,1    ;DeltaY * 2
        sub     bx,si   ;DeltaX * 2 - DeltaY * 2 (used in loop)
        add     si,bx   ;DeltaX * 2 (used in loop)
;
; Set up initial bit mask & draw initial pixel.
;
        out     dx,al
```

Listing 12.3 continues

Listing 12.3 *continued*

```
        xchg    byte ptr [di],ah
                        ;load latches and write pixel, with bit mask
                        ; preserving other latched bits. Because
                        ; set/reset is enabled for all planes, the
                        ; value written actually doesn't matter
        jcxz    Line2End ;done if there are no more pixels
                        ; (there's always at least the one pixel
                        ; at the start location)
LineLoop:
;
; See if it's time to advance the X coordinate yet.
;
        and     bp,bp           ;see if error term is negative
        jns     ETermAction     ;no, advance X coordinate
        add     bp,si           ;increment error term & keep same
        jmp     short MoveYCoord ; X coordinate
ETermAction:
;
; Move pixel mask one pixel (either right or left, depending
; on MOVE_LEFT), adjusting display-memory address when pixel mask wraps.
;
if MOVE_LEFT
        rol     al,1
        sbb     di,0
else
        ror     al,1
        adc     di,0
endif
        out     dx,al   ;set new bit mask
        add     bp,bx   ;adjust error term back down
;
; Advance Y coordinate.
;
MoveYCoord:
        add     di,EVGA_SCREEN_WIDTH_IN_BYTES
;
; Write the next pixel.
;
        xchg    byte ptr [di],ah
                        ;load latches and write pixel, with bit mask
                        ; preserving other latched bits. Because
                        ; set/reset is enabled for all planes, the
                        ; value written actually doesn't matter
;
        loop    LineLoop
Line2End:
        endm

;****************************************************************
; Line-drawing routine.                                         *
;****************************************************************

        public  _EVGALine
_EVGALine       proc    near
        push    bp
        mov     bp,sp
        push    si      ;preserve register variables
        push    di
```

Listing 12.3 *continues*

Listing 12.3 continued

```
        push    ds
;
; Point DS to display memory.
;
        mov     ax,EVGA_SCREEN_SEGMENT
        mov     ds,ax
;
; Set the Set/Reset and Set/Reset Enable registers for
; the selected color.
;
        mov     dx,GC_INDEX
        mov     al,SET_RESET_INDEX
        out     dx,al
        inc     dx
        mov     al,[bp+Color]
        out     dx,al
        dec     dx
        mov     al,ENABLE_SET_RESET_INDEX
        out     dx,al
        inc     dx
        mov     al,0ffh
        out     dx,al
;
; Get DeltaY.
;
        mov     si,[bp+Y1]      ;line Y start
        mov     ax,[bp+Y0]      ;line Y end, used later in
                                ;calculating the start address
        sub     si,ax           ;calculate DeltaY
        jns     CalcStartAddress ;if positive, we're set
;
; DeltaY is negative -- swap coordinates so we're always working
; with a positive DeltaY.
;
        mov     ax,[bp+Y1]      ;set line start to Y1, for use
                                ; in calculating the start address
        mov     dx,[bp+X0]
        xchg    dx,[bp+X1]
        mov     [bp+X0],dx      ;swap X coordinates
        neg     si              ;convert to positive DeltaY
;
; Calculate the starting address in display memory of the line.
; Hardwired for a screen width of 80 bytes.
;
CalcStartAddress:
        shl     ax,1    ;Y0 * 2 ;Y0 is already in AX
        shl     ax,1    ;Y0 * 4
        shl     ax,1    ;Y0 * 8
        shl     ax,1    ;Y0 * 16
        mov     di,ax
        shl     ax,1    ;Y0 * 32
        shl     ax,1    ;Y0 * 64
        add     di,ax   ;Y0 * 80
        mov     dx,[bp+X0]
        mov     cl,dl   ;set aside lower 3 bits of column for
        and     cl,7    ; pixel masking
        shr     dx,1
        shr     dx,1
```

Listing 12.3 continues

Listing 12.3 continued

```
        shr     dx,1    ;get byte address of column (X0/8)
        add     di,dx   ;offset of line start in display segment
;
; Set up GC Index register to point to the Bit Mask register.
;
        mov     dx,GC_INDEX
        mov     al,BIT_MASK_INDEX
        out     dx,al
        inc     dx      ;leave DX pointing to the GC Data register
;
; Set up pixel mask (in-byte pixel address).
;
        mov     al,80h
        shr     al,cl
;
; Calculate DeltaX.
;
        mov     bx,[bp+X1]
        sub     bx,[bp+X0]
;
; Handle correct one of four octants.
;
        js      NegDeltaX
        cmp     bx,si
        jb      Octant1
;
; DeltaX >= DeltaY >= 0.
;
        LINE1   0
        jmp     EVGALineDone
;
; DeltaY > DeltaX >= 0.
;
Octant1:
        LINE2   0
        jmp     short EVGALineDone
;
NegDeltaX:
        neg     bx      ;|DeltaX|
        cmp     bx,si
        jb      Octant2
;
; |DeltaX| >= DeltaY and DeltaX < 0.
;
        LINE1   1
        jmp     short EVGALineDone
;
; |DeltaX| < DeltaY and DeltaX < 0.
;
Octant2:
        LINE2   1
;
EVGALineDone:
;
; Restore EVGA state.
;
        mov     al,0ffh
        out     dx,al   ;set Bit Mask register to 0ffh
```

Listing 12.3 continues

Listing 12.3 *continued*

```
        dec     dx
        mov     al,ENABLE_SET_RESET_INDEX
        out     dx,al
        inc     dx
        sub     al,al
        out     dx,al    ;set Enable Set/Reset register to 0
;
        pop     ds
        pop     di
        pop     si
        pop     bp
        ret
_EVGALine       endp

_TEXT   ends
        end
```

CHAPTER 13

Still-Higher 256-Color VGA Resolutions

The eagle-eyed among you may notice that this chapter is installment number 14, while the last was installment number 12. Where the heck did installment number 13 go?

It's not that I'm superstitious; rather, installment 13 presented performance-timing software, and, because it was excerpted from another book of mine, it isn't reprinted here. Since graphics programming wasn't directly discussed in installment 13 (although performance and graphics are of course related), you're not missing out on anything about the EGA and VGA.

In this installment, which rounds out the book, we return to the topic of undocumented high-resolution 256-color modes, this time going all the way up to the maximum 256-color resolution, 360 by 480. After I presented 320-by-400 256-color mode in installment 10 and mentioned that there was a 360-by-480 256-color mode, there was quite a reader demand for information about that higher-resolution mode—I even got a letter from West Germany asking for a column on 360-by-480 programming!

Who am I to fight the tide? Personally, I still prefer the safer and more flexible 320-by-400 256-color mode, but "On Graphics" is a joint effort with the readers, who have spoken clearly. Besides, after spending the bulk of "On Graphics" thus far focusing on data paths and display memory, it's an interesting change to discuss monitor timings, an understanding of which is required for setting up 360-by-480 256-color mode.

This last chapter of the book should make you realize two things: First, you should realize how much you now understand about the VGA. The amount of knowledge required to merely comprehend 360-by-480 256-color mode is staggering, and you've learned a great deal more about the VGA's data paths that doesn't even show up in this chapter.

Second, you should realize how much more there is to learn about the VGA. In many ways, VGA programming is more difficult than any other sort of programming, especially when good performance is required. On the other hand, the rewards of VGA programming are many and immediate. Run the code that accompanies this article, and set your mind loose on what you might do with all that color and all those pixels. . . .

Gosh, isn't graphics programming *fun?*

Installment 14: In which we crank standard VGAs up to 360-by-480 256-color resolution, exceeding IBM's official 256-color resolution by a mere 170 percent, and also look at a way to pin down that ever-present bugbear of PC graphics programming—performance.

Several installments ago, we learned how to coax 320-by-400 256-color resolution out of a standard VGA. At the time, I noted that the VGA was actually capable of supporting 256-color resolutions as high as 360 by 480, but I didn't pursue the topic further, preferring to concentrate on the versatile and easy-to-set 320-by-400 256-color mode instead.

I got more feedback on that installment than on any other in a long time, illustrating once again that nothing fascinates graphics programmers like superior color–resolution combinations (especially undocumented ones). One particularly useful item came from John Bridges, who sent along a complete mode-set routine for 360-by-480 256-color mode, which he has placed into the public domain. John writes, "I also have a couple of freeware (free, but not public domain) utilities out there, including PICEM, which displays .PIC, .PCX, and .GIF images, not only in 360 by 480 by 256 but also in 640 by 350 by 256, 640 by 400 by 256, 640 by 480 by 256, and 800 by 600 by 256 on SuperVGAs. PICEM is in version 1.9b." (I've edited the quote slightly; John sent the information via MCI Mail, which tends to induce the dropping of certain parts of speech and punctuation.)

In this column, I'm going to combine that mode-set code with appropriately modified versions of the dot-plot code from the earlier 256-color installment and the line-drawing code from two installments back. Together, those routines will make a pretty nifty demo of the capabilities of 360-by-480 256-color mode.

I'll also look at Paradigm's Inside! Turbo C performance-analysis software. While that's not directly related to graphics, on the PC—with its limited processor power and bizarre graphics adapters—assembly, performance, and good graphics go hand in hand. Timing software like Inside! Turbo C, used regularly, can teach you more about creating good graphics programs than any number of books and articles. Why? Because every graphics program has unique performance characteristics, and only by measuring can you determine true performance.

In sum, we'll be exploring both higher 256-color resolution and ways to improve performance. That's a neat package, for we'll be approaching graphics from both ends: better appearance and better performance. Let's get started!

Extended 256-Color Modes

When last we left 256-color programming, we had found that the standard 256-color mode, mode 13h, which officially offers 320-by-200 resolution, actually displays 400, not 200, scan lines, with line doubling used to reduce the effective resolution to 320 by 200. By tweaking a few of the VGA's mode registers, we converted mode 13h to a true 320-by-400 256-color mode. As an added bonus, that 320-by-400 mode supports two graphics pages—a distinct improvement over the single graphics page supported by mode 13h. (However, we also learned how to get *four* graphics pages at 320-by-200 resolution, should that be needed.)

I particularly like 320-by-400 256-color mode for two reasons: It supports two-page graphics, which is very important for animation applications, and it doesn't require changing any of the monitor-timing characteristics of the VGA. The mode bits that we changed to produce 320-by-400 256-color mode are pretty much guaranteed to be the same from one VGA to another, but the monitor-oriented registers are less certain to be constant, especially for VGAs that provide special support for the extended capabilities of various multiscanning monitors.

All in all, those are good arguments for 320-by-400 256-color mode. However, the counter-argument seems compelling as well: Nothing beats higher resolution for producing striking graphics. Given that, and given that John Bridges was kind enough to make his mode-set code available, I'm going to look at 360-by-480 256-color mode next. However, bear in mind that the drawbacks of this mode are the flip side of the strengths of 320-by-400 256-color mode: only one graphics page, and the need to modify monitor-oriented registers. Also, this mode has a peculiar and unique aspect ratio, with 480 pixels vertically (as many as high-resolution mode 12h) and only 360 horizontally. That makes for fairly poor horizontal resolution and sometimes-jagged drawing. On the other hand, the resolution is better in both directions than in mode 13h, and mode 13h also has an odd aspect ratio; so, it seems a bit petty to complain.

The single graphics page isn't a drawback if you don't need page flipping, of course, and so there's not much to worry about there: If you need page flipping, don't use this mode. The direct setting of the monitor-oriented registers is another matter.

I don't know how likely this code is to produce problems with clone VGAs in general; however, I did find that I had to put a Video Seven VRAM VGA into "pure" mode—where it treats the VRAMs as DRAMs and exactly emulates a plain vanilla IBM VGA—before 360-by-480 256-color mode would work properly. Now, that particular problem was due to an inherent characteristic of VRAMs and shouldn't occur on Video Seven's Fastwrite adapter or any other VGA clone. Nonetheless, 360-by-480 256-color mode is a good deal different from any standard VGA mode, and while the code in this article runs perfectly well (in my experience), I can't guarantee its use on any particular VGA–monitor combination, unlike 320-by-400 256-color mode. Mind you, 360-by-480 256-color mode *should* work on all VGAs—there are just too many variables involved for me to be certain. Feedback from readers with broad 360-by-480 256-color experience is welcome.

The above notwithstanding, 360-by-480 256-color mode offers 64 times as many colors and nearly 3 times as many pixels as the original Color/Graphics Adapter color-graphics mode, making startlingly realistic effects possible. No mode of the VGA, documented or undocumented (at least none that I know of), offers a better combination of resolution and color—even 320-by-400 256-color mode has 26 percent fewer pixels. In other words, 360-by-480 256-color mode is worth considering. Let's have a look.

360-by-480 256-Color Mode

I'm going to start by showing you 360-by-480 256-color mode in action, after which we'll look at how it works. I suspect that once you see what this mode looks like, you'll be more than eager to learn how to use it.

Listing 13.1 [presented at the end of the chapter] contains three C-callable assembly language functions. As you'd expect, **Set360x480Mode** places the VGA into 360-by-480 256-color mode. **Draw360x480Dot** draws a pixel of the specified color at the specified location. Finally, **Read360x480Dot** returns the color of the pixel at the specified location. (This last function isn't actually used in the example program in this article, but it is included for completeness.)

Listing 13.2 [presented at the end of the chapter] contains a modification of the Turbo C line-drawing code I discussed back in chapter 12. The code has been altered to select 360-by-480 256-color mode and to cycle through all 256 colors that this mode supports, drawing each line in a different color.

The first thing you'll notice when you run this code is that the speed of 360-by-480 256-color mode is pretty good, especially considering that most of the program is implemented in C. In general, drawing in 360-by-480 256-color mode can sometimes actually be *faster* than in the 16-color modes, because the byte-per-pixel display-memory organization of 256-color mode eliminates the need to read display memory before writing to it to isolate individual pixels.

The second thing you'll notice is that exquisite shading effects are possible in 360-by-480 256-color mode; cone-shaped sections of lines blend into one another remarkably smoothly, even with the default palette. The VGA allows you to select your 256 colors from a palette of 256,000; so you could, if you wished, set up the colors to produce less detail but still-finer shading. (We'll get to reprogramming the palette someday—there's so much to do with the VGA!)

The one thing you may not notice right away is just how much detail is visible on the screen, because the blending of colors tends to obscure the superior resolution of this mode. Each of the four rectangles displayed measures 180 pixels horizontally by 240 vertically. Put another way, each *one* of those rectangles has two-thirds as many pixels as the entire mode-13h screen; in all, 360-by-480 256-color mode has 2.7 times as many pixels as mode 13h! As mentioned above, the resolution is unevenly distributed, with vertical resolution matching that of mode 12h but horizontal resolution barely exceeding that of mode 13h. But resolution is hot stuff, no matter how it's laid out, and 360-by-480 256-color mode has the highest 256-color resolution you're likely to see on a standard VGA.

Now that we've seen the wonders of which our new mode is capable, let's take the time to understand how it works.

How This 256-Color Mode Works

In discussing 360-by-480 256-color mode, I'm going to assume that you're familiar with the discussion of 320-by-400 256-color mode presented in Chapter 10; if not, read that chapter before continuing. The two modes have a great deal in common, but I don't want to bore faithful readers and use up this always-too-small space by repeating myself.

Three-hundred-sixty-by-four-hundred-eighty 256-color mode is essentially 320-by-400 256-color mode, but stretched in both dimensions. Let's look at the vertical stretching first, since that's the simpler of the two.

480 Scan Lines: A Little Slower

There's nothing particularly unusual about 480 scan lines—standard modes 11h and 12h support that vertical resolution. The number of scan lines has nothing to do with either the number of colors or the horizontal resolution; so, converting 320-by-400 256-color mode to 320-by-480 256-color mode is a simple matter of reprogramming the VGA's vertical control registers—which control the scan lines displayed, the vertical sync pulse, vertical blanking, and the total number of scan lines—to the 480-scan-line settings and setting the polarities of the horizontal and vertical sync pulses to tell the monitor to adjust to a 480-line screen.

Switching to 480 scan lines has the effect of slowing the screen-refresh rate. The VGA always displays at 70 Hz *except* in 480-scan-line modes; there, owing to the time required to scan the extra lines, the refresh rate slows to 60 Hz. (VGA monitors always scan at the same rate horizontally; that is, the distance across the screen covered by the electron beam in a given period of time is the same in all modes. Consequently, adding extra lines per frame requires extra time.) A rate of 60 Hz isn't *bad*—that's the only refresh rate the EGA supports—but it does tend to flicker a little more and so is a little harder on the eyes than 70 Hz.

360 Pixels Per Line: No Mean Feat

Converting from 320 to 360 pixels per scan line is more difficult than converting from 400 to 480 scan lines per screen. None of the VGA's graphics modes supports 360 pixels across the screen—or anything like it; the standard choices are 320 and 640 pixels across. However, the VGA *does* support the horizontal resolution we seek—360 pixels—in 40-column text mode, and a two-times multiple—720 pixels—in 80-column text mode.

Unfortunately, the register settings that select those horizontal text-mode resolutions aren't directly transferable to graphics mode. Text modes display nine dots (the width of one character) for each time information is fetched from display memory, while graphics modes display just eight dots per display-memory fetch. (Although it's a bit confusing, it's standard terminology to refer to the interval required for one display-memory fetch as a "character," and I'll follow that terminology from now on.) Consequently, both modes display either 40 or 80 characters per scan line; the only difference is that text modes display more pixels per character. Given that graphics modes *can't* display nine dots per character (there's enough information for only eight 16-color pixels or four 256-color pixels in each memory fetch, and that's that), we'd seem to be at an impasse.

The key to solving this problem lies in recalling that the VGA is designed to drive a monitor that sweeps the electron beam across the screen at exactly the same speed no matter what mode the VGA is in. If the monitor always sweeps at the same speed, how does the VGA manage to display both 640 pixels across the screen (in high-resolution graphics modes) and 720 pixels across the screen (in 80-column text modes)? Good question. The answer is that the VGA has, not one, but *two* clocks on board, and one of those clocks is just enough faster than the other clock so that an extra 80 (or 40) pixels can be displayed on each scan line.

In other words, there's a slow clock (about 25 MHz) that's usually used in graphics modes to get 640 (or 320) pixels on the screen during each scan line, and a second, fast clock (about 28 MHz) that's usually used in text modes to crank out 720 (or 360) pixels per scan line. In particular, 320-by-400 256-color mode uses the 25 MHz clock.

You can probably see where I'm headed: We can switch from the 25-MHz clock to the 28-MHz clock in 320-by-480 256-color mode to get more pixels. Since it takes two clocks to produce one 256-color pixel, we'll get 40 rather than 80 extra pixels by doing this, bringing our horizontal resolution to the desired 360 pixels. (This has the side effect of driving VGA memory a bit faster than in any BIOS mode. Theoretically, this could cause memory to function improperly; however, I haven't encountered any such problems, and, given that 360-by-480 mode is fairly widely used, there doesn't seem to be cause for concern.)

Switching horizontal resolutions sounds easy, doesn't it? It's not. There's no standard VGA mode that uses the 28-MHz clock to draw eight rather than nine dots per character, and so the timing parameters have to be calculated from scratch. John Bridges has already done that for us, but I want you to appreciate that producing this mode took some work. The registers controlling the total number of characters per scan line, the number of characters displayed, the horizontal sync pulse, horizontal blanking, the offset from the start of one line to the start of the next, and the clock speed all have to be altered to set up 360-by-480 256-color mode. The function **Set360x480Mode** in Listing 13.1 does all that, as well as setting up the registers that control vertical resolution.

Once all that's done, the VGA is in 360-by-480 mode, awaiting our every high-resolution, 256-color graphics whim.

Accessing Display Memory

Setting up for 360-by-480 256-color mode proved to be quite a task. Is drawing in this mode going to be as difficult?

No. In fact, if you know how to draw in 320-by-400 256-color mode, you also know how to draw in 360-by-480 256-color mode; the conversion between the two is a simple matter of changing the working screen width from 320 pixels to 360 pixels. In fact, if you were to take the 320-by-400 256-color pixel-reading and -writing code from Chapter 10 and change the **SCREEN_WIDTH** equate from 320 to 360, those routines would work perfectly in 360-by-480 256-color mode. (The program as a whole would also have to be changed to use a 360-by-480 256-color mode set before it would work properly.)

The organization of display memory in 360-by-480 256-color mode is almost exactly the same as in 320-by-400 256-color mode (which was covered in detail in Chapter 10). Each byte of display memory controls one 256-color pixel, just as in mode 13h. The VGA is reprogrammed by the mode set so that adjacent pixels lie in adjacent planes of display memory. Look back at Figure 10.1, which shows the organization of the first few pixels on the screen. The bytes controlling those pixels run cross-plane, advancing to the next address only every fourth pixel. The address of the pixel at screen coordinate (x,y) is

$$address = [(y \times 90) + x] / 4$$

and the plane of a given pixel is

$$plane = x \bmod 4$$

A new scan line starts every 360 pixels, or 90 bytes, as shown in Figure 13.1. This is the major programming difference between the 360-by-480 and 320-by-400 256-color modes: In the 320-by-400 mode, a new scan line starts every 80 bytes.

The other programming difference between the two modes is that the area of display-memory mapped to the screen is longer in 360-by-480 256-color mode—which is only common sense, given that there are more pixels in that mode. The exact amount of memory required in 360-by-480 256-color mode is 360 times 480, or 172,800, bytes. The more perceptive among you will note that that's more than half of the VGA's 256Kb memory complement, which means that page-flipping is out. However, there's no reason you couldn't use that extra memory to create virtual screens larger than 360 by 480, which you could then scroll around, if you wish. (Horizontal smooth panning may not be possible, owing to the unusual pixel formatting of 360-by-480 mode. I haven't tried it, however; if any of you out there have tried 360-by-480 256-color smooth panning, please let me know how it worked.)

That's really all there is to drawing in 360-by-480 256-color mode. From a programming perspective, this mode is no more complicated than 320-by-400 256-color mode once the mode set is completed, and it should be capable of good performance given some clever coding. It's not particular easy to implement bitblt, block-move, or fast line-drawing code for either of the extended 256-color modes, but it *can* be done—and it's worth the trouble. Even the small taste we've gotten of the capabilities of these modes shows that they put the traditional CGA, EGA, and (in many cases) even VGA modes to shame.

Measuring Performance

Graphics and performance go hand in hand on the PC. Given the relatively low performance of both the PC and standard PC graphics hardware, high-performance graphics code is a must. In the last installment, I presented a timer for analyzing code performance in detail at a relatively low (close to the hardware) level. That timer is excellent if you want to try to figure out if it's faster to increment a register twice or add 2 to the register, but more-sophisticated tools are needed to identify time-critical code in the context of whole programs and to analyze and improve the performance of algorithms and functions.

Inside! Turbo C (the exclamation point is part of the name), from Paradigm Systems, Inc. (P.O. Box 152, Milford, MA 01757 508-478-0499, $125), is one such performance-analysis tool—and it's a good one. Inside! automatically uses the debugging information Turbo C generates to produce a function-by-function performance profile, which quickly reveals which functions are candidates for optimization. You can then zero in on the truly time-critical code by having Inside! analyze performance at a source-line level or by requesting a performance analysis of one or more specific events.

The best thing about all this is that it doesn't require any particular effort. You don't much need to think about what part of your program to optimize—all you need to do is read over the performance profiles Inside! generates. That, in turn, saves an enormous amount of guesswork, experimentation, and wasted optimization. Basically, Inside! makes it easy to ask the question "Where is my program spending its time?" Once you start asking that question, it's astonishing how often you'll find that it's possible to eliminate huge chunks of execution time.

Inside! is oriented toward use with C rather than assembly language programs. You can analyze assembly language code with Inside! (although a bug in TASM 1.0, which should be fixed in TASM 1.1, makes MASM a better choice right now), but that's more easily done with assembly code that's part of a C program than with stand-alone assembly

Fig. 13.1

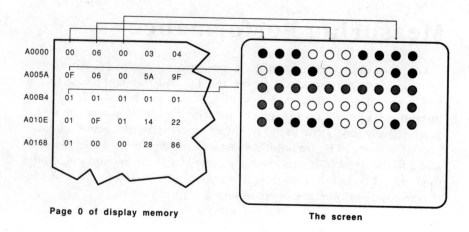

Page 0 of display memory   The screen

language. I *was* able to analyze stand-alone assembly language, mind you, but the manual doesn't provide much information, and it took me a good bit of fiddling around to get things working. Still, few substantial programs are written entirely in assembly language (who has the time to waste writing initialization code and the like in assembly language?), and sizable C–assembly language hybrid programs are exactly the sort of programs for which the ability of Inside! to produce easily interpreted performance statistics is most useful.

Inside! is simple to use and reliable. Paradigm has encountered and dealt with some hairy performance-analysis problems that I wouldn't have cared to figure out for myself, such as running in virtual-8086 environments, which intercept interrupts in sometimes unpredictable ways. Inside! is not quite perfect, however. For one thing, the manual (like most) could use some work: There's no index, and the examples could be explained in considerably more detail. On the other hand, there's a tremendous amount of useful technical information packed into less than 100 pages, if you're willing to work a bit to understand it.

The only other problem I encountered with Inside! is that it doesn't handle very large programs. Understand that I mean *very* large programs: The program I couldn't analyze with Inside! requires a minimum of 540Kb free to run. I don't know of anything else that can analyze this program, either, so that probably isn't a fair criticism. That program is one I co-wrote, however, and I very much wanted to use Inside! on it, but the two packages just couldn't fit into memory together. At any rate, the people at Paradigm have workarounds for analyzing all but the most severely memory-constrained programs and are working on using overlays, expanded memory, and the like to eliminate the problem in the next release.

All in all, Inside! Turbo C is a must-have tool for C programmers concerned with performance. That's particularly true because Inside! makes it so easy for programmers to raise their optimization sights from individual statements and instructions to the algorithm–function level, where the greatest potential savings often await, and to identify efficiently code that's worth optimizing.

Versions of Inside! for Microsoft C, Turbo Pascal, and other compilers are also available.

In Conclusion

For now, we've come to the end of the 256-color rainbow. So far as I know, there aren't any more 256-color modes hiding in the standard IBM VGA. Of course, there are several *SuperVGA* 256-color modes around, and the 8514/A—with a 1024-by-768 256-color mode—is coming on strong. (Look for hardware-compatible clones of the 8514/A soon; when those become widely available and prices drop, the move to the next PC-graphics standard may well begin in earnest.) If there's enough reader interest in either SuperVGA modes or the 8514/A, I'll cover them; for now, though, I'll keep on keeping on with the VGA. Next time, I'll look into the potent combination of the VGA's split-screen and panning features, and in the not-too-distant future, I'll move on to drawing circles, ellipses and the like . . . and drawing them fast, as always.

See you next time.

Listing 13.1

```
; Turbo C tiny/small/medium model-callable assembler
; subroutines to:
;       * Set 360x480 256-color VGA mode
;       * Draw a dot in 360x480 256-color VGA mode
;       * Read the color of a dot in 360x480 256-color VGA mode
;
; Assemble and link with the program of Listing 13.2 with a command
; line like:
;
;       tcc lst13-2 lst13-3.asm
;
; (requires Turbo C and either TASM or MASM).
;
; Assembled with TASM 1.0.
;
; Updated 6/30/89.
;
; The 360x480 256-color mode set code and parameters were provided
; by John Bridges, who has placed them into the public domain.
;
VGA_SEGMENT     equ     0a000h  ;display memory segment
SC_INDEX        equ     3c4h    ;Sequence Controller Index register
GC_INDEX        equ     3ceh    ;Graphics Controller Index register
MAP_MASK        equ     2       ;Map Mask register index in SC
READ_MAP        equ     4       ;Read Map register index in GC
SCREEN_WIDTH    equ     360     ;# of pixels across screen
WORD_OUTS_OK    equ     1       ;set to 0 to assemble for
                                ; computers that can't handle
                                ; word outs to indexed VGA registers

;
_DATA   segment public byte 'DATA'
;
; 360x480 256-color mode CRT Controller register settings.
; (Courtesy of John Bridges.)
;
vptbl   dw      06b00h  ; horz total
        dw      05901h  ; horz displayed
        dw      05a02h  ; start horz blanking
        dw      08e03h  ; end horz blanking
        dw      05e04h  ; start h sync
        dw      08a05h  ; end h sync
        dw      00d06h  ; vertical total
        dw      03e07h  ; overflow
        dw      04009h  ; cell height
        dw      0ea10h  ; v sync start
        dw      0ac11h  ; v sync end and protect cr0-cr7
        dw      0df12h  ; vertical displayed
        dw      02d13h  ; offset
        dw      00014h  ; turn off dword mode
        dw      0e715h  ; v blank start
        dw      00616h  ; v blank end
        dw      0e317h  ; turn on byte mode
vpend   label   word
_DATA   ends
;
; Macro to output a word value to a port.
;
OUT_WORD        macro
```

Listing 13.1 continues

Listing 13.1 *continued*

```
if WORD_OUTS_OK
        out     dx,ax
else
        out     dx,al
        inc     dx
        xchg    ah,al
        out     dx,al
        dec     dx
        xchg    ah,al
endif
        endm
;
_TEXT   segment byte public 'CODE'
        assume  cs:_TEXT, ds:_DATA
;
; Sets up 360x480 256-color mode.
; (Courtesy of John Bridges.)
;
; Call as: void Set360By480Mode()
;
; Returns: nothing
;
        public _Set360x480Mode
_Set360x480Mode proc    near
        push    si                  ;preserve C register vars
        push    di
        mov     ax,12h              ; start with mode 12h
        int     10h                 ; let the bios clear the video memory

        mov     ax,13h              ; start with standard mode 13h
        int     10h                 ; let the bios set the mode

        mov     dx,3c4h             ; alter sequencer registers
        mov     ax,0604h            ; disable chain 4
        out     dx,ax

        mov     ax,0100h            ; synchronous reset
        out     dx,ax               ; asserted
        mov     dx,3c2h             ; misc output
        mov     al,0e7h             ; use 28 mHz dot clock
        out     dx,al               ; select it
        mov     dx,3c4h             ; sequencer again
        mov     ax,0300h            ; restart sequencer
        out     dx,ax               ; running again

        mov     dx,3d4h             ; alter crtc registers

        mov     al,11h              ; cr11
        out     dx,al               ; current value
        inc     dx                  ; point to data
        in      al,dx               ; get cr11 value
        and     al,7fh              ; remove cr0 -> cr7
        out     dx,al               ;    write protect
        dec     dx                  ; point to index
        cld
        mov     si,offset vptbl
        mov     cx,((offset vpend)-(offset vptbl)) shr 1
@b:     lodsw
```

Listing 13.1 *continues*

Listing 13.1 *continued*

```asm
        out     dx,ax
        loop    @b
        pop     di              ;restore C register vars
        pop     si
        ret
_Set360x480Mode endp
;
; Draws a pixel in the specified color at the specified
; location in 360x480 256-color mode.
;
; Call as: void Draw360x480Dot(int X, int Y, int Color)
;
; Returns: nothing
;
DParms  struc
        dw      ?               ;pushed BP
        dw      ?               ;return address
DrawX   dw      ?               ;X coordinate at which to draw
DrawY   dw      ?               ;Y coordinate at which to draw
Color   dw      ?               ;color in which to draw (in the
                                ; range 0-255; upper byte ignored)
DParms  ends
;
        public _Draw360x480Dot
_Draw360x480Dot proc    near
        push    bp              ;preserve caller's BP
        mov     bp,sp           ;point to stack frame
        push    si              ;preserve C register vars
        push    di
        mov     ax,VGA_SEGMENT
        mov     es,ax   ;point to display memory
        mov     ax,SCREEN_WIDTH/4
                                ;there are 4 pixels at each address, so
                                ; each 360-pixel row is 90 bytes wide
                                ; in each plane
        mul     [bp+DrawY] ;point to start of desired row
        mov     di,[bp+DrawX] ;get the X coordinate
        shr     di,1            ;there are 4 pixels at each address
        shr     di,1            ; so divide the X coordinate by 4
        add     di,ax   ;point to the pixel's address
        mov     cl,byte ptr [bp+DrawX] ;get the X coordinate again
        and     cl,3            ;get the plane # of the pixel
        mov     ah,1
        shl     ah,cl   ;set the bit corresponding to the plane
                                ; the pixel is in
        mov     al,MAP_MASK
        mov     dx,SC_INDEX
        OUT_WORD                ;set to write to the proper plane for
                                ; the pixel
        mov     al,byte ptr [bp+Color]  ;get the color
        stosb                   ;draw the pixel
        pop     di              ;restore C register vars
        pop     si
        pop     bp              ;restore caller's BP
        ret
_Draw360x480Dot endp
;
; Reads the color of the pixel at the specified
```

Listing 13.1 *continues*

Listing 13.1 *continued*

```
; location in 360x480 256-color mode.
;
; Call as: int Read360x480Dot(int X, int Y)
;
; Returns: pixel color
;
RParms  struc
        dw      ?       ;pushed BP
        dw      ?       ;return address
ReadX   dw      ?       ;X coordinate from which to read
ReadY   dw      ?       ;Y coordinate from which to read
RParms  ends
;
        public  _Read360x480Dot
_Read360x480Dot proc    near
        push    bp      ;preserve caller's BP
        mov     bp,sp   ;point to stack frame
        push    si      ;preserve C register vars
        push    di
        mov     ax,VGA_SEGMENT
        mov     es,ax   ;point to display memory
        mov     ax,SCREEN_WIDTH/4
                        ;there are 4 pixels at each address, so
                        ; each 360-pixel row is 90 bytes wide
                        ; in each plane
        mul     [bp+DrawY] ;point to start of desired row
        mov     si,[bp+DrawX] ;get the X coordinate
        shr     si,1    ;there are 4 pixels at each address
        shr     si,1    ; so divide the X coordinate by 4
        add     si,ax   ;point to the pixel's address
        mov     ah,byte ptr [bp+DrawX]
                        ;get the X coordinate again
        and     ah,3    ;get the plane # of the pixel
        mov     al,READ_MAP
        mov     dx,GC_INDEX
        OUT_WORD        ;set to read from the proper plane for
                        ; the pixel
        lods    byte ptr es:[si] ;read the pixel
        sub     ah,ah   ;make the return value a word for C
        pop     di      ;restore C register vars
        pop     si
        pop     bp      ;restore caller's BP
        ret
_Read360x480Dot endp
_TEXT   ends
        end
```

Listing 13.2

```
/*
 * Sample program to illustrate VGA line drawing in 360x480
 * 256-color mode.
 *
 * Compiled with Turbo C 2.0.
```

Listing 13.2 *continues*

Listing 13.2 *continued*

```
 *
 * Must be linked with Listing 13.1 with a command line like:
 *
 *     tcc lst13-2 lst13-1.asm
 *
 * By Michael Abrash.  6/2/89.
 * Updated 6/30/89.
 */
#include <dos.h>                     /* contains geninterrupt */

#define TEXT_MODE       0x03
#define BIOS_VIDEO_INT  0x10
#define X_MAX           360     /* working screen width */
#define Y_MAX           480     /* working screen height */

extern void Draw360x480Dot();
extern void Set360x480Mode();

/*
 * Draws a line in octant 0 or 3 ( |DeltaX| >= DeltaY ).
 * |DeltaX|+1 points are drawn.
 */
void Octant0(X0, Y0, DeltaX, DeltaY, XDirection, Color)
unsigned int X0, Y0;            /* coordinates of start of the line */
unsigned int DeltaX, DeltaY;    /* length of the line */
int XDirection;                 /* 1 if line is drawn left to right,
                                     -1 if drawn right to left */
int Color;                      /* color in which to draw line */
{
    int DeltaYx2;
    int DeltaYx2MinusDeltaXx2;
    int ErrorTerm;

    /* Set up initial error term and values used inside drawing loop */
    DeltaYx2 = DeltaY * 2;
    DeltaYx2MinusDeltaXx2 = DeltaYx2 - (int) ( DeltaX * 2 );
    ErrorTerm = DeltaYx2 - (int) DeltaX;

    /* Draw the line */
    Draw360x480Dot(X0, Y0, Color);   /* draw the first pixel */
    while ( DeltaX-- ) {
        /* See if it's time to advance the Y coordinate */
        if ( ErrorTerm >= 0 ) {
            /* Advance the Y coordinate & adjust the error term
               back down */
            Y0++;
            ErrorTerm += DeltaYx2MinusDeltaXx2;
        } else {
            /* Add to the error term */
            ErrorTerm += DeltaYx2;
        }
        X0 += XDirection;               /* advance the X coordinate */
        Draw360x480Dot(X0, Y0, Color);    /* draw a pixel */
    }
}

/*
 * Draws a line in octant 1 or 2 ( |DeltaX| < DeltaY ).
```

Listing 13.2 *continues*

Listing 13.2 *continued*

```
 * |DeltaY|+1 points are drawn.
 */
void Octant1(X0, Y0, DeltaX, DeltaY, XDirection, Color)
unsigned int X0, Y0;          /* coordinates of start of the line */
unsigned int DeltaX, DeltaY;  /* length of the line */
int XDirection;               /* 1 if line is drawn left to right,
                                 -1 if drawn right to left */
int Color;                    /* color in which to draw line */
{
   int DeltaXx2;
   int DeltaXx2MinusDeltaYx2;
   int ErrorTerm;

   /* Set up initial error term and values used inside drawing loop */
   DeltaXx2 = DeltaX * 2;
   DeltaXx2MinusDeltaYx2 = DeltaXx2 - (int) ( DeltaY * 2 );
   ErrorTerm = DeltaXx2 - (int) DeltaY;

   Draw360x480Dot(X0, Y0, Color);   /* draw the first pixel */
   while ( DeltaY-- ) {
      /* See if it's time to advance the X coordinate */
      if ( ErrorTerm >= 0 ) {
         /* Advance the X coordinate & adjust the error term
            back down */
         X0 += XDirection;
         ErrorTerm += DeltaXx2MinusDeltaYx2;
      } else {
         /* Add to the error term */
         ErrorTerm += DeltaXx2;
      }
      Y0++;                          /* advance the Y coordinate */
      Draw360x480Dot(X0, Y0,Color);  /* draw a pixel */
   }
}


/*
 * Draws a line on the EGA or VGA.
 */
void EVGALine(X0, Y0, X1, Y1, Color)
int X0, Y0;    /* coordinates of one end of the line */
int X1, Y1;    /* coordinates of the other end of the line */
unsigned char Color;    /* color in which to draw line */
{
   int DeltaX, DeltaY;
   int Temp;

   /* Save half the line-drawing cases by swapping Y0 with Y1
      and X0 with X1 if Y0 is greater than Y1. As a result, DeltaY
      is always > 0, and only the octant 0-3 cases need to be
      handled. */
   if ( Y0 > Y1 ) {
      Temp = Y0;
      Y0 = Y1;
      Y1 = Temp;
      Temp = X0;
      X0 = X1;
      X1 = Temp;
   }
```

Listing 13.2 *continues*

Listing 13.2 *continued*

```c
    /* Handle as four separate cases, for the four octants in which
       Y1 is greater than Y0 */
    DeltaX = X1 - X0;      /* calculate the length of the line
                              in each coordinate */
    DeltaY = Y1 - Y0;
    if ( DeltaX > 0 ) {
        if ( DeltaX > DeltaY ) {
            Octant0(X0, Y0, DeltaX, DeltaY, 1, Color);
        } else {
            Octant1(X0, Y0, DeltaX, DeltaY, 1, Color);
        }
    } else {
        DeltaX = -DeltaX;                   /* absolute value of DeltaX */
        if ( DeltaX > DeltaY ) {
            Octant0(X0, Y0, DeltaX, DeltaY, -1, Color);
        } else {
            Octant1(X0, Y0, DeltaX, DeltaY, -1, Color);
        }
    }
}

/*
 * Subroutine to draw a rectangle full of vectors, of the
 * specified length and in varying colors, around the
 * specified rectangle center.
 */
void VectorsUp(XCenter, YCenter, XLength, YLength)
int XCenter, YCenter;    /* center of rectangle to fill */
int XLength, YLength;    /* distance from center to edge
                            of rectangle */
{
    int WorkingX, WorkingY, Color = 1;

    /* Lines from center to top of rectangle */
    WorkingX = XCenter - XLength;
    WorkingY = YCenter - YLength;
    for ( ; WorkingX < ( XCenter + XLength ); WorkingX++ )
        EVGALine(XCenter, YCenter, WorkingX, WorkingY, Color++);

    /* Lines from center to right of rectangle */
    WorkingX = XCenter + XLength - 1;
    WorkingY = YCenter - YLength;
    for ( ; WorkingY < ( YCenter + YLength ); WorkingY++ )
        EVGALine(XCenter, YCenter, WorkingX, WorkingY, Color++);

    /* Lines from center to bottom of rectangle */
    WorkingX = XCenter + XLength - 1;
    WorkingY = YCenter + YLength - 1;
    for ( ; WorkingX >= ( XCenter - XLength ); WorkingX-- )
        EVGALine(XCenter, YCenter, WorkingX, WorkingY, Color++);

    /* Lines from center to left of rectangle */
    WorkingX = XCenter - XLength;
    WorkingY = YCenter + YLength - 1;
    for ( ; WorkingY >= ( YCenter - YLength ); WorkingY-- )
        EVGALine(XCenter, YCenter, WorkingX, WorkingY, Color++);
}
```

Listing 13.2 *continues*

Listing 13.2 continued

```
/*
 * Sample program to draw four rectangles full of lines.
 */
int main()
{
    char temp;

    Set360x480Mode();

    /* Draw each of four rectangles full of vectors */
    VectorsUp(X_MAX / 4, Y_MAX / 4, X_MAX / 4, Y_MAX / 4, 1);
    VectorsUp(X_MAX * 3 / 4, Y_MAX / 4, X_MAX / 4, Y_MAX / 4, 2);
    VectorsUp(X_MAX / 4, Y_MAX * 3 / 4, X_MAX / 4, Y_MAX / 4, 3);
    VectorsUp(X_MAX * 3 / 4, Y_MAX * 3 / 4, X_MAX / 4, Y_MAX / 4, 4);

    /* Wait for the enter key to be pressed */
    scanf("%c", &temp);

    /* Back to text mode */
    _AX = TEXT_MODE;
    geninterrupt(BIOS_VIDEO_INT);
}
```

Index

More Computer Knowledge from Que

C Programming Guide, 3rd Edition

by Jack Purdum, Ph.D.

Hands-on practice sessions lead you step-by-step through the fundamentals of C programming. This Que classic features useful information on the ANSI C standard, common C commands, and proper syntax. A valuable resource!

Order #850
$24.95 USA
0-88022-356-1, 456 pp.

C Programmer's Toolkit

by Jack Purdum, Ph.D.

Ready-to-run subroutines highlight this task-oriented book/disk set for intermediate to advanced level programmers. Presents useful functions not found in an ANSI standard library and shows you how to design library functions. A code-intensive text!

Order #992
$39.95 USA
0-88022-457-6, 500 pp.

C Quick Reference

Developed by Que Corporation

Gain instant access to the essential commands and functions of C programming! This compact, portable reference is ideal for desktop or laptop computer users!

Order #868
$7.95 USA
0-88022-372-3, 160 pp.

Turbo C Programming

by Alan C. Plantz, et al.

An excellent guide to advanced Turbo C programming! This outstanding Que text presents detailed information on the Turbo C Professional 2.0 environment, including the Turbo Assembler and the Turbo Debugger.

Order #936
$22.95 USA
0-88022-430-4

Using Turbo Pascal
by Michael Yester

An excellent introduction to Turbo Pascal 5.5! This combination of tutorial and reference teaches you the fundamentals of the Pascal language and protocol, plus disciplined programming techniques.

Order #883
$21.95 USA
0-88022-396-0, 724 pp.

Turbo Pascal Advanced Techniques
by Chris Ohlsen and Gary Stoker

Dozens of inside tips and professional programming techniques make this a powerful programming reference for the Turbo Pascal environment! Helps you push Turbo Pascal 5.5 to its greatest potential.

Order #945
$22.95 USA
0-88022-432-0, 600 pp.

Turbo Pascal Programmer's Toolkit
by Tom Rugg and Phil Feldman

Programming experts Rugg and Feldman provide dozens of Turbo Pascal programs and subprograms in this useful book/disk set complete with ready-to-run applications. Includes routines for input/output, sorting and searching, and data manipulation. Covers Turbo Pascal through Version 5.5!

Order #978
$39.95 USA
0-88022-447-9, 650 pp.

Turbo Pascal Quick Reference
Developed by Que Corporation

Find the information you need—immediately—with Que's *Turbo Pascal Quick Reference*! A compact guide to essential Turbo Pascal operations!

Order #935
$7.95 USA
0-88022-429-0, 160 pp.

DOS Programmer's Reference, 2nd Edition
by Terry Dettmann

Updated for DOS Version 4! This combination of reference and tutorial discusses DOS functions, BIOS functions, and using DOS with other programming languages—including C, BASIC, and assembly language. Must reading for experienced applications programmers!

Order #1006
$27.95 USA
0-88022-458-4, 850 pp.

DOS and BIOS Functions Quick Reference
Developed by Que Corporation

Covers BIOS functions and DOS through Version 4. This handy reference helps you find the information you need about basic programming operations—fast!

Order #932
$7.95 USA
0-88022-426-6, 160 pp.

Using Assembly Language
by Allen Wyatt

Look to Que's *Using Assembly Language* for thorough coverage of all assembly language concepts! This text explains how to develop, manage, and debug subroutines; access BIOS and DOS services; and interface assembly language with Pascal, C, and BASIC.

Order #107
$24.95 USA
0-88022-297-2, 746 pp.

SQL Programmer's Guide
by Umang Gupta and William Gietz

Pre-eminent SQL authorities Gupta and Gietz present the definitive book for SQL programming. Covers SQL fundamentals, including queries, virtual tables, indexes, variables, database utilities, and function calls.

Order #881
$29.95 USA
0-88022-390-1, 302 pp.

Using QuickBASIC 4

by Phil Feldman and Tom Rugg

A complete, hands-on guide to improving your QuickBASIC programming skills! A special step-by-step tutorial gets you up and running in minutes, and the text also includes practical tips, techniques, and a handy Instant Reference.

Order #845
$19.95 USA
0-88022-378-2, 713 pp.

QuickBASIC Advanced Techniques

by Peter Aitken

This informative book is a powerful resource for experienced programmers! Covers the advanced uses of QuickBASIC through Version 4.5 and contains dozens of tips, techniques, and programming code examples.

Order #944
$21.95 USA
0-88022-431-2, 600 pp.

QuickBASIC Programmer's Toolkit

by Tom Rugg and Phil Feldman

An easy-to-use book/disk set, designed to increase user productivity instantly. Includes a comprehensive library of practical QuickBASIC subprograms in ready-to-run form. Subprograms are designed as building blocks for complete programs—custom fit for your needs!

Order #982
$39.95 USA
0-88022-450-9, 650 pp.

QuickBASIC Quick Reference

Developed by Que Corporation

Put the essential QuickBASIC commands and functions at your fingertips with this handy reference. A compact, portable guide to QuickBASIC 4 fundamentals.

Order #869
$7.95 USA
0-88022-373-1, 160 pp.

Free Catalog!

Mail us this registration form today, and we'll send you a free catalog featuring Que's complete line of best-selling books.

Name of Book _____

Name _____

Title _____

Phone (____) _____

Company _____

Address _____

City _____

State _____ ZIP _____

Please check the appropriate answers:

1. Where did you buy your Que book?
   - [ ] Bookstore (name: _____)
   - [ ] Computer store (name: _____)
   - [ ] Catalog (name: _____)
   - [ ] Direct from Que
   - [ ] Other: _____

2. How many computer books do you buy a year?
   - [ ] 1 or less
   - [ ] 2-5
   - [ ] 6-10
   - [ ] More than 10

3. How many Que books do you own?
   - [ ] 1
   - [ ] 2-5
   - [ ] 6-10
   - [ ] More than 10

4. How long have you been using this software?
   - [ ] Less than 6 months
   - [ ] 6 months to 1 year
   - [ ] 1-3 years
   - [ ] More than 3 years

5. What influenced your purchase of this Que book?
   - [ ] Personal recommendation
   - [ ] Advertisement
   - [ ] In-store display
   - [ ] Price
   - [ ] Que catalog
   - [ ] Que mailing
   - [ ] Que's reputation
   - [ ] Other: _____

6. How would you rate the overall content of the book?
   - [ ] Very good
   - [ ] Good
   - [ ] Satisfactory
   - [ ] Poor

7. What do you like *best* about this Que book?

   _____
   _____

8. What do you like *least* about this Que book?

   _____
   _____

9. Did you buy this book with your personal funds?
   - [ ] Yes   [ ] No

10. Please feel free to list any other comments you may have about this Que book.

    _____
    _____
    _____

que

Order Your Que Books Today!

Name _____

Title _____

Company _____

City _____

State _____ ZIP _____

Phone No. (____) _____

Method of Payment:

Check [ ]   (Please enclose in envelope.)

Charge My: VISA [ ]   MasterCard [ ]
American Express [ ]

Charge # _____

Expiration Date _____

Order No.	Title	Qty.	Price	Total

You can **FAX** your order to **1-317-573-2583**. Or call **1-800-428-5331, ext. ORDR** to order direct.

Please add $2.50 per title for shipping and handling.

Subtotal _____

Shipping & Handling _____

Total _____

que

NO POSTAGE
NECESSARY
IF MAILED
IN THE
UNITED STATES

BUSINESS REPLY MAIL
First Class Permit No. 9918   Indianapolis, IN

Postage will be paid by addressee

11711 N. College
Carmel, IN 46032

NO POSTAGE
NECESSARY
IF MAILED
IN THE
UNITED STATES

BUSINESS REPLY MAIL
First Class Permit No. 9918   Indianapolis, IN

Postage will be paid by addressee

11711 N. College
Carmel, IN 46032

4905

POWER GRAPHICS PROGRAMMING— THE DISK

☐ **YES!** I want to get all of the code listings in this book on disk. Please rush me my copy of the Michael Abrash **Power Graphics Programming** disk today!

Programmer's Journal
The Resource Journal for IBM Micro Programmers

☐ **YES!** I want to take a look at *Programmer's Journal* and save some money too. Please sign me up for the **Que Books/Programmer's Journal** subscription special, a full year of **PJ**, (6 issues) for only $17.95, a savings of 10% off our regular discount price!

SATISFACTION GUARANTEED

For faster service call toll free:
1-800-234-0386

NAME _____

COMPANY _____

ADDRESS _____

CITY _____ STATE _____

ZIP _____ PHONE _____

All orders must be prepaid. Offer good in U.S. only. Call 503-747-0800 for prices outside the U.S.

☐ *Power Graphics Programming* disk: $14.95   ☐ Check enclosed
☐ *Programmer's Journal* subscription: $17.95   ☐ Visa/MC   Amount $ _____

☐☐☐☐–☐☐☐☐–☐☐☐☐–☐☐☐☐ ☐☐–☐☐
Expire Date

Signature _____

BUSINESS REPLY MAIL

FIRST-CLASS MAIL   PERMIT NO. 44   EUGENE, OR

POSTAGE WILL BE PAID BY ADDRESSEE

Programmer's Journal

P. O. Box 30160

Eugene, OR 97403-9976

NO POSTAGE
NECESSARY
IF MAILED
IN THE
UNITED STATES

BUSINESS REPLY MAIL

FIRST-CLASS MAIL   PERMIT NO. 44   EUGENE, OR

POSTAGE WILL BE PAID BY ADDRESSEE

Programmer's Journal

P. O. Box 30160

Eugene, OR 97403-9976